Forbidden City, USA

Chinese American Nightclubs, 1936-1970

Lily Pon on the cover of a Forbidden City program (mid-1940s). Photo by Romaine.

Forbidden City, USA

Chinese American Nightclubs, 1936-1970

Arthur Dong

DeepFocus Productions, Inc., Los Angeles, California

Dudley Lee (1940s). Photo by Romaine.

Contents

Foreword

by Lisa See

CHINATOWN GIRL

ABOVE: Dottie Sun and Mary Mammon are the subjects of this AP Feature Service story about the modern Chinatown woman (June 14, 1942).

Arthur Dong has a passion: Chinese American nightclubs and the dancers and singers who performed in them. In the 1980s, he found entertainers—many of whom time had forgotten—and interviewed them. Through his research and by asking the right questions, he captured the memories of the men and women who lived through the glamorous Chinese American nightclub era—what some scholars have dubbed the "Chop Suey Circuit"—and allowed them to tell their stories in their own words with their own brand of funny, brassy, clever showbiz humor.

In San Francisco in the late 1930s, the Depression still lingered. People had lost money, their jewelry, their homes. Families had arrived from Oklahoma, fleeing the Dust Bowl. The most unfortunate stood in breadlines. Despite all this, a sense of optimism in anticipation of the Golden Gate International Exposition, which would open on Treasure Island on February 18, 1939, began to lift the entire city. In the year or so leading up to the opening of the exposition, astute business leaders in Chinatown grabbed this moment to launch a "Shine for '39" campaign, which was designed to clean up the enclave, open new businesses, and welcome the many visitors who would come from across the country and from around the world to visit the fair. Part of this campaign included the establishment of several nighteries along Chinatown's Grant Avenue that would appeal to "mainstream" customers. Wilbert Wong opened the Li Po cocktail lounge; Andy Wong opened the Chinese Sky Room. And then there was Charlie Low, who, on December 22, 1938, would open the first Chinese American nightclub in the country *outside* of Chinatown.

But who would perform in these clubs? Certainly not the young women who'd been born and raised in the neighborhood. They'd been told never to show their arms or legs in public, never to show their teeth when they smiled, never to venture far from traditional family values and customs. Here is where the real genius of the nightclub owners emerged. They hired young women who'd grown up outside the restrictions of Chinatown. Many of the women who became chorus girls and headliners were from Arizona, Hawaii, and states in the Midwest. They literally broke the mold for what an Asian girl could or should do.

In these pages, you will see that these performers were hardly passive victims of racial and sexual stereotypes. For some, working at the clubs marked the attainment of a lifelong dream—to sing and dance in front of an audience—while for others, the job was practical—a way to make a living and support their families. For a lucky few, these jobs were a stepping stone that led to working at other nightclubs on the road, performing in other countries, or having their acts recorded for film and, later, television. Arthur has embellished all these stories—again, told by the performers themselves—with what is arguably the largest private collection of photographs and memorabilia from Chinese American nightclubs in existence. How fortunate we are that he is sharing his passion with the rest of us.

ABOVE: The marquee of Chinatown's first cocktail lounge, the Chinese Village, can be seen in this J. K. Piggott postcard of San Francisco's Grant Avenue (ca. 1937).

So put on some music from the 1930s and 1940s, start turning the pages of this remarkable volume, and step into the intoxicating and magical world of the Chinese American nightclub scene. Enjoy! ●

Lisa See is the author of several *New York Times* bestsellers, including *Snow Flower and the Secret Fan, Peony in Love, Shanghai Girls,* and the memoir *On Gold Mountain,* about her Chinese American family. Her newest novel, *China Dolls,* is set in Chinese American nightclubs during the 1930s and '40s.

Preface

by Arthur Dong

One of my favorite childhood adventures was walking through the Stockton Street Tunnel. It began in San Francisco's Chinatown and led to what we Toisan people called "Mahkeit Guy" (Market Street, downtown). Just outside the end of the tunnel, in the upscale area of Union Square, was where I first stumbled upon the Forbidden City in the 1960s.

What struck me then were the photos of nightclub acts from the 1940s that were still on display. I don't recall exactly who was in those black-and-white stills, but I do remember that this was the first time I saw Chinese American performers dressed in glamorous taffeta gowns, swing-style suits with wide lapels, and skin-baring showgirl costumes. I had seen those kinds of outfits before in old Hollywood musicals, but they were almost never worn by entertainers who looked like me.

It's odd that I didn't venture in—I was a pretty nervy kid. Maybe it was because the club had become an adults-only place, where shows like the all-Chinese "Gershwin Revue" had been replaced by exotic dancers. In any case, I walked on, and so ended my first encounter with Chinese American nightclubs.

By the 1980s I had become a filmmaker, and during the course of some research, I spotted an article on dancer Jadin Wong that mentioned she had performed at the Forbidden City. My old memories of the nightclub reawakened, I headed out to New York City to meet Jadin. I stayed with my longtime friend Kevin Gee, only to discover that his stepfather was none other than Charlie Low, the impresario who had created the Forbidden City. Coincidence?

Jadin was seventy-two and delightfully outrageous. I'm the son of traditional working-class immigrants, and she was so unlike the sewing factory women I had grown up around; during our first meeting, she modeled her new bathing suit and asked my opinion of her cleavage (well-defined and firm, by the way). As it happened, Jadin's former

ABOVE, LEFT: Grant Avenue between Pine and Bush Streets once boasted three Chinese American nightclubs on a single block. This postcard shows the Chinese Sky Room and Club Shanghai marquees (1947). Photo by John D. "Snappy" Goodrich.
RIGHT: Cover from a Kubla Khan program (mid-1940s). The Kubla Khan was at the corner of Grant Avenue and Bush Street, on the same block as the Chinese Sky Room and the Club Shanghai.

dance partner, Jackie Mei Ling, was in town too. He turned out to be a tall, witty gay Chinese man with an elegantly coiffed head of white hair. What stories they told!

I set out to investigate this Chinese American club scene they raved about, but my initial research turned up few leads on the Forbidden City or any of the other Chinese American nightclubs that thrived during the 1940s and '50s. In conversations with Chinatown elders, they disparaged the clubs as immoral houses of prostitution better left forgotten. Some cultural critics and feminists I met criticized the images projected by the female performers, calling them exploitative, with sexist and racist undertones. They didn't see any reason to bring such imagery back into focus. As for mainstream entertainment historians, these nightspots were apparently not noteworthy enough to merit documentation.

That left oral histories as the key to unlocking this untold story. Starting from my connection to Charlie Low via Kevin, I branched out and located more than one hundred entertainers and club staffers. The spirit and audacity of the performers were a revelation. After all, I was Chinese American, an independent filmmaker, and gay—not exactly a winning combination of mainstream values (especially in the 1980s)—and, notwithstanding the political, cultural, and social critiques about the clubs, I was inspired by this earlier generation who defied societal norms to pursue their show business dreams.

ABOVE: On August 18, 1988, filmmaker and author Arthur Dong gathered Chinese American nightclub veterans for a reunion at the Oakland home of singer Frances Chun. Back (l–r): Lily Pon, Stanley Toy, Lenna Chan, and Bob Chan. Middle: Jackie Mei Ling, Larry Ching, Jade Ling, Arthur Dong, Fay Ying (Mary Watson), and Frank Huie. Front: Dottie Sun (Murray), Charlie Low, Frances Chun (Kan), Paul Wing, and Mary Mammon (Amo). Photo by Zand Gee.

BACKGROUND: Detail from a Forbidden City ad (ca. 1964).

After four years of interviewing and collecting archival material, I produced the documentary *Forbidden City, USA*, focusing on Charlie's club. All along, I wanted to write a companion book, knowing that a fifty-six-minute film could never capture all the stories, ephemera, and photos I had amassed. These memories, postcards, menus, snapshots, programs, and meticulously crafted studio photos magically transported me to an era before my time, a time I yearned to be a part of in all the senses: the looks, the sounds, the feels, the smells, the tastes (*wor siu opp,* anyone?).

Yet, the materials that I've chosen for this book aren't meant to be purely nostalgic anecdotes and souvenirs. They are historical accounts and cultural art, where the storytellers and creators—the performers, photographers, and graphic designers—have passed on a wondrous legacy.

Besides my private collection (which has continued to grow, even to this day), I've included items from scrapbooks that have been lovingly preserved by the families of club veterans including Andy Wong, David Sum, Dorothy Toy, Dottie Sun, Fong Wan, Frances Chun, Ivy Tam, Mai Tai Sing, Paul Wing, and Tony Wing. I thank them for their generosity and for trusting me with such treasured keepsakes.

ABOVE: Forbidden City performers (l–r): Diane Shinn, Elizabeth Jean, Lily Pon, Ginger Lee, Dottie Sun, and Connie Parks (ca. 1955). Photo by Milton Mann Studios.

OPPOSITE: The Tai Sings: Mai Tai Sing and Wilbur Tai Sing (ca. 1942). Photo by Romaine.

Thanks also to Lorraine Dong, co-writer of this book's essay (and my sister), who never gave up on the notion that this twenty-five-year effort would actually become a reality. But this book's physical reality wouldn't be possible if it weren't for designer Zand Gee, who shared my delight in working with such remarkable stories and fabulous images. Thanks, Zand! And I can't complete this paragraph without a few appreciations: to fellow "Chop Suey Circuit" enthusiast Lisa See, whose foreword has set the perfect kickoff for the chapters to come, and to editorial consultant Oliver Wang and copy editor Lisa K. Marietta, whose keen expertise of the written word have provided much valued guidance on this, my first book.

Mostly, though, I'd like to dedicate this book to my parents, Don and Zem Ping Dong. In the 1930s and '40s, they carried out courageous acts of defiance in their own right when they took steps to circumvent racially discriminatory U.S. immigration policies in order to start a new life in America. Their accomplishments have been a lifelong inspiration that have taught me the principles of perseverance and hard work. Without their bravery and example, I would not be here to fulfill this dream that you are reading. ●

Romaine

Chinese American Nightclubs, 1936–1970

by Arthur Dong and Lorraine Dong

Chinese Sky Room performers: Vicky Lee,
second from the right, others unidentified
(ca. 1950). Photo by Romaine.

Out of the Rubble: Creating the Modern Chinatown

San Francisco's Chinatown was literally reinvented from the ashes of disaster. The infamous 1906 earthquake and fire almost completely wiped out the original twelve-block Chinatown, which had been located near the city's center since the mid-nineteenth century. Anti-Chinese forces seized the opportunity and tried to purge a community they saw as a cultural and racial blight on the city, planning to relocate Chinatown to Hunters Point, on San Francisco's geographic margins: out of sight and presumably out of mind.

Chinese leaders shrewdly countered with plans of their own. They persuaded city officials that Chinatown could be rebuilt into a tourist destination, abetting the city's effort to bring back much-needed revenue. What arose was Chinatown as we know it today, with its pagoda-topped buildings and crimson-coated doorways—architectural details largely unique to American Chinatowns versus actual towns in China. This new Chinatown, from its conception, was meant to be a fantasy space, faking the exotic as a way to lure in an eager, unsuspecting public.

Americans were already accustomed to treating the Chinese as spectacles. As early as the 1830s, Chinese women with bound feet toured the United States as part of circuses and variety shows. The Cantonese opera troupe Hong Took Tong became a huge crossover hit in San Francisco in the 1850s, setting up shop in the city's one-thousand-seat American Theatre and performing to packed audiences seven shows a week. A half century later, China-born acrobat and magician Long Tack Sam traveled to major cities with his splendidly costumed troupe.

Skewing toward a broader Western milieu, the rise of vaudeville by the late 1800s saw a number of Chinese American performers on playbills. Although their exoticism was still accentuated, these entertainers nevertheless began to carve out a place on American

OPPOSITE: A late 1930s postcard view of San Francisco's Grant Avenue. The back text reads: "Pagoda-like structures line the streets and strange foods are displayed in the shop windows." Scenic View Card Company.

LEFT: "In Frisco: Give me her weight in opium and she is yours" reads the cover caption from this novel by Chuck Connors (J. S. Ogilivie Publishing Company, 1906). ABOVE, TOP: Chinatown tourists (1880s). Photo by R. J. Waters. BOTTOM: *The Evening Post*, San Francisco, December 27, 1901: "...it has been recognized for years that Chinatown, with its filth and vice, stands a constant and active menace to the health and morals of the people."

THE SLAVE DENS OF CHINATOWN

ABOVE: The Chinatown Knights band included future Chinese Sky Room impresario Andy Wong, third from left (1930s).

OPPOSITE: Early Chinese American singers are featured in sheet music of the period (clockwise from top left): Anna Chang, 1929; Harry "Honorable Wu" Haw, 1925; the Chung Hwa Four, 1918 (inset photo enlarged for visual clarity); Chee Toy, 1914.

stages with their interpretations of Western culture. Popular acts included the Chung Hwa Four, a barbershop quartet; female vocalists Anna Chang and Chee Toy; singer and actor Harry "Honorable Wu" Haw; and the Musical Mandarins, called "China's Greatest Jazz Band" even though it originated in California.

Post-quake San Francisco Chinatown aimed for a different kind of entertainment, catering mostly to visitors to the neighborhood. Following a trend in the city, the district became the home of several dine-and-dance clubs, such as the Mandarin Cafe, the New Shanghai Cafe, and the Grand View Hotel's rooftop Chinese Tea Garden, whose brochure promised "a taste of China with all the delightful Chinese dishes, the pleasure of having attractive and demure Chinese girls serving, and an ideal place for dancing." Among the bands that supplied dance music at the Chinese Tea Garden were two Chinese American groups: the Musical Mandarins and the Chinatown Knights (more on the latter to come). In due course, these dine-and-dance clubs' heyday was short-lived, and by the late 1930s their names had largely disappeared into memory. But the spaces they left behind would find new tenants soon enough. ●

LEFT: The Musical Mandarins toured the vaudeville circuit from 1927 to 1929. L–R: David Sum, Ed Chin, Wayne Tom, Gum Loew, and Harry Wong. ABOVE: Advertisement for the Musical Mandarins' appearance at the Los Angeles dance palace Solomon's (ca. 1927–1929).

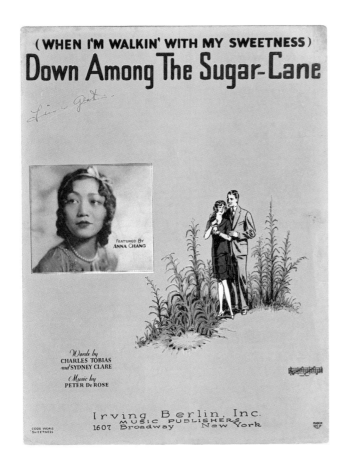

San Francisco Chinatown Dine-and-Dance Clubs

CHINESE TEA GARDEN, 605 Pine Street

MANDARIN CAFE, 400 Grant Avenue

NEW SHANGHAI CAFE, 453 Grant Avenue

TOP RIGHT: The New Shanghai Cafe, site of the future Club Shanghai nightclub (postcard postmarked September 24, 1934). BELOW: The Mandarin Cafe, site of the future Kubla Khan nightclub (clockwise): Postcard, Curt Teich and Company; club exterior; club postcard (Curt Teich postcard 1926; other two items 1920s).

MANDARIN CAFE, 400 GRANT AVE., SAN FRANCISCO, CALIFORNIA.

MANDARIN CAFE

Bush and Grant   San Francisco   Garfield 6464

"The only and finest Restaurant of its kind in the world"

Dine and Dance

Chinese and American Menus

Business Luncheon **.60** 11 to 2:30	Table d'Hote **Dinner** **$1.25** 5 to 8:30	Afternoon Tea **.50** 2:30 to 5

After Theater Supper Specials
A la Carte at all hours

Dancing

Music by
Mandarin Orchestra
Tea Dance Saturday Afternoon 2:30 to 5

The Famous Yee Woo Yuen Trio
12 to 2 Daily, Sunday 5 to 7

Booths, Private Dining Rooms, Mah Jong Parlors
and Banquet Halls for Every Occasion
Peking's "Forbidden Palace" and the Famous
"Hangchow Tea Garden" are Reproduced

ENTRANCE TO GRAND VIEW HOTEL AND CHINESE TEA GARDEN

COZY CORNER IN THE BRIGHT CHEERFUL CHINESE TEA GARDEN

Ideal for Banquets as above picture shows, with room large enough to accommodate many couples for dancing—The picture below illustrates how much pleasure is awaiting those who wish to pass an enjoyable evening dancing. The Paganini Violin Orchestra supplies the latest dance music at the will of the guests.

Real Wholesome Fun Awaits the Visitors to the Chinese Tea Garden

THE MANAGEMENT invites special supper dance parties. The management is prepared to take care of special dinner dance parties with either Chinese or American dishes. Phone **China 1156** a day in advance in order to insure best service.

AFTERNOON TEA for that out-of-town friend or a special party for the kiddies at the Chinese Tea Garden offers novelty and real wholesome enjoyment. The kiddies can dance to the entrancing music of the famous Paganini Violin Orchestra.

CASHIER'S DESK WITH SODA FOUNTAIN IN FRONT

THE BEAUTIFUL PEACOCK WINDOW MAKES A PICTURE BACKGROUND

The Grand View Hotel's Chinese Tea Garden was the site of the future Chinese Sky Room nightclub.

Clockwise: Brochure (early 1920s); postcard, Curt Teich and Company (1927); postcard back (1927); postcard, Stanley A. Piltz Company (postmarked November 20, 1936).

From Village to City: Chinatown's Nightlife Evolution

ABOVE: Charlie Low at his Chinese Village cocktail lounge (ca. 1936).

OPPOSITE, TOP: The Cathayans in Watsonville, California (l-r): David Sum, Dudley Lee, Frances Chun, Joseph Sum, Fred Wong, G. Lee, Ted Lee, Ed Jung, Bob Wong, Fred Wong, Bill Chan, Willie Lee, Ed Quon, Ken Lee, and Fred Young (September 5, 1938). MIDDLE LEFT: Chinese Skyroom ad with Andy Wong (1940s). MIDDLE RIGHT: The Cathayans, with Dudley Lee at the mic, far right (late 1930s). BOTTOM: The Chinatown Knights, with Andy Wong, third from left (mid-1930s).

Of the various characters who came in and out of San Francisco's Chinese American nightclub scene, few were more colorful than Charles "Charlie" P. Low. Born in Nevada as the youngest of seven children, Low arrived in the Bay Area in 1922 at age twenty-one. He displayed a talent for business, initially in real estate, and then in stock trading. His new wealth gave the young Chinese American considerable mobility in a city where being Chinese was often a liability; when white landlords refused to rent him property in the mid-1920s, Low bought the corner of Powell and Washington and built his own five-story Low Apartments instead. The 1929 stock market crash nearly wiped out Low's early fortunes, but the end of Prohibition in 1933 laid the foundation for his next venture: the Chinese Village, Chinatown's first cocktail bar.

"Chinese people don't drink hard liquor," or so Low was warned by the Chinatown establishment. They thought the bar was doomed to fail and condemned it as immoral, going so far as to ban Chinese women from patronizing it. Low shrugged off the criticisms: "The old-fashioned Chinese in Chinatown had no foresight," he complained. "They're satisfied in their little herb business, run it for maybe thirty, forty years, but I'm a little different." In the end, the Chinese Village's success didn't require heavy neighborhood patronage; it was the "white trade" that buoyed the bar's business. They came partially for the alcohol but also for the in-house entertainment: pianist and singer Li Tei Ming, who would eventually become the second of four Mrs. Charlie Lows.

As the Chinese Village enjoyed standing-room-only business on a regular basis, a new Chinatown quickly emerged. After the Chinese Village's start on November 12, 1936 (incidentally the same day the San Francisco–Oakland Bay Bridge opened), it was followed by the Chinese Pagoda, the Jade Palace, the Twin Dragon, the Ricksha, and two bars that survived into the twenty-first century: Li Po and the Buddha Lounge. Chinatown nightlife was spicing up and Low crowed, "Chinatown itself had to swallow the words they predicted against me."

Even though the bar was successful, Low was dissatisfied. The space was small and he wanted something grander, a place where he could entertain his friends and business associates in style. Li Tei

Ming had larger ambitions too—a bigger stage for herself—and she urged Low to open a nightclub, one stocked not only with Chinese staff and cooks but also Chinese entertainers. It would be a premier showcase for Chinese American talent from Chinatown and beyond.

The potential had been there all along. The Chinatown population had for many years filled ballroom dancing venues; neighborhood organizations like the YWCA also organized regular dances that drew a Chinese crowd. By the late 1930s, Chinatown boasted two homegrown dance orchestras, the Cathayans and the Chinatown Knights. The latter included a trumpet player named Andy Wong, who, in 1937, joined with family members to take over the Grand View Hotel's rooftop Chinese Tea Garden, where his band had performed. The plan was to convert the space into Chinatown's first full-fledged nightclub—complete with a floorshow. Renamed the Chinese

Sky Room, Wong's new venture opened on New Year's Eve of 1937, a fitting date to usher in the Chinese American nightclub era.

Wong was first, but Low was in hot pursuit with his own nightclub plans. And not surprisingly, his ambition was too big for Chinatown—literally. He couldn't find a location grand enough in the neighborhood, so he looked elsewhere in the city, eventually landing at 363 Sutter Street, between Stockton and Grant. The space had once held the Aladdin Studio Tiffin Room, a tearoom that had already exploited a Chinese motif and Chinese waitresses. Its location was perfect in many ways: close to Chinatown, yet also a mere block from downtown's fashionable Union Square, giving the club an added sense of elegance. It also soothed the delicate nerves of white tourists who thought Chinatown proper was filled with opium dens and hatchet-wielding tong members. Symbolically, the

location mirrored Low's crossover vision for the club: neither fully Chinese nor white but straddling both realms.

All he needed now was a name, and Low delivered a beauty: Forbidden City. He chose to name the club after the emperor's compound in Beijing, where no commoner could ever expect to enter. Low himself once joked to the press, "My babies [showgirls] are forbidden to say 'Yes.'" When he was a special guest on the Arthur Godfrey CBS radio show in New York, he explained, "Mr. Godfrey, my beautiful Oriental girls—look but don't touch!"

In reality, recruiting showgirls proved to be no laughing matter. Both Low and Wong found that if Chinese elders had moral misgivings about a bar peddling hard liquor, they absolutely balked at the idea of a club where their daughters would wear makeup and false eyelashes while dancing in flesh-baring costumes. Male performers also drew derision, being labeled as "sissies," a thinly veiled code for homosexual. When these nascent clubs began to advertise for talent auditions, local Chinese Americans hesitated to answer the call.

Dancer Jadin Wong, who was part of the Forbidden City's original lineup, remembered, "We used to get letters—Chinese people telling us that we should be ashamed of ourselves doing what we do for a living, dancing in a nightclub, showing our legs. They looked upon us as loose characters and whores. Now, if we were whores, we wouldn't have to work that hard to get very little money from Charlie Low!"

In the City by the Bay, it was Low's club that became forbidden, at least for conservative Chinese locals. Undeterred, Low simply recruited talent from outside San Francisco. Jadin Wong, for example, came from Stockton; others came from smaller California cities such as Marysville, Isleton, Salinas, and Visalia. Farther-flung entertainers hailed from Oregon, Arizona, Massachusetts, and even Hawaii. Walton Biggerstaff, who choreographed and produced shows at most of the Chinese American clubs in the San Francisco Bay Area, admitted: "But one of the tricks was you never hired the girls as dancers. You hired them as waitresses, and within two or three nights you kind of coax them to take a lesson with me, as I had my own studio."

Though the Forbidden City and other clubs would bill their entertainers as part of an all-Chinese revue, in reality the casts were drawn from across the Asian diaspora, with those of Japanese, Korean, and Filipino descent all passing for Chinese. The ultimate example may have been Gonzalo Anthony Lagrimas, who was of Portuguese, Spanish, Filipino, and Chinese heritage. He had initially created for himself the stage name "Tony Costa," but when he came to Forbidden City, Low convinced him to dye his hair black, use makeup to alter his eyes, and bill himself as "Tony Wing."

Despite Low's enthusiasm, things didn't go quite as planned when the Forbidden City opened on December 22, 1938. For all Low's efforts, his venture foundered in the beginning. Business was so poor that Low could barely cover rent and electricity bills; paychecks for staff and performers were overdue. What helped turn things around was Low's discovery of a young undergrad attending the University of California, Berkeley: Noel Toy. She had already been working as a model at the Candid Camera, an attraction at the Golden Gate International Exposition on Treasure Island, earning thirty-five dollars a week by letting customers take pictures of her in various "artistic" poses in the nude.

In 1940, Low persuaded Toy to work at the Forbidden City as a "Chinese Sally Rand," a reference to one of San Francisco's most famous burlesque dancers of the era. Unlike Rand, though, Toy lacked formal dance training; initially, her famous bubble dance mostly involved her simply walking around with a giant latex balloon. Jadin Wong, one of the club's more seasoned talents, felt sorry for her and tried to teach Toy some choreography. It may not have mattered, though: male patrons flocked to the club to see a naked Chinese woman perform, eager to confirm the perverse rumors about the genital differences between Asian and white women. It was an unsavory cocktail of racism and sexism, but it was also lucrative. Business soared.

It was at this moment that club manager Frank Huie invited a friend from *Life* magazine to stop by. That led to the magazine publishing a three-page spread on the Forbidden City in their issue dated December 9, 1940. Jadin Wong scored a full-page picture of her "Dance of the Moon Goddess," while other photos showcased Li Tei Ming singing "When Irish Eyes Are Smiling," and, of course, Toy's bubble dance. The magazine hailed the Forbidden City as "the No. 1 all-Chinese nightclub in the U.S.," passing over competitor Andy Wong's Chinese Sky Room. Within weeks, the club went from being desperate for business to needing to turn people away, having captured the imagination of an international audience. Huie remembers: "We had three shows a night and some people get in there at six o'clock and wouldn't get to see the show until eleven o'clock, the last show. We clocked twenty-two hundred [patrons] a day. And the bar was, not to exaggerate, four deep all night long!" ●

OPPOSITE, TOP AND MIDDLE: The Aladdin Studio Tiffin Room, "San Francisco's Most Distinctive Oriental Show Place" and the city's first supper club. Decorated with a Chinese motif, it occupied the future site of the Forbidden City nightclub (postcards, ca. 1921–1925). BOTTOM: Forbidden City opening night ad (December 22, 1938).

ABOVE, TOP: Producer/choreographer Walton Biggerstaff leads a rehearsal at the Chinese Sky Room with (l-r) Robin Wing, unidentified, Vicky Lee, unidentified, unidentified, and Julianne Lew (1940s). Photo by Ivan Essayan. BOTTOM: Noel Toy was discovered by Charlie Low while working as a model for the Candid Camera concession at the Golden Gate International Exposition on Treasure Island (1939).

FOLLOWING PAGES: Noel Toy lifts bubbles *and* business for the Forbidden City, as in this article from *Carnival Show* magazine (March 1941). Mary "Butchie" Ong, Jessie Tai Sing, Kim Wong, and Helen Kim are featured in *Beauty Parade* magazine (November 1943).

EAST GOES WEST

Noel Tay, the featured bubble dancer of the floor show, makes a big hit.

Despite Mr. Kipling, East Meets West in "The Forbidden City" Night Club in San Francisco, and a Gay Time Is Had by All

MAID 'N CHINA

This Chinese doll would make a swell ad for Dresden China. Isn't she Dresden the cutest costume?

Here's Tessie Tai Sug. We wonder if she inspired the famous song, "Chow Mein(y) times Have I said I loved You?"

A New Slant on Beauty

Meet Mary Ong, who dances at Charlie Low's "Forbidden City" in Frisco. Mary's smile proves that she's right Ong the "beam."

For centuries, the Chinese have been great entertainers and just to show you that the standards haven't changed—except for the better—here's a bunch of lovely China dolls. They've all made their mark in show business from 'Frisco to New York, and they're as precious as anything from the Ming Dynasty. In fact, when they Ming, then zing go the strings in your heart. Just a bunch of Toys and gals together. And it's not Occidental that these Orientals are tops in loveliness and talent. Now we can understand why the Chinese built a great wall around China—they probably didn't want to let these eyefulls go. But here they are, Professor, so strike up the band and play that Mandarin, and never mind that play-as-you-go plan. Yowsa gents, if you wanna be right, go Wong!

Horticultural note: Put two Chinese peaches together and you get a pip of an Oriental pair. They're Kimg Wong and Helen Kim of the "Wongettes." They're Wong-derful!

A Razzle-Dazzle Situation: Rise of the Nightclubs

If Chinatown critics had previously hoped for the nightclubs' demise, savvy copycats now couldn't act fast enough to capitalize on their success. Wong and Low had paved the way and were soon joined by other would-be Chinese American "nitery kings" like Wilbert Wong (Li Po and Club Mandalay) and Eddie Pond (Dragon's Lair and Kubla Khan—the latter taking over the old Mandarin Cafe dine-and-dance space).

Then there was herbalist and restaurateur Fong Wan. He presented floorshows at his venue across the bay in Oakland, the New Shanghai Cafe, as early as 1936, although not exclusively all-Chinese. The club featured dancer Jadin Wong one month before she opened the Forbidden City. In 1940, Wan expanded his club and added the Shanghai Terrace Bowl next door with its forty-foot dome to accommodate Chinese acrobats. Wan also acquired the Club Shanghai in San Francisco (which was previously the New Shanghai Cafe dine-and-dance club), and he would even partner with Andy Wong to operate the Chinese Cellar after-hours bistro. Wong himself had his own mini-empire, adding the Club Lido in North Beach and the short-lived Shangri-La nightclub to his Chinese Sky Room.

The rate of new club openings was so rapid that it outpaced the talent pool, and venues had to compete for the same entertainers. Some dancers and singers worked for two or three different clubs on the same night, dashing from one stage to another. Dancer Jade Ling reveled in the flurry: "There were lots, lots of clubs here; the place was jumping. Sky Room, Kubla Khan—I worked them all. In fact, I was doing a single at Forbidden City and doubling at Kubla Khan; I was doing both."

Meanwhile, the San Francisco Chinese clientele was turning out too. Whatever their initial skepticism or misgivings, some patronized the new nightclubs out of curiosity and many came because they simply wanted to have an entertaining evening on the town. It was quite the switch for this newly popular scene, run entirely by Chinese Americans. Where they had once been sideshow freaks, Chinese Americans were now entertainment moguls in San Francisco.

Much as the post-quake rebuilders of San Francisco's Chinatown had hoped, the neighborhood had become a popular tourist destination, and nightclubs played a key role within that framework. Besides the shows, clubs offered other attractions, whether souvenirs to bring home or a taste of "Chinese food you'll never forget!" as the Club Shanghai menu once boasted. (Just to cover all the bases, clubs offered two different menus: one for Chinese food and another for classic American fare.)

Still, the primary draw at the nightspots remained the all-Chinese entertainment revues. Depending on the club, a typical show lasted forty-five minutes, with a mix of chorus lines, singers, dancers, and a novelty act, such as an acrobat or magician. The Forbidden City prided itself on its elaborate thematic productions, many created by Walton Biggerstaff. A Washington state native, Biggerstaff found that whenever he suggested doing a Chinese-themed show, Low subtly rejected the idea in favor of productions with a more Western edge, among them "The Summertime Revue," "A South American Holiday," and "The Gay '90s Revue."

The rise of these Chinese American nightclubs necessitated a delicate dance of their own. Tourists wanted a taste of the exotic, and club owners and entertainers were happy to oblige, recognizing the value of self-Orientalization as a marketing and performance strategy. Yet, they also wanted to prove their American chops. While most of the entertainers stuck strictly to Western outfits, some would take the stage in modified traditional Chinese garb, or use props like fans and gongs and adopted monikers like "the Chinese Bing Crosby," "the Chinese Sophie Tucker," and "the Chinese Frank Sinatra." Once the public took the bait, however, the performers revealed that not only could they sing and dance in the Western mode but they were also just as American as the audience.

Few others perfected that switcheroo as deftly as the husband-and-wife dance team of Toy and Wing (Dorothy Toy and Paul Wing). The duo, sometimes sold as "the Chinese Fred Astaire and Ginger Rogers," had already traveled the world professionally before joining the Chinese American nightclub circuit. One of their more popular routines began with them in elegant Chinese gowns, which they would strip off a few beats into the music to reveal Toy shimmering in a classic taffeta evening gown and Wing all tuxedo-ed up. Rather than the expected fan or ribbon dance, the two would perform a ballroom or tap number, much to the audience's surprise. As Palo Alto–born Wing said, "It was a novelty because we were Oriental. But still we considered ourselves Americans, doing American dancing and trying to be as good competitively, if not better [than white Americans]."

San Francisco Chinatown tour guide Bill Nowak recalls, "It was kind of like a half-and-half—[patrons] expected something more mystical like out of the Orient, and then they got this emcee that's popping the jokes, and Charlie [Low] would say, 'Hi, fellows, how you doin'? Come on in.' And people would be astonished. They felt at home; they loved it. And the mystery was gone—it was like a sigh of relief. It was a razzle-dazzle situation." ●

OPPOSITE, TOP: Lt. Allen Lim and Lilly Chow Lim (front right of table), celebrate their wedding at the Forbidden City (August 1, 1943). BOTTOM: Dragon's Lair ad featuring dancer Mei Lan (photo replaced for visual clarity) (March 18, 1944).

ABOVE: Lion's Den ad (1940s); Kubla Khan ad (ca. 1944); Club Shanghai ad (October 1949).

FONG WAN PRESENTS
San Francisco's Biggest
NITE CLUB SHOW

EXOTIC DANCE TEAM
TALENTED SONGSTERS
MYSTIC MAGICIANS
TERRIFIC ACROBATS

Acrobats and magicians were crowd-pleasers at the clubs alongside singers and dancers. Clockwise from top left: The Mandarins, acrobats, photo by Romaine. The Young China Troupe, acrobats (bottom and middle row); Professor Lee Tai King, magician and fortune-teller (in black garment); May Lee, singer (top left); and the Tai Sings, dancers (top row). The Ah Hings, magicians (photo by Romaine). The Sing Lee Sing Trio, acrobats, photo by Bruce Chin (all photos 1940s).

OPPOSITE: A member of the Young China Troupe performs at the Club Shanghai (1950s). Photo by Ton W. Lee.

The Golden Era: World War II

ABOVE, TOP: Andy Wong, far right, and performers from the Chinese Sky Room raise funds for the USO (1940s). Photo by Grau. BOTTOM: Frances Chun instructs US Army service members on the art of using chopsticks, at the Forbidden City (Signal Corps US Army photo, 1940s).

When the bombing of Pearl Harbor pushed the United States into World War II, the Bay Area became central to the greater war effort. Ports and shipyards operated overtime, the number of war-related factories tripled, the workforce doubled. Servicemen also came in droves, as San Francisco was the last port of call before they shipped off into the Pacific theater. That meant another 1.5 million people moving through the bay for the duration of the war. At times, housing space was so limited that theaters opened their doors to give soldiers and others a place to sleep for the night.

While the war invigorated many industries, the entertainment sector surged in particular. For one, wartime rationing limited the number of consumer goods for purchase, so people shifted their spending to entertainment. Second, for servicemen on the eve of deployment, time spent at nightclubs, theaters, and bars made for a pleasurable distraction from the reality of impending combat and possible death.

The Chinese American community had already been involved in the greater war effort for years, helping raise money through Rice Bowl benefit events to support the Chinese fight against Japanese aggression. Once the United States committed itself to the war, Chinese American entertainers began to donate their talent and celebrity status to the cause. Performers traveled with USO shows and tours, entertained servicemen locally at military bases, and participated in fundraising drives. The military inducted some Chinese American entertainers while others went off to work in the shipyards. At the clubs, performers paid special attention to service members in the audience, sitting and drinking with them between shows, trying to ease their minds from the thought of going overseas to fight.

If World War II fueled business for the Chinese American nightclubs, it also created unexpected racial dilemmas for the talent. Those of Japanese descent found themselves turned away from businesses that were caught up in anti-Japanese sentiment. As a result, many Japanese Americans changed their surnames to Chinese-sounding ones in order to work. That included entertainers Jack Soo (née Suzuki) and Helen and Dorothy Toy (née Takahashi, although Dorothy maintains that "Takahashi" was simply too long and impractical to use in show business).

For Dorothy Toy, her attempts at racial passing had severe consequences when RKO Radio Pictures learned she wasn't exactly who she said she was. Not only did she and her partner, Paul Wing, lose a Hollywood film contract after officials learned that Toy was actually Japanese, but given that she was performing on the West Coast during World War II, she was subject to immediate internment with other Japanese Americans. In order to avoid that fate, she and Wing left the region to start their careers over again.

Toy and Wing were in good company on the road, being two among many Chinese American entertainers who toured extensively in the United States during the 1940s. One popular stop was the China Doll in New York City—the only known club that advertised an all-Chinese cast but was not also owned by Chinese Americans. Started by Tom Ball in 1946, and with shows produced by Donn Arden—the man credited with creating the Las Vegas showgirl persona—the China Doll gave Chinese American performers a place to branch out and showcase their talents in front of a worldwide audience in the Big Apple.

Even then, it was not an easy career. As with most nightclub acts, regardless of ethnicity, Chinese American performers were usually only booked for one-night stands or limited engagements—call it the "Chop Suey Circuit." They had to leave behind the relative security and familiarity of the Chinatown ethnic enclave and dive into the full-blown complexities, contradictions, and prejudices of society in the rest of the country.

The South proved especially challenging, as Chinese American performers confronted stark segregationist rules. Neither black nor white, they didn't know how to respond to separated movie theaters and drinking fountains. One time, singer Toy Yat Mar boarded a segregated public bus and recalled her confusion: "I looked in the rear, I looked to the front. Fortunately there was something open in the middle of the bus...so I sat down. But nobody sat down beside me....They probably had the same thought: 'What is it? It's not white. It's not black.'" Meanwhile, others like Paul Wing discovered that if Japanese people could pass for Chinese, the opposite held true too. He remembered people in the South calling him "Jap" when they saw him on the streets, not realizing they had applauded the same person on stage the night before.

These experiences on the Chop Suey Circuit reminded Chinese American entertainers of their own precarious position in a country wracked by racial inequality. Yet, by going on the road, they were also serving as informal ethnic ambassadors, helping to shift white and black perceptions of Chinese Americans. Dancer Mary Mammon recalls, "When we arrived at some of the small towns, they were even more surprised. I mean, they liked the Chinese people, it seemed, but they pictured them in just certain types of occupations." If the old stereotype was that the Chinese lacked rhythm or talent, these performers altered those beliefs after entertaining audiences with their "razzle-dazzle." Mammon: "We educated the American public to what another race could be." ●

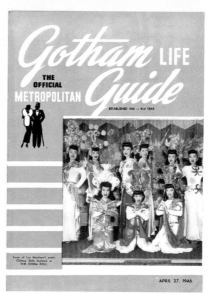

ABOVE, TOP: Performers on the road (l–r): Dottie Sun, Larry Chan, Mary Mammon, unidentified, Jade Ling, Jackie Mei Ling, unidentified, Mai Tai Sing, and Wilbur Tai Sing (mid-1940s). BOTTOM: The cast of New York City's China Doll nightclub are featured on the cover of *Gotham Life* magazine (April 27, 1946).

FOLLOWING PAGES: Lee Mortimer's write-up about the "Yellow Peril" in *Real Screen Fun* magazine (February 1942). Along the top are photos taken at the Chinese Sky Room; owner Andy Wong is featured in the second photo from the left. The article reports that the Forbidden City opened prior to the Chinese Sky Room, however the Chinese Sky Room opened December 31, 1937, and the Forbidden City opened December 22, 1938. Additionally, Noel Toy attended the University of California, Berkeley, not the University of Southern California.

NEW SLANT ON

THE CHINESE QUESTION POSES A NEW PROBLEM FOR THE YOUNG MEN OF MANHATTAN AS ALLURING ASIATICS CAPTURE THEIR HEARTS

Glamorous JADIN WONG was rushed here from the Coast at the behest of Leon and Eddie's. She enjoys the distinction of being half of the first Chinese dance team. MISS WONG'S specialty is a rhumba number, done in Spanish costume.

IF YOU should ask any one of the feminine half of New York what she thinks about the Oriental situation the answer would be, "I don't like it."

But she wouldn't be thinking about politics.

The truth is that the so-called "Yellow Peril" already has engulfed New York. But nicely.

What has happened is this: Some of America's best known swains and wolves have discovered the allegedly superior charms of pretty Oriental damsels and now every Asiatic gal in show business is getting a terrific rush from the guys of the Cafe Society set.

Of course this really is nothing new, because what few American-born Chinese girls there have been in show business up until now, always have found that most of their gentlemen friends were Caucasians. There is, of course, no racial distinction between whites and Orientals, with Asiatics having entree to the nicest places.

In fact one of show business' most celebrated friendships, which lasted through the years, was between lovely Anna May Wong, of the films, and George Jean Nathan, brilliant dean of the drama critics.

Until recently, however, there have been few Oriental gals in the theater world, because of the conservatism of their old folk. The shifting of the spot-light of world affairs to the Orient, has awakened an interest in everything Asiatic, so greater inducements were made to young Chinese to enter show business and within the past few years there has been a veritable flood of slant-eyed dancers, singers, comics and even striperoos.

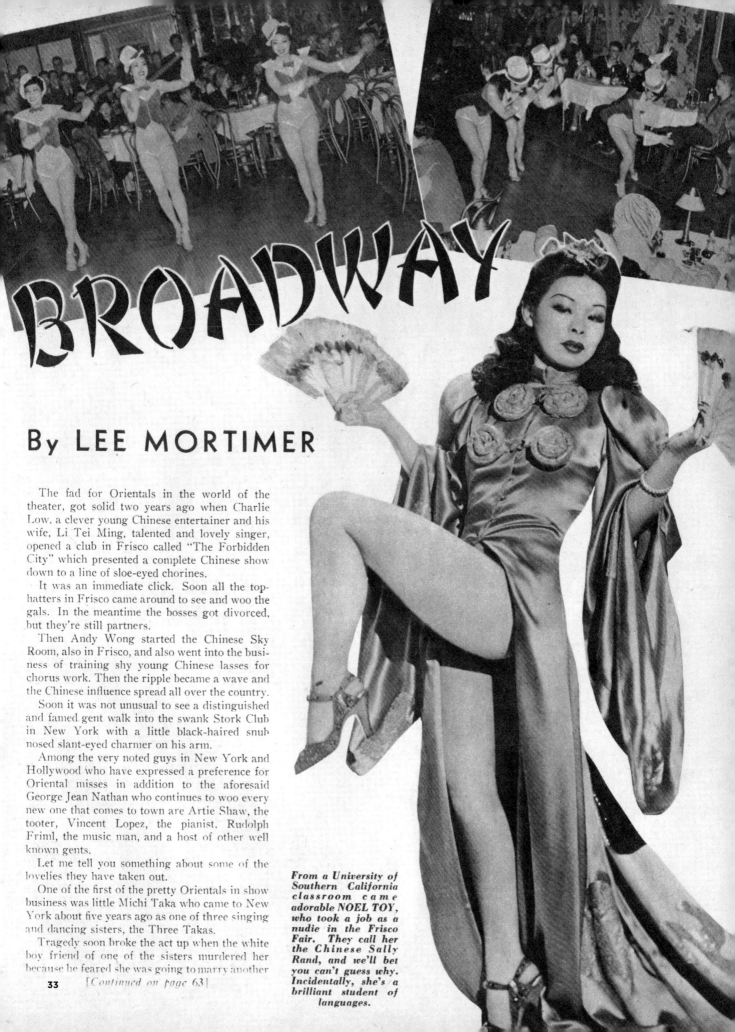

BROADWAY

By LEE MORTIMER

The fad for Orientals in the world of the theater, got solid two years ago when Charlie Low, a clever young Chinese entertainer and his wife, Li Tei Ming, talented and lovely singer, opened a club in Frisco called "The Forbidden City" which presented a complete Chinese show down to a line of sloe-eyed chorines.

It was an immediate click. Soon all the top-hatters in Frisco came around to see and woo the gals. In the meantime the bosses got divorced, but they're still partners.

Then Andy Wong started the Chinese Sky Room, also in Frisco, and also went into the business of training shy young Chinese lasses for chorus work. Then the ripple became a wave and the Chinese influence spread all over the country.

Soon it was not unusual to see a distinguished and famed gent walk into the swank Stork Club in New York with a little black-haired snub nosed slant-eyed charmer on his arm.

Among the very noted guys in New York and Hollywood who have expressed a preference for Oriental misses in addition to the aforesaid George Jean Nathan who continues to woo every new one that comes to town are Artie Shaw, the tooter, Vincent Lopez, the pianist, Rudolph Friml, the music man, and a host of other well known gents.

Let me tell you something about some of the lovelies they have taken out.

One of the first of the pretty Orientals in show business was little Michi Taka who came to New York about five years ago as one of three singing and dancing sisters, the Three Takas.

Tragedy soon broke the act up when the white boy friend of one of the sisters murdered her because he feared she was going to marry another

[Continued on page 63]

33

From a University of Southern California classroom came adorable NOEL TOY, who took a job as a nudie in the Frisco Fair. They call her the Chinese Sally Rand, and we'll bet you can't guess why. Incidentally, she's a brilliant student of languages.

Twilight of the Nightclubs: A Slow Dance

As World War II was a boom time for the nightclubs, the end of the war brought about the opposite result. Effective April 1, 1944, the federal government raised the 5 percent cabaret tax to a huge 30 percent. The impact was immediate and devastating, in some cases tripling operating costs. Club owners reacted by cutting their most flexible expense: the entertainment. Nightclubs canceled floorshows, replaced parquets with dining and drinking spaces, and laid off performers by the thousands. The American Guild of Variety Artists (AGVA) estimated that within a month of the new tax, half of the country's singers, dancers, and other entertainers had lost their jobs or were in danger of losing them.

Unfortunately, the cabaret tax was merely the first of many blows that fell upon the Chinese American nightclub industry. The rush to open a flood of copycat venues watered down the market as a whole, spreading audiences thin. Unionization of staff and entertainers helped protect worker interests but further chipped away at owner profits.

More profoundly, the end of the war massively redirected spending priorities as millions of veterans returned home eager to start families and find some stability; money once freely spent on entertainment was now being saved for homes, cars, and appliances, including a new black-and-white device called the television, which seduced people to stay at home instead of head out on the town.

Meanwhile, San Francisco nightlife was going through its own transformations. In the 1950s, the Beat Generation took over, especially in the North Beach area that bordered Chinatown, leading to a spate of bohemian shops, galleries, restaurants, and coffee houses. By the end of the 1950s, the rise of rock 'n' roll crowded out nightclub musicians in favor of discotheque DJs. Then in the 1960s, the topless-dancer era lit up North Beach in neon, with Carol Doda's Condor Club leading the pack. Grant Avenue was once the premier destination for tourists looking for the exotic; now it was Broadway, just outside of Chinatown's borders, that promised a glimpse of the forbidden.

Club entrepreneurs including Charlie Low, Andy Wong, and Fong Wan kept pursuing new schemes in hopes of staying profitable. In the 1950s, Low and Wong built partnerships with local bus companies to bring tourists to their world-famous venues. Singer Toy Yat Mar laments how the clubs "depended on Gray Line Tours: their salvation, their bread ticket." The Chinese Sky Room surged back during this time, thanks

to the efforts of Dorothy Toy, who took charge of the Sky Room's entertainment, which now included an amateur strip night. Said Toy: "I built that place up so they had three buses coming every night and they had so much business. We were taking the business away from Broadway." Unfortunately, Toy's labors were ultimately all for naught; just as the Sky Room was enjoying a recovery, Wong was forced to shutter the club after losing his lease in 1964, much to everyone's surprise.

At the Forbidden City, visitors trickled through the doors, but not even Charlie Low could recreate the club's previous zeitgeist. Mar pointed out one of the problems: "These people [tour line customers] were just a one-shot deal: businessmen from Dubuque, Iowa, and Omaha, Nebraska." Unlike the earlier generation of patrons who were loyal to the Forbidden City for its retinue of talent, tour customers had no investment in any particular venue; the Forbidden City was just one snapshot stop of many.

In 1962, Low, now in his sixties, was ready to sell the Forbidden City and ease into retirement. A few people from the nightclub contemplated buying it, and in the end, dancer Coby Yee and her family members became the new owners. The tour buses kept coming, and the club added exotic dancers to their lineup, cashing in on the popularity of the topless craze. Eventually, Yee and her partners moved on to other opportunities and the Forbidden City finally closed its doors in 1970. ●

Images from the final years at the Chinese Sky Room and Forbidden City.

OPPOSITE, TOP: Chinese Sky Room postcard, with (l–r) Cynthia Fong, Vi Wong, Kimiko, Paul Wing, Dorothy Toy, Bebe Lim, and Arlene Wing (1960s). BOTTOM: *Pal Joey* (Columbia Pictures, 1957) filmed a scene at the Chinese Sky Room with Frank Sinatra. Unfortunately, the scene was cut from the finished movie and outtakes have yet to surface. This cover photo from the *International Sinatra Society* magazine (August 1997) shows Sinatra and Sky Room dancers during a production break. Clockwise from top: Jean Kakano, Lynne Wong, Vicki Ching, Bebe Lim, Frank Sinatra, Pat Chin, and Barbara Yung.

ABOVE (l–r): "Charlie's Finale?" article from the *San Francisco Examiner* picturing (l–r) Arlene Wing, Charlie Low, Yuki Cho, and (bottom) Noel Toy. (December 15, 1962); a Forbidden City ad featuring new owner Coby Yee (February 1964); backstage at the Forbidden City, dancers Arlene Wing, left, and Sisko Borges wear bunny costumes from the sixties. Photo by Bill Cogan.

Our Own Place: Staking a Claim

ABOVE, TOP: *Flower Drum Song* movie lobby card, with Nancy Kwan, front (Universal International Pictures, 1961). BOTTOM: Jack Soo and Cely Carrillo on the Chicago Playbill cover for the Shubert Theater's production of *Flower Drum Song* (March 1961).

For many Chinese Americans, especially those whose families arrived after the 1965 Immigration Act, these nightclubs were part of a community's forgotten history. At best, some might have seen a quasi-accurate depiction of the club scene in the 1961 movie version of Rodgers and Hammerstein's *Flower Drum Song*. Appropriately enough, cast as the 1961 film's Low-like nightclub owner was actor Jack Soo, a former Chinese Sky Room and Forbidden City entertainer. Soo wasn't the only future Hollywood star who had honed his or her craft in Chinatown clubs: so did actors Sammee Tong, James Hong, Robert Ito, and, most famously, Pat Morita. And then there's 1960s superstar Nancy Kwan, who, although not a veteran of the clubs, co-starred with Jack Soo to portray a nightclub dancer in the *Flower Drum Song* film. Taking the connection nearer to the present, there's David Henry Hwang's 2002 Broadway revision of the musical, which continues to be performed today.

Perhaps the greatest legacy of the nightclubs wasn't in these mainstream crossovers, however. For those who grew up in and around the scene, it represented a crucial coming-of-age for a generation of American-born Chinese. Before that time, the rest of America saw the Chinese as perpetual foreigners, strange and incomprehensible. Closer to home, traditional Chinese families thought show business was morally questionable and professionally risky. As later chapters in this book will detail, the performers at these nightclubs sought to challenge these misconceptions. Part of an overwhelmingly American-born community, they wanted to assert their own American identity. Low himself, never shy about burnishing his accomplishments, boasted, "I proved to [white people] that we were on an equal basis. I put the talent of the Oriental people on the silver platter. I tore down the race barrier in that way."

But the most lasting impact may have been on the performers themselves, and not just the ones who were part of the Chinatown nightclub circuit but those who were inspired by these men and women who dared stake a claim to an entertainment career. Singer Frances Chun summed up the nightclub experience: "When Forbidden City opened, it was really the first place we could call our own—our own place to show off all the Oriental talents. It was hard, you know. It wasn't easy. But somewhere along the line there's always someone to help you break the ice, to give you a chance, to prove yourself—then you're fine. But you have to be given that chance." ●

Frances Chun at the Kubla Khan (late 1940s).
INSET: Frances Chun performs at the world premiere of the documentary *Forbidden City, USA*, Palace of Fine Arts, San Francisco (November 15, 1989). Photo by Bob Hsiang.

39

Interviews

AUTHOR'S NOTE: The following interviews were conducted for the documentary *Forbidden City, USA*. They are primarily with people who worked at the Forbidden City nightclub during the 1940s, the peak period for Chinese American nightclubs (although they worked at other clubs as well, from the late 1930s to the '60s). The interviews have been edited for clarity and flow.

LEFT: Larry Ching at the Forbidden City, with fellow performers (l–r) Mai Tai Sing, Jade Ling, Diane Shinn, unidentified (early 1940s).

Charlie Low—Both Kept His Wife and Let Her Go

Clever These Chinese! Mr. Low, the Night Club Genius, Didn't Mind When Pretty Li Tei Ming Divorced Him, But She Was Too Good to Lose As a Torch Singer, So He Paid Her More Salary Instead of Alimony and Still Gives the Orders

CHARLIE LOW, American-born Chinese wonder man, shocked his countrymen in San Francisco's Chinatown by opening the first cocktail bar in their midst.

When other bars began to blossom all around him, Charlie thought up a bigger and better shock, namely, a Chinatown night club, called "The Forbidden City" after the sacred inner precincts of Peking.

"East is East and West is West, and never the twain shall meet," wrote Rudyard Kipling, but he didn't know about "The Forbidden City," where East meets West with a bang.

Charlie built his night club by adding shock to shock, bang to bang.

Shock A was Li Tei Ming, the owner's wife and a rarity if there ever was one—a Chinese torch singer!

Miss Ming, of whom more will be said in a minute, was the cornerstone of "The Forbidden City."

Then, poring over the "take," Charlie decided that a new shock was needed (shock addicts are not unlike other kinds of addicts: the dose always has to be increased).

So next appeared not only Miss Ming but also a chorus line of beautiful Chinese girls—the first all-Chinese chorus in history and, to put it mildly, a wow.

In China itself it was only comparatively recently that women were allowed to appear in public spectacles at all and when they did they had to act with the greatest dignity and decorum.

Which distinguished them from Charlie's chorus. These girls didn't hide their oomph under a bushel and they accounted for another big boom in the business—followed in due time by another slump.

Something really terrific was needed now, and once more a resourceful Charlie turned up with the goods, in the person of Joy Ching, a lovely Chinese gal who didn't mind in the least doing a Sally Rand—with or without bubbles.

She, too, was an historical first, a giraffe like the farmer who, on seeing a giraffe for the first time remarked: "There ain't no such animal," the customers just sat and stared.

A lot of them still feel this way about Miss Ching, but some of the native Chinese aren't sure but that Charlie has done the impossible by topping her with still another shock.

The sight that makes them wonder seems comparatively tame to a Western eye; it's that of Charlie himself and Li Tei Ming, his torch singer, hobnobbing at the microphone, or one of the tables.

And the reason Eastern eyes goggle at

with a party of friends, she happened to drop into his cocktail bar.

The moment Charlie learned that she had been singing with Earl Carroll and on the RKO circuit, he invited her to do a number for his clients. She was such a hit that he decided it might be worth while to explore the situation further.

Six months later the exploration ended in a wedding.

A slight difference of opinion promptly made itself felt between the newlyweds. Marriage to Li Tei Ming, it seemed, meant giving up her career, settling down and having children.

Charlie, for his part, confessed to dreams of a houseful of children, but he was not anxious to have them materialize on him—not for a while at any rate.

Li Tei Ming couldn't figure a way out of

in hard cash, and he has a clear title to the night club.

Meanwhile, he loyally stands by at the microphone and leads the applause when she sings. Their only concession to criticism has been to refrain from going out on dates together.

the impressive list of his activities includes engineering, law, merchandising, real estate, brokerage, politics, golf and polo—and he's been a success at all of them.

Born and brought up in the small frontier town of MacDermitt, Nevada, about 40 years ago, he picked up his three R's in the local ...

So he Chinese and, are shock, t

Ville become Chines

Charlie Low, Chinese Edition of the American Dream, in One of His Many Activities—Master of Ceremonies At His "Forbidden City" Night Club.

Even More Intriguing to a Chinese Eye Than Joy Ching's Dance, Is the Sight of Charlie and Li Tei, His Ex-Wife, Hobnobbing at the Microphone.

Joy Bubble All-Chi At Cha Where With Be

boa for gly we Chi

Charlie Low's
FORBIDDEN CITY

Charlie Low

1901–1989, Owner, Forbidden City

Excerpts from interviews conducted on
November 25, 1985; December 2, 1985; and September 23, 1988.

I was married four times. My first wife passed away, the other three ended up in divorce, and now I live with a Korean girl half my age. I can't live with them or without them. I met four of the prettiest girls in the country and I have one living here. She's in the bedroom now. She's around forty, a lovely girl. And I'll soon be eighty-five.

My first wife was Minnie Louie. She was the belle of the San Joaquin Valley, a Fresno girl. I married her around 1931. Within a year and a half she passed away, meningitis, came back from the Chinese theater and that was the end of it. Imagine, I've been going to her grave for some fifty-odd years. I was there within the last three months. She's buried in Woodlawn.

Then I married Li Tei Ming—she was a singer—and then later on we divorced. My third wife was Betty Wong. She was from New York, and that didn't last too long. Ivy Tam was my third wife—fourth, fourth, you're right. She was the belle of Hong Kong; her mother and dad were very popular. And she worked in the Forbidden City too, I might add. First she was in the chorus line and later on she kind of helped me manage the place. She was very handy, very likeable. She could do practically anything. She had a lot of friends and she could make friends quickly.

I was an Oriental—not much education—but I could do things that the college boys could not do in respect to getting business and maintaining it and broadening it. Maybe through just the way I look, just the way I talk—that is called charm. I'd meet a guy and talk with him a few minutes or a nice-looking woman...she'll remember me a thousand years! With [only] an eighth-grade education, I've dealt with famous people. I met some of the biggest people in America in my place: Adlai Stevenson. Pat Brown. Earl Warren, Chief Justice. Well, you can't rub elbows with higher people in the United States, [but] I'd walk up to them— I can talk about anything to them.

The world of sports? I'm quite versed. Business? Insurance? Real estate? I was manager of the stock and bonds exchange from 1927 to 1929. Branch manager for Russell Caldwell and Company Investments, and they were members of the San Francisco exchange, associated with the New York Stock Exchange. No matter what those people wanted to talk about, I'd know something about what they were talking about. Although I might not have the vocabulary of a college professor, I don't need that, I have other charms that invite praise—natural ones.

OPPOSITE: Article from *The American Weekly* (May 24, 1942). BACKGROUND: Details from a Forbidden City menu (1940s).

ABOVE, TOP: Charlie Low is interviewed by the author at his home in the Low Apartments, San Francisco Chinatown (November 25, 1985). Photo by Arthur Dong. BOTTOM: Charlie Low photo (1940s), autographed to the author.

I did things that Orientals have never thought to do. First [Chinese] polo player the world has ever known was Charlie Low the Oriental guy. I raced a string of thoroughbreds with reputation, raced in all the major tracks in California: the Santa Anita, the Hollywood Park. I was accepted everywhere: Del Mar, Bay Meadows, and so forth. And then I broke harness horses. No Oriental living had driven horses—I have. Those are the reasons I was more outstanding. I hate to say this—sounds egotistical, it's true.

It's in black and white: "Playboy of the Eastern World." Oh, yeah, there was a big story written about me in *True: The Man's Magazine*. "Playboy of the Eastern World" was the title of the story. There's your proof—big story. It was about my ranch and my summer home and my polo ponies, my pheasants, and so forth. Quite a story, written by Dugal O'Liam.

I am from McDermott, Nevada. I was born June 9, 1901. McDermott, Nevada, is eighty miles directly north of Winnemucca, Nevada, Humboldt County. I was born the seventh child of a family of seven. And since all these years have passed, they have all passed away; I am the only living soul of the Low family clan. My

BELOW: Article from *True: The Man's Magazine* (September 1947). Top right photo: Charlie Low performs at the Forbidden City's "Gay '90s" show; caption reads: "Among night club novelties, Charlie introduced the communal-singing mike." Other photos shot at Forbidden Acres, Low's estate in Pleasanton, California. Bottom right photo (l–r): Dottie Sun, Charlie Low, Vicky Lee, and Diane Shinn; caption reads: "His 'babies' romp at Forbidden Acres, luxurious Low estate on a hilltop."

Good-time Charlie—himself a rare bird in several enviable ways —fondles a prize Sea Bright bantam rooster on his home bar.

Playboy of the Eastern World

BY DUGAL O'LIAM

San Francisco's Charlie Low is the Oriental Billy Rose, complete with swimming pool and cheesecake. But did Billy Rose ever own polo ponies?

Among night club novelties, Charlie introduced the communal-singing mike.

Listed as a four-goal man on the San Francisco polo team, he'll settle for two.

His "babies" romp at Forbidden Acres, luxurious Low estate on a hilltop.

You climb a wide stairs from Sutter Street in downtown San Francisco. Your nose takes in an incense so suggestive that it would bounce a jaded Oriental potentate over the Great Wall of China. Your feet sink into the green velvet carpeting up to your Oxford tops.

At the top of the stairs you meet an atmosphere of mysterious expectancy and several entrancing visions of femininity with ebony hair piled fantastically above demure olive features. These almond-eyed Venuses move past you in gowned grace that reveals only pulchritudinous perfection.

They will be on their way, no doubt, to a fifty-foot bar decorated with the most wondrous Siamese fighting fish

you ever beheld, all glaring ominously from crystal insets in the gleaming teakwood. There they'll probably have a lime coke, but nothing stronger. They'll be members of the chorus in the night club named Forbidden City, which is where you'll be.

After you follow them into the bar and listen dazedly to their soft, low voices, you may take time for a look around. You'll find the lights in the lounge very subdued with bartenders to match and the customers sitting comfortably in deep, upholstered chairs, acting pleased and decorous. Beyond a tier of windows you will see the main dining room and $150,000 worth of Chinese-motif decora-

tion with a *piece de resistance* consisting of a golden joss, or Chinese idol, backed by a bulbous moon of alternating rose and jade.

About this time a little guy, 5-feet-5 and stocky, dressed in soft gray gabardine suit and hand-painted tie with blue background, may swim into your ken and, whether he knows you or not, greet you with "Ah-low, ow-yoo?" and a semicircular grin.

You'll observe no wrinkles on his brown features, no gray in his blue-black, carefully barbered hair. You will notice that his eyes twinkle youthfully and that his step is as springy as a sponge cake. You'll learn eventually that he's Charlie Low, owner of the most fabulous Chinese cabaret in the world, polo player, sulky-racing champion, game-bird fancier, philanthropist and general Man-About-Chinatown and other points.

You may also learn that, although he looks 35, he actually is 46 and admits it and that he is in the night-club business because he grew weary of being fleeced in Occidental booby traps and watching others louse up the master-of-ceremonies profession. You'll find that he's his own m. c., a smooth dancer, fair harmonizer and a sort of Billy Rose of Cathay-in-America. As a top night-life showman, he picks performers, among whom his principal male singer is likely to be the Chinese Frank Sinatra and his leading female vocalist the Chinese Kate Smith, or something.

After a while, when you get back to your drinking because the little ladies have gone off to get ready for the floor show, you hear a fanfare from the orchestra beneath the golden joss, and there will be Charlie out on the floor in Colonna mustache and Steve Brodie suit wrestling with a microphone and urging one and all to enjoy his Chinese Gay Nineties Revue, plus the enchanting talents of his damsels in specialties.

He has the *savoir-faire* of a Chevalier, although he giggles incessantly because he's enjoying his own entertainment and giving his customers their money's worth, which will probably bring them back again. He smiles constantly at his babies, as he terms all his chorus girls, whom he likes and makes his special pets.

About now, eight black-eyed delicacies wearing those Empire State Building coiffures and nothing else worth mention-

dad was born and raised in the village in Canton and he came over here at the age of three, and that was one hundred fifty years ago or more. And then he worked on the railroads—mining and so forth. And one time he worked for Miller [and] Lux, the land and cattle company. They are big landowners; they own property from the Canadian border to the Mexican border. My dad wasn't educated, no chance for education.

Then he came down to San Francisco and met my mother. My mother was a San Francisco–born Chinese girl from the Chu family. Her mom and dad came from China. When she married she had to go up to the mountains. Frontier days, she had no choice; the husband took her with him. Then my mother and dad started a little store. The year was 1885, started the store in McDermott, Nevada, which is eighty miles off the railroad.

Because my dad had small connections with Miller [and] Lux—foremans and ranchers and so on—he had access to sell merchandise to the cowboys and cowhands. And then we ran a peddling wagon: three-quarter-ton Studebaker wagon with a covered top and all locked cases of merchandise. So we had a little bit of everything—tobacco, candy, dried goods, boots and shoes—everything that the ranchers and cowboys would need. And my dad would go peddling from one ranch to the other, made a living that way. It grew larger and larger and we sold it in 1921.

So for thirty-five, thirty-six years my dad and mother lived in the wilderness up there in the mountains, eighty miles off the railroad. We used to get our mail twice a week by stagecoach, and everything that was sold in the town of McDermott was freighted in by mule team. There's no doctor in McDermott even. A lot of times during those years I would run a little delivery; I would take injured people from the ranches to the town of Winnemucca for medical care. Oh yeah, I made quite a bit of money running an auto service; I'd go way up in the canyons to pick up these injured people.

I was considered one of the best drivers in northern Nevada because it was very difficult, there were no roads. You think there're roads like now? Cow paths, high centers, and rocks and everything. And your tires, you think you'd have tires mounted like today? Pincher tires. Take the tire off and repair it and pump it up yourself in these dusty mountain roads. Rocks and everything. Hardship, hardship.

Those years during my early life, the Chinese men wore pigtails. I can remember the day my dad cut his queue off. I would say 1908 or '07; he died in 1909. We were the only Chinese family within the radius of a couple of hundred miles. That's very remote country. Very few Chinese survived up there because you're the only ones. But there were possibly one hundred in Winnemucca, Nevada, mostly men. They worked as cooks or so forth in the summer months during the haying time, at all these ranches.

ABOVE, TOP: Charlie Low dons traditional Chinese clothing and writes calligraphy in this publicity photo taken at the Forbidden City (1940s). BOTTOM: Low with his polo ponies, Tar Baby and American Girl. Photo by Moulin Studios (1940s).

MANDARIN CAFE

Bush and Grant Ave.   Garfield 6464

Wednesday, Aug. 19th, 1925

TODAY'S SPECIALS

Oyster, Shrimp Cocktail	.40
Lobster Cocktail	.60
Cream of Tomato	.25
Consomme	.15
Chicken Halibut or Sole	.75
Pork Chops, Breaded	.65
Crab Egg Foyoung	.65
Capon Fricassee	.85
Chicken a la King	1.00
Almond Chicken Chop Suey	1.00
Roast Squab, Chinese Style	1.10
Subgum Chicken Chow Mein	1.00
Prime Ribs of Beef	.75
Beef Chop Suey	.70
Roast Chicken	.85
Mashed Potatoes	.15
Baked Potato	.25

DINNER 1.25
5 to 8:30

Cantalope en Supreme

Cream of Tomato
Consomme, Julienne

Mammoth Dills

Broiled River Salmon, Brown
Butter
Lobster Egg Foyoung

Chow Mein, Mandarin
Roast California Chicken,
Currant Jelly

Roast Sirloin of Beef
Grilled Dinner Steak,
Hollandaise
Fine Cut Chicken Chop Suey

Corn on Cob Brown Garnets
Hearts of Lettuce a la Russe

Strawberry Short Cake
Orange Sherbert
American Cheese

Tea Milk Postum Coffee

LUNCHEON .60
11 to 2:30

Scotch Broth
Hearts of Lettuce 1000 Island

(Choice of one)
Egg Foyoung
Fried Rex Sole, Meuniere
Bacon and Eggs, Country Style
Paprika Veal Cutlet, Egg
Noodles
Ox Tail Saute, Vegetables

Chow Mein or Chop Suey
Baked Potatoes
Mashed Squash

Stewed Prunes
French Pancake
Ice Cream and Assorted Cakes
Swiss Cheese

Milk Coffee Postum Tea

(The above Luncheon with
Half Squab Chicken, $1.25)

DESSERT, SALADS, DRINKS,

Club Sandwich	.50
Chicken Salad Sandwich	.40
Combination Salad	.40
Fruit Salad	.40
Chicken Salad	.50
Strawberry Shortcake	.25
Pies, per cut	.15
Cakes, per cut	.15
Watermelon	.15
Cantaloupe	.15
Ice Cream	.15
Sundaes	.25
Ginger Ale or Beer	.25
Coffee, per cup	.10
Tea, Postum	.15

For Other Items see a la Carte Menu

ABOVE: The Mandarin Cafe interior and menu, from a postcard menu (1920s). Charlie Low waited tables at the Mandarin Cafe when he first arrived in San Francisco. The dine-and-dance club would eventually become the Kubla Khan nightclub.

There was a Paiute tribe of Indians at Fort McDermott—that was a huge Indian reservation just six miles from downtown McDermott, Nevada. They would buy from us because we were Orientals, and Paiute look something like we do. And they would feel more at home when they came into our store than in the white stores or the Basque stores.

My mother spoke Paiute very fluently. I myself picked up a lot of stuff because you do it through waiting on the trade. They wouldn't know what to call the article in English, so they'd keep repeating it in Paiute, and sooner or later you'd find out what they need, what they want—Pidgin English. Our biggest trade was from the Paiute Indians, and they were very handy and they did our washing and cut the wood— sagebrush wood that we'd burn during the winter months. They were a handy people to have around, and very peaceful, nice people.

I can speak Cantonese fluently because of my mother and my dad. And then naturally, we being Chinese, we ate Chinese food at home every day in McDermott. We had a big garden and we would grow our own. All right, now, we had a big place: we had eighty-eight acres and wells and gardens and everything. And we raised chickens, a lot of chickens, milk cows, and horses and pigs. We had pigpens and pigeons. We were almost self-sustaining, and a lot of the stuff was dried and kept.

And then we'd get our ingredients that we put in different dishes from San Francisco—the dried stuff, like black beans and so forth, and Chinese canned goods—a lot of that. And then we'd open it up and mix it with vegetables—whether it be pork or beef; a lot of pork and beef up there—that's beef country.

Now, during those years, that era, there was a lot of race prejudice. Imagine, the Indians don't have a race prejudice, it's the whites; the whites go back to the white store to buy. There was really never any real protests or outright prejudice against us, they just didn't buy from us, that's all. We would feel it that way.

But we were very lucky. My mother and dad were well liked by the two leading families of that community. Mr. and Mrs. Alfred E. Wilkinson had a ranch up there, the Tenmar Ranch. They were very influential and very well liked. And over here was the justice of the peace, William Miner; he and Mrs. Miner were also very fond of my mother and dad. It was through those two avenues that nobody else dared to intimidate us in those ways—because the two leading families of that valley, which was called Quinn River Valley, were my dad and mother's best friends.

I went through grammar school from first grade through the eighth grade. There were never more than sixteen or eighteen kids in the school—every year the same ones. [It was a] little schoolhouse: two Chic Sale toilets [outhouses] in the back and over there was the barn for the horses. The children had to come from the little ranches three, four miles away and they'd come on horseback or little buggy, and horses would have to be put in the barn during those few hours of school. Imagine one little schoolroom from first grade to the eighth, all those years. And we literally had only one teacher that taught all those grades and her name was Vern Hayward. I remember quite well.

My brothers and sisters would get along pretty good. They would go to the town dances every now and then; on Saturday night there would be a dance. They didn't date much. I don't think my sisters wanted to date white people; there weren't many eligible young men then. My mother kept them pretty much secluded. Those were matchmaking days. My mother managed to get pictures of available sons-in-law and so forth and she screened them. And through some such method, dates were made and marriages performed—they married and went away.

ABOVE: Charlie Low (far right) in the 1930s, with unidentified men.

My oldest brother was married by matchmaking, no dating. I didn't date either. There were very few people around there—the whole valley, maybe a hundred people—there was no one to date. A couple of ranchers, a couple of cowboys, lots of Indians—that's the population.

My brother Henry and I—he was fourteen months older than I—went to visit my sister who was married to a merchant in St. Louis. But really it was across the Mississippi River, East St. Louis. He had the Paris fashion shop in St. Louis and they had a home out in Forest Park, and Henry and I stayed there one winter. He went to the University of Washington in St. Louis and I went to the YMCA school of auto mechanics. We got a touch of city life.

When we got back to our little store in McDermott, Nevada, we weren't satisfied. A little town [like] McDermott, if you wanted some ice cream, you'd have to go buy some ice and freeze it and ten hours later you'd have to crank it to make it—it's for the birds! We wanted to keep going, so we talked our mother into selling everything and moving away. We insisted we were old enough now and would like to branch out a bit. She was getting old and we convinced her she should live in the city, where there's a doctor. My dad died at the age of sixty-three and we finally sold our store and our property and everything to a Basque named Joanna Kavy.

We moved to San Francisco in the spring of 1922. We came in a Buick touring car. The roads were kind of remote in those days; it took only two days, one day from McDermott to Reno. We'd drive to Winnemucca and I think we stayed all night in Winnemucca.

We liked seeing the Chinese and the few Chinese restaurants—there weren't a lot of Chinese restaurants in San Francisco in '22. I worked as a waiter for a Chinese restaurant called the Mandarin a few years during the time 1922 to '25. [The Mandarin Cafe was a dine-and-dance venue that would eventually house the Kubla Khan nightclub.]

A Home to Live In

'Typical' S.F. Apartment Is Discovered at Last

Charles Low Home Called Dream Come True; Colors Taken From Orchid

By ELIZABETH LAWRENCE

When a gentleman has the numerous accomplishments of San Francisco's Charles P. Low, nothing is surprising. Charlie Low is one of the west's most famous hosts—both professionally and privately. He is well known as a successful business man in the realistic realms of insurance, real estate and finance. For many years he was one of the Bay area's most celebrated polo players. Now he is polishing up his golf.

Among Charlie Low's more exotic accomplishments is an ability to converse—and fluently—in Piute, the Indian language common to that section of northern Nevada where he was born. The Low family were prominent business people there from 1885 to 1922.

Charles Low is that truly typical San Franciscan . . . cosmopolitan . . . sophisticated . . . warmly appreciative of the color and culture of his adopted city. But a sophisticate compassionately aware of the needs of others. As his efforts in behalf of the city's most famous foreign quarter—Chinatown—long have proclaimed.

CONNOISSEUR——

Now to this list of accomplishments must be added one more. That of artist . . . connoisseur . . . collector of beautiful things . . . AND interior decorator.

For in the last eight months, Mr. and Mrs. Low have remodeled

Mrs. Low gives to smaller, upholstered sectional which fills a window in the den-like music room which adjoins the living room.

Here Joyce Low, aged 10, follows the adventures of her favorits television friends. The blond wood TV set is on casters so it can be moved about the room. A blond spinet is a planned purchase—to replace the charming walnut piano now used in this intimate part of the large room.

Mr. and Mrs. Low supervised the design of all furniture custom-made for them. Personally they chose each ornament. Everything from the 200 year old Ming vase, used as a lamp base, to a piece of carved jade, no larger than a coin, which is suspended on a miniature teak stand.

Treasures of the apartment are the series of embroidered Chinese silk panels framed and used as pictures. These show the delicate mauve, lilac, orchid and plum hues which provided Mrs. Low with her color scheme.

Most ingenious are the special storage areas given a home which

DELICATE HUES—The favorite color of Mrs. Charles P. Low is purple. It is theme color for her San Francisco home where a delicate range of the plum, lilac and magenta tones are background hues for custom designed furniture of black glass and carved crystal. Mrs. Low is shown above seated upon a magenta sectional large enough for fifteen guests. Curtains, wall to wall carpeting and cei[l]... in a single orchid, Mr. and Mrs. Low redecorated their ... They applied custom-blended paint themselves; personal every object in their home, which formerly was two separa[te] ...ents. Cocktail table is a modern abstract design in crysta[l]. A 200 year old Ming vase has been wired to serve as back of sectional.

—Photo by San Francisco E[xaminer]

Charlie Low built his own modern apartment building in San Francisco's Chinatown when he faced housing discrimination in the city. TOP: The *San Francisco Examiner* reports that Betty Wong, Mrs. Charlie Low #3 and a club performer, is "seated upon a magenta sectional large enough for fifteen guests" (March 5, 1950). BOTTOM: The Low Apartments at the corner of Powell and Washington Streets, where the building still stands in 2014 (photo ca. 1941).

The main thing was the difficulty in getting a nice place to live; we could not get a decent place to live. First thing that entered into my mind, and my mother's too, I suppose, is that living in San Francisco was so congested, so bad. We come from the country; we lived in spacious places in Nevada. God, twenty acres, a hundred acres...a lot of room. But not in San Francisco.

Now there comes the prejudice: when you go around and apply for a place to rent, they would have signs out, "Apartment for Rent" or "Flat for Rent," but when you applied, they'd look through the door peephole or open the door and see that you're Oriental and literally slam their door in your face. And it's the god's truth, it's happened. A lot of these old Italian people—just ordinary flats, you know; high society people wouldn't rent or even think of living in this neighborhood. But we had no choice.

We lived on 952 Jackson Street for a few years. Chinese owned this particular building on Jackson Street, and when we found out we rented it. And that was a five-, six-room flat. It was fairly nice. It was livable. Then we were on Wentworth Place for a year or two. That isn't Chinatown. Wentworth was pretty nice too; it was livable. Chinese were also living up there in that area. We were used to clean and spacious places, so instead of Grant Avenue and alleys like Spofford Alley, we were up there a little bit and that was a small advancement.

I said to my mother, "Why don't we build our own? We'll be the

46

landlord; let us turn the horse around a bit. We got to do something about it." And we did. So that's how the Low Apartments was born. The Low Apartments sits on two lots and they were in probate and had never been built on since the 1906 fire of San Francisco. So I went ahead and located the owner and so forth, and to make a long story short, bought the lots.

It took us a little over a year to complete everything, from the day we wanted to buy the lot to the completion of the building. January 7, 1927, that's when we finished. Moved in January 7, 1927, and have been here since. The same phone number, sixty years, apartment 51. Had a lot of parties. We were the first ones to build a nice building. It was my mother's money but it was my legwork. Six-story steel-frame building with all the modern conveniences: breakfast nooks and bathrooms and everything else, hardwood floors—very modern. And as it stands today, sixty years later, it's one of the better buildings in Chinatown, where I now live: six-story building and we have thirty apartments. My mother died at the age of sixty-seven after seven to nine years of peaceful living in this building before she passed away— high blood pressure and diabetes.

Immediately after the housewarming—quite a few parties—a fellow named John Wong, who had an insurance firm and employment office, took me in as a partner. I immediately became half owner of this little office; we sold insurance and so forth, handled a lot of insurance on Grant Avenue. And then we had an employment agency. A lot of Orientals were employed in different restaurants and hotels and summer resorts and so forth—immediately went into that. We furnished a lot of fine crews to all those summer resorts in California and northern Nevada for many years. I might say that we had a fine insurance and real estate business in Chinatown, and we handled all the permits for all the Chinese rice wines. Finally, I bought him out and then it was Charles Low Company. It wasn't just one project—project after project.

We were very popular then, even among the Chinese people. We were a welcome addition to the "400 society" of Chinese people; we were invited to all the Chinese parties. Joe Shoong of National Dollar Stores was the king man during that era; he'd invite us to their home and everything. We'd invite him to our apartment and we'd always have a first-class party: live music, three pieces, all kinds of food and liquor and everything. We did things in good style because our heritage demanded it, warranted it.

Never a dull moment! There had not been any bars in Chinatown proper since the fire—1906, the earthquake fire of San Francisco—so

Charlie Low broke barriers in 1936 when he opened the Chinese Village, the first bar in San Francisco's Chinatown. TOP: Low, left, entertains at the Chinese Village (l–r): Cynthia Dong, Mrs. Hayne Hall, Dr. Collin Dong (a partner for the bar), and bartender Hubert Wong (Wide World Photos, November 26, 1936). BOTTOM: Detail from an ad for the Chinese Village (March 1941).

ABOVE: Forbidden City ad featuring Li Tei Ming, a singer and Mrs. Charlie Low #2 (March 1941).

I thought the time would be right to open one, and I did. I opened the first Chinese cocktail bar ever in Chinatown of San Francisco. It took us two or three weeks to build the place, and we opened the same day the Bay Bridge opened [November 12, 1936]. The address is 702 Grant Avenue, and the name of the place is the Chinese Village. Most successful. Dr. Collin Dong had a small financial interest; Dr. Margaret Chung had a small interest. [Dong and Chung were among the first Chinese American physicians to practice in the United States.]

Oh, I had a lot of criticism about it. The old-fashioned Chinese in Chinatown have no foresight. They're satisfied in their little herb business, run it for maybe thirty, forty years, but I'm a little different. I try, step by step, to advance. The Chinese people would say the Chinese people don't drink hard liquor; if they do, they do it at home—and they were totally wrong. Although our trade was not all Oriental, part of it was Oriental, but we catered mostly to the white trade, the trade from the street, so to speak. Mostly Caucasians, some Chinese.

My wife [Li Tei Ming] sang in the lounge, and we had a girl who played the piano and she sang, entertained. It was a small version of a nightclub. And we furnished quite a bit of entertainment, and that caught on and worked out beautifully. In my place it was standing room only. That [bar] was the very first, and within twenty-four months, there were ten other Chinese bars in San Francisco. OK, then following that, all of the cities in California of any consequence had Chinese bars. So I was really instrumental in starting that business. It became a huge business. So Chinatown itself had to swallow the words that they predicted against me.

I got the idea of opening a Chinese nightclub. The idea came through me visiting all the other Caucasian or Spanish or Italian nightclubs in San Francisco. They were all doing good business, and I said, "Why can't I do it? If they could do it, I can do it." San Francisco and other states as well as other cities had not seen a Chinese nightclub with an all-Chinese floorshow, and the time was ripe for something like that. They could go to many nightclubs with other types of white performers in their shows, but to see an all-Chinese show in a Chinese nightclub was something different. Ha ha! Always trying to think faster than the next guy!

My basic clientele would be Caucasian; I catered to the white trade, the American trade. [I told them] if you want to see something different, you've got to come. I felt that I was doing the public, doing Mr. and Mrs. America, a favor by being able to present a show that was different, and to advance the Chinese girls. Not to have them like the old-fashioned days, all bundled up and four, five pairs of trousers and so forth—I wanted to do it in a modern way. We can't be backwards all the time; we gotta show the world that we're on an equal basis. And Chinese girls baring their legs...they have limbs as pretty as anybody else, so somebody has got to break the ice and do it. "I've never seen an

Charlie Low's **FORBIDDEN CITY**
AMERICA'S GREATEST CHINESE NIGHT CLUB!

ADE AND JACKIE MEI LING

TOY YAT MAR • LARRY CHING

THE WING BROS.

DOTTY SUN

BETTY WONG

CHARLIE LOW

ABOVE: Forbidden City postcard (mid-1940s).

Oriental show, I've never seen the legs of an Oriental girl. Let's go!"—that is running though the mind of Mr. and Mrs. John Public.

I married this girl, Li Tei Ming, who was a pretty, lovely, and talented singer. And I said to her one day, "I want to open a nightclub, honey. What do you think about it?"

"Oh honey, Daddy, oh, it's hard work; you're cutting off a big chunk there. I don't know whether you could chew it or not—although you're very active and likeable, and have a nice personality and everything."

I said, "Oh honey, the challenge is very tempting—for you to do your part as a wife and help me, I think we can."

"Do as you wish and I'll do my part. I'll help you as much as I can and I'll sing in the show."

"Well, that's part of it already."

And I said to my wife, "Li, honey, I'm going to look around, find a good location. I'm going to open a nightclub. I'm going to make a lot of money. And the name," I said, "I got it: Forbidden City. I've lived in Detroit, Chicago, and St. Louis for a few years, and every Chinese restaurant is named Canton, Shanghai, Tientsin, and so forth. But none of them Forbidden City: the inner city in Peking where royalty only lived. You've got to be king or queen; all the treasure of the country of China is housed in Forbidden City in Peking."

TOP: Page from a Forbidden City program (l-r): Mae Dong, Rose Chan, Walton Biggerstaff, and Hazel Jay (ca. 1942). MIDDLE: Forbidden City program featuring the Tai Sings, Jessie Tai Sing and Wilbur Tai Sing (ca. 1942). BOTTOM: Charlie Low greets Duke Ellington (1940s).

She says, "Not bad. It's catchy. Anything forbidden is catchy." That's how Forbidden City was born.

I found the location on Sutter Street, 363 Sutter Street, which is in San Francisco, two and a half blocks from Union Square, between Stockton and Grant Avenue. That was outside of Chinatown. I tried to get it in Chinatown, but no building was large enough to house the nightclub I had in mind. I opened it in 1938, December 31. [An ad shows an opening date of December 22, 1938.]

I knew there wasn't a lot of Chinese talent because I would go to different shows where they had vaudeville and not too many acts. I knew I would have a lot of trouble, a lot of hard work recruiting a good Chinese floorshow. At one time I had a big act, husband and wife, a good American team on the American stage: Harry Barris and Loyce Whiteman. I've had talent of different nationalities, it's true, that's one incident. And we had a band and they played for us year in and year out; Joe Marcellino's band was with me for quite a few years. And Joe's brother, Muzzy Marcellino, was one of Art Linkletter's best friends and performers. But the overall picture was the Oriental revue.

I've got to have two singers, a boy singer and a girl singer, and we'd give them three chorus lines. Then I'd have a dance team and then a novelty act, like an acrobat or magician. Pretty well-balanced; that would be my format. Show after show it was more or less on that pattern.

But I'd have to give [Walton] Biggerstaff the credit for helping me put Forbidden City on the map; he set all the routines for my chorus line. We would change the shows every six or eight weeks, and new routines and new costumes for all the chorus line. He's a fine choreographer and he worked with his heart; he was there at Forbidden City for many years, upwards of fifteen to eighteen years, and I give him a lot of credit. He had to come up with something new all the time, and I was very pleased. However, I did have other choreographers for a short period of time in between because twenty-four years [of running a club] is a long time.

The most important act that I ever had at Forbidden City was this ballroom team, the Tai Sings, Wilbur and Jessie. They were comparable to the two leading teams in America; they were comparable to the DeMarcos [and] Veloz and Yolanda. They performed three times a night for quite a few years in the early forties, for six to eight years. My ex-wife, Li Tei Ming, pretty clever girl, she used to do a take-off on Will Rogers. She'd spin a little rope and dish out patter. For an Oriental girl to do that you gotta go a long way and get the laughs and get the respect and the entire feeling of the act.

Larry Ching from Honolulu, fine voice. Now they're two Larrys: One is Larry Chan, he's the Chinese Bing Crosby. Good-looking young kid, softer stuff. Larry Ching could sing the heavier stuff, nice voice. This guy had the better voice, Ching did. Chan was more of the hot stuff, rock 'n' roll. But both had contributed their talents to Forbidden City.

Jackie [Mei Ling] was a dancer, ballroom team. He had different female dancers that danced with him that formed a team. Jackie did his part at Forbidden City, did a fine job. I liked Jackie—worked on and off for me for many years. We readily became a little family; geez, these kids are just like my children. From our bartender to the cooks in the kitchen, busboys, performers in the show—we were one big, happy family.

No place in Europe can you go see a prettier girl than Noel Toy. She was born and raised in Inverness, just over in Marin County, and she was young and beautiful. She was a coed at UC [Berkeley] and she was in the Candid Camera concession of the Treasure Island Fair, 1939 to '40 [the Golden Gate International Exposition], and I signed her up in '41 when the fair closed. [Noel Toy appeared in Forbidden City ads as early as November 1940.] And she became my Chinese Sally Rand. In her presentation, instead of fans—Sally Rand was very famous in those days with her fans from the Chicago Fair—instead of copying that, I used a bubble, a four-foot bubble. It was made of rubber—the balloon dance—but these balloons were big balloons. I don't know why I bought them, but anyway, she would bounce these around—nude, mind you. And we had some good lights, a kind of diffused light, and the presentation was lovely.

Pretty girls dancing, what's wrong with that? My girls were thinly clad, dancing on the dance floor. Although I had nudity in my show, it was done nicely, no vulgarity. It was the highest plane. Everything we've done—everything, I'll emphasize—I've done in good taste. Beyond reproach. That's dance culture, I call it. You understand what I mean?

Forbidden City was the leader of all those other little nightclubs that existed. Sure, they had the right to exist and so forth, but I had the lion's share of publicity and business combined. I gave the public a better show. My personal appearance, it was far reaching, that's why they came there. I used to perform in the "Gay '90s" show. I'd sing with the boys in the trio and I would always dance in the Florodora Sextet. All my friends got a kick out of me on the floor, all dressed up with a gay '90s suit and a handlebar moustache pasted on my upper lip. All my friends enjoyed it and couldn't help but laugh. If I didn't do a thing, they'd enjoy it!

My club itself, the premises, was better than [the others]. Most attractive—the decor and everything...that had a lot to do with it. [Li Tei Ming] did a lot of the painting on art glass. We had a fellow, Bill Jones, an artist, do the walls. We had to drag him. Walls and everything were done by this Caucasian artist—I liked his ideas. But back to my wife, Li Tei Ming, she painted a lot of flowers and little maidens dancing and everything on art glass that was being used in the bar next to the settees. And my publicity was unsurpassed—much publicity. Everything that I did myself connected me with Forbidden City, and Forbidden City is me—Charlie Low himself—that's the reason why.

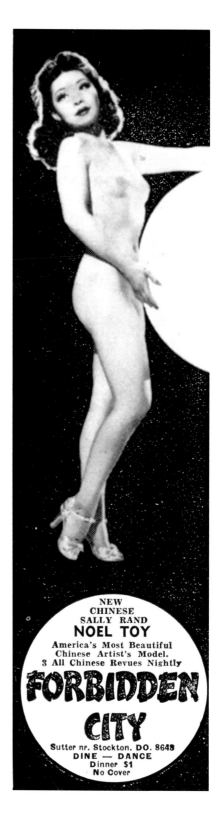

NEW
CHINESE
SALLY RAND
NOEL TOY
America's Most Beautiful
Chinese Artist's Model.
3 All Chinese Revues Nightly

FORBIDDEN
CITY

Sutter nr. Stockton. DO. 8643
DINE — DANCE
Dinner $1
No Cover

ABOVE: Forbidden City ad features Noel Toy, the "New Chinese Sally Rand" (November 1940).

TOP (l–r): Betty Wong, Charlie Low, and Vicky Lee (1940s). MIDDLE: *Pic* magazine reports: "Orientals strut the latest Harlem jitterbug numbers and Cuban Congas with equal ease" (November 12, 1940). BOTTOM: Forbidden City ad featuring Charlie Low (July 1947).

I was the guest of Arthur Godfrey on the CBS show in New York. I was being interviewed by him on the CBS stage, and one thing I said made the whole theater, thousands of people, roar. Godfrey asked what was so forbidden about my place, and I said, "Mr. Godfrey, my beautiful Oriental girls—look but don't touch!" And everyone in the theater roared. You see, look, all this is national stuff. Glamorized the Chinese girl, did I not?

All the important people, I would say, all the top movie stars in Hollywood came to Forbidden City because it caught on. And these people in Hollywood that were in the movies and well known came to Forbidden City to see what I had to offer. People like John Wayne, Charlie Chaplin, and oh, so many. Bill Kaufman was head of the East-West Shrine Game and every year he saw to it to reserve the space for me to entertain the east squad. Year after year, they would come to Forbidden City because they had never seen anything like it in the East, because it did not exist in the East. And not only that, all the coaches of the various universities would come and I had the opportunity to meet some of the finest coaches in the universities in the country, year after year.

Peak would be during World War II. That's the influx of all the army; [San Francisco] is the point where they would embark for foreign soil. We had to have the man hold the rope out there to let so many in at a time. Little by little, business dropped. Cycles work in the entertainment and restaurant world. For so many years, certain types are popular and pretty soon they fade out. Something new comes along, which is only natural.

I was there for twenty-four years and I was kind of getting a little bit tired and I thought I had a chance to sell the club. The people that bought it from me literally begged me to sell them the place when I was ready to sell. Time to retire, but I was interested in other things in life too. And sure enough, before the Christmas of '61, we made a deal and I sold it. December 1961. I owned Forbidden City for twenty-four years, emceed the show literally three times a night for at least twenty-two of the twenty-four years that I owned it. After I sold it to Coby Yee, she ran it for five to six years. So Forbidden City existed for thirty years. [The *San Francisco Examiner* reported that Low sold the club in December 1962 (see article on page 35). Coby Yee and partners date the club's final closure at 1970.]

My health was good then and it's good now. And I was only sixty at that time; today, eighty-four and a half. For a short while I was handling the Oriental business for the Harold's Club in Reno. I would run the Greyhound buses from here to Reno and I had a nice, new office in Chinatown and sold tickets and routed the buses to Reno. I did that for a while. I'm a very restless, adventurous person. Even now at the age of eighty-four and six months, I don't just lay in bed and rot, I do something.

ABOVE: Forbidden City's "Gay '90s" cast: Back (l–r): Dottie Sun, Ginger Lee, Paul Wing (top), Larry Chan, Lily Pon, and Elizabeth Jean. Front (l–r): Diane Shinn, Charlie Low, and Connie Parks (ca. 1955). Photo by Milton Mann Studios.

I'm working now; I'm working for the Oaks Club card room. I work as a prop player, meaning I fill in the games when it's needed. When the game's filled up, I get up. And I'm getting paid for that. Low-ball games in Emeryville. That's a big industry, the card room in California. I have worked for them on and off for fifteen years. I get paid so much a day and I use my own money, so win or lose, it's my own, and I'm being paid to work seven and a half hours, five days a week. Right now, I make $320 a week, take-home pay after taxes, which is something to do. I have a lot of fun; I get paid to play cards.

I think I played a very important part in tearing down the race prejudice here in America, so to speak. Through my coming in contact with the American people I proved to them that we were on an equal basis. I educated the American people [about] the talent of the Oriental people; I put on the silver platter all good Oriental talent that they could see nowhere else. I tore down the race barrier in that way. And the show, the dinner, and the environment in my place proved very successful. Although I'm old as the hills, I enjoyed that life. I was young and adventurous. ●

Arthur –
Thanks for the fond
memories of the yesteryears
They were the greatest!
Love
Dottie

Dottie Sun (Dorothy Sun Murray)

1919–2007, Dancer

Excerpts from interviews conducted on
February 12, 1986, and October 1, 1988.

Butchie [Mary Ong] and I went up to Forbidden City to see a girlfriend rehearse. We went to see Bertha Hing. The lady instructor asked us to pull up our dresses: "Lift up your skirts, girls. Let me take a look at your legs. OK, come on, rehearse them!" We looked at each other and said, "Why not?" For kicks, "Why not?" So we did. [After that,] we started to take ballet lessons because [the choreographer] Mr. [Walton] Biggerstaff was just six blocks away from our house, and we became chorus girls. That's the way our career started. Doesn't sound very true, does it [*laughs*], but that's how it happened! We weren't very experienced dancers, we were just mediocre dancers; I always felt like I had two left feet. To the public we were cute. [*Laughs*] We got away with murder, to tell you the truth!

We started rehearsing and then we would go back to Sammy's to work split shift. Do you know who Sammy Yee is? The judge? A Chinese judge. He owned a restaurant on Polk Street. We had these horrible, grinding hours and we had to work morning shift—work as waitresses—'cause we needed a job. Then we would go at nighttime [to the Forbidden City] and we would come to work with bags under our eyes. Sammy says, "For Christ's sake, you girls, why don't you quit this job? I can get somebody to work." Sammy was so good to us—a friend of the family. So we quit after a year or two; we were just dragging around.

I'm from a little town in the [Sacramento] Delta; I was from a ranch, from Isleton. My father was from Coulterville. My father's store is still standing there; it's in Mariposa County, an old mining town. My great-grandfather built [the store]. It's an old museum [now], sort of a historical place. My father's name is still there: Sun Sun Wo Company.

[When I was growing up], in my days we had segregation. That was Walnut Grove, Locke, and Courtland [California]. We went to school on school buses. My sisters went through it; I went through it. Except high school. High school was the only time we were not segregated, just grammar school. The Chinese, the Japanese, and the Filipinos were in one school. The white and the colored were in one school. The Orientals were segregated. Isn't that funny?

I hated it. Oh, the Japs outnumbered the Chinese real badly. They were mean, they were horrible. Everything was: "Japan's gonna do this to you," "Japan's Hirohito's gonna do this to you." The Japs picked on me and everything. It wasn't because of the war, they were just hateful. They

OPPOSITE: Dottie Sun photo (1940s), autographed to the author. Photo by Romaine.

ABOVE, TOP: Dottie Sun is interviewed by the author at her Sacramento home (February 12, 1986). Photo by Arthur Dong. BOTTOM (l–r): Lily Pon, Dottie Sun, Mary Mammon, and Rose Chan are featured in *Laff* magazine: "A bunch of Wong numbers who are certainly all right…" (June 1948).

Whirling like dervishes, the Tai Sings make a Chinese tail spin.

Page 12

ABOVE: A page from *Peek* magazine shows Dottie Sun performing "Little Egypt" at the Forbidden City (December 1942). INSET: Forbidden City performers (l–r): Fay Ying, Mary Mammon, Dottie Sun, Rose Chan, unidentified, Hazel Jay, Lily Pon, and Mae Dong (1940s). Photo by Romaine.

were terrible; I will never forget it. Japanese Americans. The old people drummed it into the children's heads.

We rode the bus with white friends. When they got to the school they stopped the bus on the white side and we walked over to our side. Of course, the Orientals had a smaller school, smaller buildings, although we had our own basketball courts and baseball diamonds. But they're smaller. Like, instead of having two or three baseball diamonds or so, we had one.

But the funniest thing was the black people went to the white school—that's what got us. Now, isn't that the funniest damn thing? And then segregation made an about-face—they would hate the coloreds now. I don't know why they did that. Now they did away with it. But imagine in those days...segregation. I had to accept it; you had to go to school.

When I was sixteen, I moved to San Francisco and finished my high school there, and after high school, I went to work. Butchie—she and I were living in the same apartment building—she came from Arizona and she didn't know anybody.

[At the Forbidden City] I was pegged to do comic numbers—a half-assed comedian. I'd step out of the chorus to do comedy to fill in, like a substitute. I don't know, I just fell into it, I guess; I just started horsing around. Someone said, "Oh, keep it in, keep it in." I did one number, it was "Cockeyed Mayor." I would cross my eyes like that. [*Demonstrates*] Of course I don't do it very long because it hurts my eyes. And every time the song would mention the Cockeyed Mayor of Kaunakakai, I would cross over like that [*demonstrates*] so you'd see the white of my eyeballs [*laughs*], like that. It looks ridiculous, doesn't it?

I would kind of do a parody of "Little Egypt"—that was for the "Gay '90s" show. I did the tune of *Song of India*, sort of like a belly dance. But I didn't do a belly dance, I just did a regular comedy dance, like a snake dancing, but I'd use my hands like a snake. You know how the hands make the shape of a snake, and how the snake would come after you and you'd go like that. [*Lurches her head toward her hand curved like a snake*] The snake would look at me and I would look at it with my eyes crossed. Biggerstaff taught me those steps.

I thought it would be funny to put a blonde wig on a hat where my snake would be attached to it. And Li-Kar was the one that designed the clothes for me. Yeah, he was the one that designed all the costumes for Finocchio's [a club featuring female impersonators], and he was the one that designed the costume and he didn't charge me one penny, he was such a doll. Charlie [Low] don't pay for any of that stuff. When you are a featured dancer he don't pay for it. Heck no. Very, very cheap.

I hate to say it, Charlie was very cheap. We didn't belong to the union. Then the union got after us—AGVA [American Guild of Variety Artists]. The boys belong to the union—the band boys—so if we did not join the union, they get into trouble; the band boys cannot play for you. Charlie just raised Cain. And the union was right there every night: "You join the union or you don't work." And Charlie said, "Well, kids, you gotta join the union." The union took all our money; I mean, forty bucks was a lot of money to pay out to the union. Heck, we didn't make that much in three weeks. Well, we had our rights, we couldn't be walked upon. If our boss demanded us to do something, we say we will report to the union. And that made him think twice. If you work overtime you get paid overtime, just like the orchestra. That's why we pay union dues.

For a while it was so dead we thought Charlie was going to lose the place. That was

BELOW, TOP: Chinese soldiers are welcomed at the Forbidden City (l–r): Frances Chun, Lt. David Mow, Yu Yeh Chun, and Dottie Sun (August 15, 1946). BOTTOM: Dottie Sun entertains at a party for Chinese American servicemen hosted by Charlie Low at his Forbidden Acres estate. Photo from the *National Police Gazette* (December 1943).

before the *Life* magazine thing came out. Charlie would never have had that advertising. Barney was the PR man and gave us this terrific write-up in *Life* magazine. All of a sudden, business; overnight, people came in buckets.

Then Charlie got wise and he started buying drinks for the press—that was very important. Like Johnny Kan [owner of Kan's Restaurant] and Herb Caen [a *San Francisco Chronicle* columnist]. Johnny Kan knew how to butter Herb Caen. I used to work for Johnny Kan 'cause he was my cousin. He said, "Dottie, if Herb Caen comes in, it doesn't matter if it's a hundred people or two, you always pick up the check." It was always on the house. That's why Herb Caen was always writing about Johnny Kan, and people read about Johnny Kan all the time, and that brought in the business. Everybody reads Herb Caen in San Francisco; that's the power of the press. I told Charlie, "You have to buy the press drinks. It's like a cop on the beat—you got to feed them."

We had a lot of servicemen and we had... would you believe we had padres come up there? They came in every time the ship came in and they become regular customers, ask for us, and we sit down and have dinner with them, have coffee with them. They come up and they dance with us. They don't drink, but they come and they spend money. And we're always glad

ABOVE: Dottie Sun, center, and Mary Mammon with unidentified men at the Forbidden City (1940s). BOTTOM: Mary Mammon (left), Toy Yat Mar, and Dottie Sun in the "Chinese Follies" show for the USO (ca. 1945).

to see them because they're such nice people.

Oh, one night during the evening show, we were doing a sort of showgirl number where we came out in scanty show costumes with the feathers and headgear. And I walked by a table in the front and there was a big family. I stood there and all of a sudden I hear my name being whispered. And I look down and there was my aunt at table length staring at me right at my, well...she sat right there and was looking right up at my belly button. I was so surprised. My aunt was very old-fashioned—I almost fainted dead! She just kind of waved at me a little bit.

And after the show I went and sat with her. She enjoyed the dinner and she was surprised that it was a very decent show, and it was the first time she had ever seen an Oriental show. And she had brought her whole family and the rest of the world too. The first thing I thought about was, "What will my relatives say?" Well, they sort of raised their eyebrows a little, but nothing was said about it. We didn't have anything risqué—except the bubble dancer. But she [Noel Toy] didn't show everything; she was covered up. They're not like American burlesque. They don't come right out and show it; it was just an illusion. Even backstage she was covered up the minute she got off; she didn't parade around so the orchestra boys could see her. She was very modest. It was a place for families and their children to come up for dinner.

I was in a trio at one time. I danced with Jackie Mei Ling and Mary Mammon and we did rather nicely as the three of us danced together. I mean, we practiced a lot. If we miss our turns it's too bad because we had to have a lot of coordination when three people had to dance together. We didn't work too long. We just worked at the Shanghai Terrace, that big place in Oakland. We performed at the Golden Gate Theater; we had an engagement there in '42—one performance. I can remember...yeah in '42, 'cause I can remember *Suspicion* was playing there.

Jackie got mad at me one time. We were rehearsing this number where I would do a slide. You know, where he does a right and a left and I go under his foot—you slide under that foot. Well, I slid too close to his foot and I knocked him over; we both landed on our derriere! His friends were in the audience. He was so mad at me, he wouldn't talk to me for days. He got real mad at me in rehearsals and he kind of threw me around and sort of got even with me, I think. He almost dropped me. But that was all right. I kind of knew it was coming. *Doink*, he threw me on the floor. [*Laughs*]

After we started, we had the opportunity to travel, so we just grabbed the opportunity to go on the road, as the expression is called. At first I went with Toy Yat Mar to Seattle on our own to do our shows, the two of us. Then Mary Mammon joined us and it sort of opened up show business as individuals instead of being in a chorus and being in one place like the Forbidden City. And then we traveled to different towns, playing one-night stands. And we had our little group and we joined different people, units. We had a manager who always managed our show and we just took it out.

And then we had the opportunity to join a USO show to go overseas, which was our greatest desire: to go entertain the boys overseas during the war, to do our part during the war. I was with USO with Mary and Toy. We had to play all the different hospitals before we could play overseas, to build up our constitution so that we would get used to—if we had to hit the war zones—to get used to seeing the boys being...the blood, whatever. Maybe we might have to go into the war zones, so we had to get used to all that.

First we went across from San Francisco to New York twice. We had to play all the hospitals, in the wards where the boys were laying in bed. And maybe we could cover six or seven wards, different wards of all different hospitals—amputees and blind people. And then in the evening we would play the auditorium where the boys were able to go to see the show in a wheelchair, or being wheeled into the audience into the auditorium in a bed that could be pushed into an auditorium. And we did a big show.

We did some shows with Ron Reagan, Frances [Chun], and I, at Travis or—I can't remember which air force base. Was it Travis or

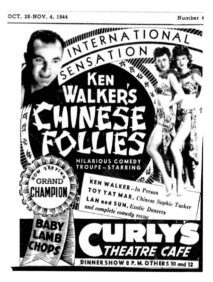

TOP: Forbidden City women in uniform: Mary Mammon (fourth from left), Dottie Sun, Jade Ling, and Toy Yat Mar with unidentified woman and men, at the Forbidden City (ca. 1945). MIDDLE: On tour with the USO (l–r): Dottie Sun, Toy Yat Mar, and Mary Mammon (ca. 1945). BOTTOM: "Chinese Follies" ad, with Ken Walker, Mary Mammon (center), and Dottie Sun (November 4, 1944).

Hamilton? I remember I was playing slot machines with Ronald Reagan in one of those places. And dinner was ready and he and I kept playing and they said, "Come on, Dottie, Ron, hurry up!" And we ran to the table and the next guy who came along hit the jackpot and Ron says, "Dottie, look what the guy did." He was really nice. So was Jane [Wyman, Reagan's wife]. He was a public relations or liaison officer at that time.

Then the war ended, but we still wanted to go overseas. That's when we were needed for the boys who were still stuck over there. We went maybe two years, three years—the South Pacific: Johnson Island, Guam, Eniwetok, Saipan, Wake Island, Midway. Everywhere we went we had ten convoys behind us. I mean, there's still Japanese in the caves, you know. Don't forget: a lot of them don't know the war is over. There are guards this way and guards that way, guarding you to go eat and back to your quarters. You can't go out; you can't go out with anybody.

• • •

I married a Scotchman. My husband and I met in Hawaii and we came back here [to California] to get married, but we couldn't on account of [laws banning] intermarriage. The only place we could get married was in Chicago or go back to Hawaii. So we went back to Hawaii. I married out of my own race.

We moved to Sacramento and we went house hunting. We went out to Southgate and my brother helped me put five hundred dollars down on a house. And they found out I was Chinese and they called me up and said, "We're sorry. We cannot accept your money because I found out you're Oriental." My husband had a fit. He said, "I am going to fight it." I says, "John, I don't want to live where I am not wanted." [The couple decided to settle in a racially mixed area of Sacramento.]

I hate to tell you what the [relatives] thought in their minds [about the marriage]. They didn't come right out, but I hate to tell you what they thought: "It won't last any more than two years." But we proved that our marriage was happy, and our marriage lasted thirty-five years, until my husband died. We had a very nice marriage; we had three lovely children.

When a dancer is a certain age, you have to give up. When you get old, people say, "God, she's still trucking down there, she looks terrible." I just thought it was time, instead of me just falling on my face. [Laughs] Show business was great: I saw the world, I was able to travel, I wasn't just stuck in one place. I met so many nice people, worked with so many people, and understand show people and what they go through. Like, say, when they're laid off of work, I know what they mean. To go without a meal, not get paid, [because] the agents don't pay them. They starve and they don't know where the next meal is coming from. I know what they're going through. It's something to write about. ●

OPPOSITE: The Mei Lings trio (l–r): Dottie Sun, Jackie Mei Ling, and Mary Mammon (ca. 1941).

Romaine

Frances Chun (Kan)

1919–2008, Singer

Excerpts from interviews conducted on
December 2, 1985; September 23, 1988; and June 14, 1989.

What we did in the thirties and forties was shocking to the Chinese community and confusing to the Caucasian people. It's a novelty to be in show business in my generation; there weren't that many of us around. Chinese were always noted as magicians, acrobats...but to be a singer and a dancer? Well, that's quite different, quite unique.

Years ago I made a demo record for a radio station when I heard they were looking for local singers. And when I got a callback after I submitted the record, I was very encouraged. So I went down to be interviewed personally. But when I got down there, the person that interviewed me—I believe he was the producer or assistant producer—was very shocked to see that I was a Chinese girl. And I guess he didn't expect that; he expected a Caucasian girl and he was very embarrassed. And then when he told me he couldn't use me, he didn't specifically say because I was Chinese, but in a very diplomatic way, and I realized what the story was. So I said to him, "Well, this is a radio program. What's the difference? How can you tell?"

So that was my experience. I thought I was very brave in saying that. [*Laughs*] Of course I thought it was unfair. But I don't know...we took those things in stride in those days. We'd try harder, that's all. We are so patient; I think we Chinese people are so patient. "So you don't want me, it's OK," you know. But it does hurt a little bit.

I came from a very musical family. My parents were born and raised in Hawaii, so my father was always playing music around the house; he played ukulele and a mandolin and guitar. So during the Depression, a lot of Hawaiian boys were stranded in San Francisco and my dad would go down, you know, on Grant Avenue, Eastern Bakery—it used to be a hangout for these Hawaiian boys who were stranded down there. He'd bring them home and they'd work for us, and at night they played music. So we were always singing and playing, kind of what you would call a Hawaiian jam session. It was just a way of life for me.

We were more Hawaiian Chinese than *Chinese* Chinese; we weren't the stereotyped *Chinese* Chinese. I know a lot of kids grew up in Chinatown without learning English until they went to school. As I remembered, we always spoke English at home here in San Francisco. I'm second-generation.

My dad had a business in Chinatown on Washington, right next to Commodore Stockton School. It's called Lun Hing and he did a lot of

OPPOSITE: Frances Chun (ca. 1935). Photo by Romaine.

ABOVE, TOP: Frances Chun is interviewed by the author at her Oakland home (December 2, 1985). Photo by Arthur Dong. BOTTOM: Frances Chun photo (1940s), autographed to the author. Photo by Gordon-Geddes, Inc.

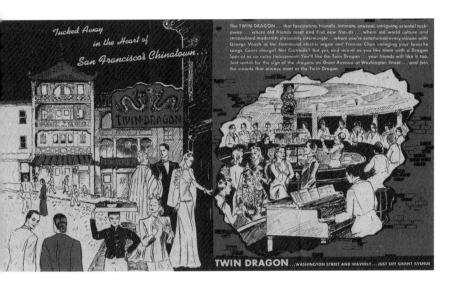

TWIN ARTISTS — No, not brother and sister; they're the Twin Dragon's cele-brated organist, George Veach, and its alluring little songstress, Frances Chun.

ABOVE, TOP: Twin Dragon cocktail bar brochure: "...that fascinating, friendly, intimate, unusual, intriguing oriental tuck-away..." (ca. 1941). BOTTOM: Twin Dragon ad featuring Frances Chun and George Veach, organist (March 1941).

OPPOSITE, TOP: Frances Chun performs with the Cathayans in Bakersfield, California. David Sum is at the piano and Fred Wong is on drums. (May 31, 1936). MIDDLE: The Cathayans perform at a gym dance (ca. 1935). BOTTOM: Frances Chun, center, with Ray Tellier and his orchestra (1941).

business with American, Caucasian people. So we had a lot of Caucasian friends, so I was exposed to the so-called American culture more.

I think you can survive in Chinatown without any contact with the outside world or American people. Chinatown is so self-contained; it's a city by itself. The Chinese were more or less by nature confined right in Chinatown. You sort of stayed in your own little area. Of course there was prejudice. To begin with, you cannot buy property outside of Chinatown. You couldn't rent beyond Nob Hill, you couldn't rent anywhere outside or anywhere in North Beach. I remember when my family lived on Powell Street and they thought that was so far, that you lived away from Chinatown.

And it was a very close-knit community in those days because there were not that many of us; everybody in Chinatown knew each other in those days. And the Chinese telephone exchange was so unique, it being a small community, the staff there actually speaks both English and Chinese and they know everybody's number and you don't even have to know the number. All you have to say is, "I want to talk to Frances Chun on Washington Street," and they'd just plug you in right away. Of course it was a great community communications center, and that's how news traveled, gossip traveled.

I don't remember being poor or it being hard. We grew up in the Depression, but I think people in Chinatown always ate; they seem to manage to survive. Because my father had a store, he was trying everything to help the people in Chinatown. He contracted Standard Oil and Shell Oil to make little souvenir things. And I remember when gasoline was only ten cents a gallon, and then you go to the station and you get a little ornament to put on your car, on your hood, for Christmas. My father would package them; he packed them by the [one-thousand-piece] lots. Well, that generated a lot of jobs for the women in Chinatown. They'd come to our store and they would take it home and put it together. And people would get paid for every thousand they'd pack in a box. I know he lost money on it—he didn't make anything—but he really helped the women in Chinatown, and a lot of people in Chinatown said my father saved them that winter because those women were so fast—they got something to do. So we all got along and slowly blended into the American culture.

Well, now that I think back to it, I think the people in my generation, we really are very lucky to be in that generation because it's such a wonderful blend of our Chinese and our American ideas. We all went to Chinese school and we all, you know, can understand Chinese—read and write. My goodness, even Saturday we went to Chinese school. [*Laughs*] But that was the way of life and we all did it. But I'm very happy for that and I think we got very great benefits. And yet, we're very Americanized.

In the early 1930s the Cathayans [band] started. One of my cousins was a trumpet player, so he would say, "I'm getting into this band called the Cathayans. Oh, you've got to come and try out and sing for us." The Cathayans stemmed from the Cathay Club. That was a very, very good club in Chinatown—social club—they were all very musically inclined. So that's how I started. I started with the Cathayans. I was still in high school; I think I was sixteen, seventeen.

David Sum was the leader. David started years ago in vaudeville, much earlier, I think in the early twenties. He was always interested in music, so he started the Cathayans. Mr. Ed Quon was the business manager, and then once in a while we would have public relations people, so it really was run like a very perfectly well-organized orchestra. We'd get paid fifty dollars for a dance, we'd spend half that on eating. The rest went for music, arrangements, and traveling expenses. But I think everybody did it because they loved music; we were just really semi-professional. I think I'm the only one that went professional.

In those days there were always dances in Chinatown. I think it's to this day still, Chinatown people are very interested in ballroom dancing, and very good at it. There were so many clubs in Chinatown, everybody had dances. Every weekend the Y would have dances. Some of them were high school dances, senior proms, and all that.

And so there were two different Chinese dance orchestras in Chinatown; there was another band called the Chinatown Knights. And we didn't just confine ourselves to Chinatown, we went all over, we worked all up and down the state of California. All the

RAY TELLIER AND HIS ORCHESTRA. 1941

fraternity dances, the out-of-town dances, we played for dances in Japantown, all the conventions in San Francisco, and we were very much in demand, I must say.

And then along came the Chinese-Japanese war, '37, '38. And they had what they called the Rice Bowl fund drives. We did a lot of that. We traveled up and down the coast, helping organizations raise money for the Rice Bowl. I'd say 80 percent of the business was Chinese. And it was a very good orchestra regardless of whether we were Chinese or not. Several bookers were trying to get us to go on the road, promote us as a professional group—we had a chance. Now David, he was going to pharmacy school, he was in college, he made his way through college playing music, and so did some of the other boys—several boys were in college. And they just couldn't stop and give it up.

Chinatown started with two, three bars. Charlie Low started the very first cocktail bar in Chinatown, and I guess he was very progressive in those days. I'd forgotten what year Chinese Village opened...'34? [It was 1936.] That was Charlie Low's very first cocktail lounge; he can take credit for that. He and, I think, several partners. It was very attractive and a perfectly nice place and didn't cater strictly to tourists—everybody went there.

And then after that there were a lot more. There was Li Po and there was Jade Palace. And they were all very nice gathering places, and they used to say, "No Chinese ever got drunk!" And there was Twin Dragons on Waverly and Washington. Right on the corner, which is now a jewelry store, right upstairs. I worked at Twin Dragons for a long time; I sang on the weekends during my school days. I wasn't of age and nobody stopped me. Funny, nobody came in to stop me!

Then the war came. I had to quit the College of Arts and Crafts because all my brothers were in the army. It was the circumstances; I didn't have a chance to finish because I had to make a living and help the family. From then on I concentrated and went on to show business, so-called legitimately.

I was told that a white band needed a vocalist; it was an all-Caucasian band. I was working at the Twin Dragons and somebody came in and said he liked my singing and would I go audition for the job that was available. So I went down to audition and I noticed I wasn't too well received by the musicians. You feel the tenseness, the tenseness in the air. And I was kind of a little bit discouraged at first.

So I went through and sang my song. And then later on the bandleader [Ray Tellier] told me himself, "You stay right there," he said, "I want to use you." But I think he got some complaint from the musicians. But I was hired and I guess he smoothed it out with the union. At the end of the season all the musicians came to me—and they were all Caucasian musicians—complimented me and said, "You did OK, kid." So that was the best feeling I had. And I really feel like, "OK, so I could cut it with the rest of the world." I worked with him for two years, I think.

TOM BALL
presents
"MAID IN CHINA"
a new revue staged and produced by DONN ARDEN
with **MING & LING**, TAI SINGS, FOUR CANTON BROS., MUI SONG, FRANCES CHUN
AND
LEE MORTIMER'S CHINA DOLLS

Costumes designed by Bob Mackintosh, executed by Mme. Berthé   Publicity: Milton Rubin
Original Music and Arrangements: Elliot Eberhard   Lyrics: Lee Morris
Music by JOSE CURBELO and JACQUES FRAZE

1- **Opening—"JADE MAID"**
with *LEE MORTIMER'S CHINA DOLLS.*
TAI SING and featuring *MUI SONG.*

2- **THE CANTON BROTHERS**

3- **FRANCES CHUN**

4- Production—"MAID IN MING" with
the China Dolls
Tobi Kei   Mae Lin   Hazel Jay   Dorothy Choy
Trudie Kim   Lu Mae   Edna Chin
Showgirls
Mae Dong   Lily Pon   Katherine Kim   Louise Leung
Featuring MUI SONG and introducing THE TAI SINGS

5- **THE TAI SINGS**

6- **MING & LING**

7- **FINALE-Chinese Circus**
with entire cast
our barker — TAI SING
our ring mistress — MUI SONG
The acrobats — THE CHINA CATS
THE NAUTCH GIRLS.

When Forbidden City opened, it was really the first place we can really call our own. Our own place to show off all the Oriental talents. In those days, there was never a place like that. When Forbidden City started, they tried to be just like everybody else—modern. And we were not, you know, anything different; it's just to show that we were able to present a package of an all-Chinese entertainment—*American* entertainment.

And everything was done in English. You know, none of that, what shall we say, "chop-chop English." But just because the fact that we were Chinese, you can't help but underlining it—it is Chinese, it's a Chinese show. It was staffed by a complete Chinese staff, but the only difference...the only thing that was not Chinese was the band.

He [Charlie Low] had a difficult time getting chorus girls. It's not easy to try and influence a Chinese girl, say, to go into dancing. You know how the Chinese idea of show business is. Dancing was kind of different from singing. I think when they're dancing, maybe their parents felt like...like Charlie Low would say, "They're showing off their bodies." With singing you don't have to worry about that.

OPPOSITE, TOP: Frances Chun with unidentified foursome at the China Doll nightclub, New York City (ca. 1946). MIDDLE: Forbidden City ad featuring Frances Chun (October 8, 1945). BOTTOM: Ad for Frances Chun's appearance at Chin's Pagoda nightclub in Buffalo, New York (ca. 1946).

ABOVE: Program from the "Maid in China" show at the China Doll nightclub, New York City, featuring (l–r) Frances Chun, the Canton Brothers, Ming and Ling, the Tai Sings (Jessie Tai Sing and Wilbur Tai Sing), unidentified (October 1946).

I don't think we were ostracized or anything like that. It's kind of shocking at first, probably, for Chinatown people to see, all of a sudden, a nightclub with chorus girls and, you know, short dresses. That was enough of a shock, but they got used to it. I think Chinese people are very adjustable. [*Laughs*]

Charlie Low really started a trend. Because after he opened Forbidden City, then other cities wanted to open [Chinese clubs]. New York opened the China Doll. And then they had a Vegas show. After that I went out and worked other clubs. I used to double. To show you how little entertainers there are, I used to double between clubs. I used to work Forbidden City and then run out of Forbidden City and work another club because they didn't have a singer. And I would dash—I'd come as far as to Berkeley at the Claremont Hotel. [At Forbidden City] we would have a doorman, you know, leave the door open and he'd wait and I'd jump into the car, come all the way to Berkeley to the Claremont Hotel, work, and dash back there.

I remember when I was in a town somewhere in Oklahoma and somebody came up to me in a club I was working in and said, "Can I touch you? I've never seen a Chinese before." And he touched me! [*Laughs*] I guess he expected us to be very different. And I remember during war, I met a soldier, and he was from the Midwest somewhere, and he said he never met a Chinese. Then they often wonder and say, "How come we can speak English?" I mean, sometimes you still meet people like that, believe it or not. But as a whole, people were very nice.

[*Laughs*] I think the first time I went down South I was with a show, and when I got to the train station...I don't know if I should say this or not. [*Laughs*] I went to the ladies room and I saw this sign that said "Black and White." So I stood there—never been exposed to the South—and I said, "Now where should I go? Where do I belong?" I was stunned for a while. I didn't know they had such things. [*Laughs*] But you learn. So I thought, "Well, I'm not black. So I must go to the white one!"

Then the war ended, and there were a lot of opportunities to travel to South America, to Europe. I decided I would become a housewife and a mother, so I stayed put and lived in Chicago.

I think show business is wonderful when you're younger. You know, it's tough, it's not an easy business—especially the traveling part. I think people think it's a very glamorous life. It is, in a way; we meet some wonderful people. It's been very educational and a very good experience for me. I always wanted to be an entertainer. I wanted to sing and I got in with the rest of them and I felt that I'm able to get into the so-called job market of the mainstream and prove to myself that I could do it, regardless of race or background. ●

ABOVE, TOP: Cast of the "Maid in China" show at the China Doll nightclub, New York City. Standing (l–r): unidentified, Four Canton Brothers member, Mai Tai Sing, Ming and Ling, Four Canton Brothers member, Wilbur Tai Sing, Jessie Tai Sing, Frances Chun, Four Canton Brothers member, unidentified, Louise Leung, Four Canton Brothers member, and Lily Pon. Front row: far right is Hazel Jay, others unidentified (ca. 1946). Photo by David Workman.
BOTTOM: Cover from *Tonight,* a magazine on San Francisco nightlife. Clockwise from top left: Frances Chun, George Jessel, Vehiari, and Carol Davis (August 1942).

OPPOSITE: Management agency flyer for Frances Chun (photo replaced for visual clarity) (mid-1940s).

PRESENTING . . .
FRANCES CHUN
America's Outstanding Chinese Song Stylist

36 Months at San Francisco's World Famous **"FORBIDDEN CITY"**

Acclaimed by

SAN FRANCISCO EXAMINER	"Frances Chun . . . a best bet."
SAN FRANCISCO CHRONICLE	"Frances Chun, Chinese Star of Song continues to pack 'em in."
SAN FRANCISCO CALL-BULLETIN	"Your favorite and mine."
SAN FRANCISCO NEWS	"Miss Chun is THE Chinese Nightingale."
ACTOR MAGAZINE	"Frances Chun, the terrific Chinese Singer is the prettiest songstress we've ever seen, and the sweetest we've ever heard."

Personal Management:
WALTON GOLDMAN
988 Market Street
Loew's Warfield Bldg.
San Francisco, California

Ivy Tam

b. 1935, Dancer, Mrs. Charlie Low #4

Excerpts from interviews conducted on
August 27 and September 29, 1988.

How did I meet Charlie? It was through a friend. When I met Charlie it was 1958 or '57, somewhere around there. I think it was end of '57. We went up to Forbidden City to see the show, and that's how we met. We went up there two or three times; then he asks me out for dinner and then we start dating. That's all. [*Laughs*] Not much to tell because after that we see each other all the time and he liked my children.

I just tell him I have a son, two years old. My daughter was in Hong Kong then; my father took her to Hong Kong because I cannot handle her, she cried all the time. So I only have Kevin [Gee] with me. And he [Charlie] said, "I'd like to meet him. Let's take him out for dinner." And then we take him along and he really, ever since then, he take him everyplace. He even take him to Disneyland by himself, you know, for seven days on vacation. He was about four years old, I think, at the time, and [Charlie] just loved him like his own. He said he never loved someone like he loved Kevin. He always say, "I can kiss him one hundred times a day." [*Laughs*]

I go up to the club a lot, you know, see the show. And I decided to stay there; every night go up there helping around, seat customers and all that. I learn how to hostess; I learn all the cocktails. Not only that, Forbidden City they serve sort of American type of Chinese food, right? I mean, they are different from Chinatown, so I learned all this and was helping the waitress and all that. When it's a very busy night like New Year's Eve or Saturday night, you know, big convention, when the waitress running around doesn't have time to take care of all the customers, I even take a piece of paper and go take orders. Get a piece of paper and do it. And sometimes I even help the cashier—take the money and check the food and go in the kitchen. I'm really all over the place.

At the time, they don't even allow women to go behind the bar; I cannot go behind the bar. But I stand there in front of the service bar and talk to Douglass, the bartender, and I learn all the drinks. I even go behind the bar to go make the drinks. I'm not allowed to, but I always stand there and watch him. I always ask questions. Who knows, maybe one of these days I have to make a living on my own. Only during show time, of course, I sit there and watch the girls dancing. At the time I think everything so fascinating.

We married in '61 or '62. What happened? I really don't know what happened. I find him—he's a very kind man, very nice man, OK? And

OPPOSITE: Ivy Tam, dancer (1960s). Photo by Romaine.

ABOVE, TOP: Ivy Tam currently performs as a founding member of the Grant Avenue Follies, a San Francisco troupe of former Chinatown nightclub entertainers (2012). Photo by Frank Jang. BOTTOM: Ivy Tam photo (1960s), autographed to the author.

ABOVE: At the Forbidden City: actor James Mason, Ivy Tam, and Charlie Low (ca. 1959).

he liked my son and then to me he's nice to everybody—not just the family, not just me, and he really is good-hearted person. You know, I feel I could depend on him, and that's why I married him. At the time I not even think about our age difference or anything like that because he was always real active. I always even tell people maybe I die before him [laughs] because he's so active!

The first wife passed away after they married for one year. And the second one was a singer at Forbidden City. She's beautiful, and I think they married for two years or so. They got divorced. But the third wife, the one with the daughter, is a showgirl in the show, and they got married. But that part I don't know because that long before me. When I met Charlie, I think at the time they divorced a long, long time.

And before he married me, before I met him, long before he married Betty [his third wife], he has ranch, he has polo team, and he play horses. He always enjoyed life. So I don't think he can save too much [money] on that [laughs]; I don't think he should be a rich man or a poor man, but he enjoyed his life. He always have something to fall back on, I guess, because the family has property and things like that.

When Charlie go anyplace, it's always first class. Like, you walk into Bimbo's, you walk into Fairmont, you walk into Venetian Room, we always have the best seat. One day he said he hasn't been to Las Vegas for long time and then he wants to go because Stardust was just built and opened a beautiful show—the Follies and all that. So he want to take me there. So he wrote a letter to Stardust to tell them, just wanted to make a reservation before we get there. And you know what we get? We get a letter back from the owner and the owner said, "I've never met you, but I heard about you." And he even get us a private plane and he tell us to take whoever we like. And we take the waitresses, I mean the crew, all the people in Forbidden City, if they like to go. We spent a night over there. And they sent a limousine to the airport pick us up. And they save for us the front-row seat. You know, all that. I mean, when you go spend all these years with Charlie, let's face it, it's hard not to miss it. So even now if I go someplace, I try to have the best before I get there.

When we start a new show we always look for girls. They rehearse every day at daytime, I always sit there and I always try to help with jewelry and costume and all that. And when new girl come in to interview for the job, we don't have too much choice; as long as they look Oriental, we take them as long as they can dance a little. First thing, the girls at Forbidden City, they start not as professional dancer; most of them not even have a dancing lesson. They go in there because they look Oriental—we need that. Like Arlene [Wing], she go to the show because she grow up after high school; she don't want to go to college. Her brother [Tony Wing] take her in. She look beautiful!

Not all the people are Chinese, because not too many Chinese girls want to be in the show. But they not actually try to tell people they are really Chinese; everybody know they are not pure Chinese. You know, especially Filipino and things like that, and everybody knows they are Filipino and they are Japanese. Like Connie Parks—everybody knows she is Japanese girl, OK? But they all have a Chinese name, like Anna Lee, like Jack Soo.

You know why Jack Soo name Jack Soo? He's Japanese. Because during the war he don't want to go into the [internment] camp and then he changed his name. But at the time Japanese don't get any work, even after the war, so they have to change their names. Like Jimmy Jay—he's Jimmy Borges, he's Puerto Rican. Like Tony Wing? You know, like Arlene Wing? They all changed to Chinese name to try to get a job because at the time only Chinese nightclubs take them. Bimbo's—they have the big production show and at the time they take all white girls.

In the show, how did I start? Well, when we start rehearsal we still need girls, but seems like nobody come to interview for the job. So, Marah Gates keep on yelling, "We need a girl, we need a girl." So I was sitting there and then Lucy, one of the waitress, said, "What you sit here for? Just go out and try it for yourself." So Marah said, "Yes, do you know how to dance?" I said, "I think so. I know how to waltz, a little tango, and rumba and all that." So she said, "OK, let me have some music and you follow me for a few steps." I remember she used the music from *Gone with the Wind,* "My Own True Love"—I think that was it. So I just follow her and I did it. And she said, "You are OK." And then I stepped into the show. But after that I take some lessons to improve myself. And so that's how I get into the show.

Oh, I love it. I love it. I'm very interested in show business. I guess it's all in me, that part. I still think so, I mean, I always have a dream; I guess every girl have a dream.

I mean even to this day I still always try to look good. You know how showgirls always look beautiful [*laughs*], so I think I'm very into it, really. That's why I think I do a pretty good job in the show, and at least people think so.

When I step into the show, of course, a lot of people say, "Why you have to do that?" [But for me] it's not, "Why have to do that?" I don't have to do that, but I enjoy it. I want to be dancing good; I want to be a showgirl. I don't want to just do something I don't know how or I'm not good at, OK?

I know at that time most people look down on showgirls, let's put it that way. That's thirty years ago, right? I mean some people—not everybody—still a lot of old-fashioned people. For me, I think it's a job. And I never look at [it like], "Oh, it's sexy," or something like that. In the

ABOVE, TOP: At the Forbidden City: Charlie Low, stepson Kevin Gee, and Ivy Tam (ca. 1959). BOTTOM: Non-Chinese performers adopted Chinese names in order to perform at the Forbidden City, including Arlene Wing (Legrimas) and Jimmy Jay (Borges) (ca. 1959).

ABOVE, TOP: Forbidden City performers (l–r): Haruyo Kanada, Anna Lea, Yuki Cho, Mary Mammon, Ivy Tam, and Lily Ogawa. (ca. 1960s). Photo by Romaine. BOTTOM: Ivy Tam on the Forbidden City dance floor (1960s).

OPPOSITE: Dancer Coby Yee (1960s). Yee and family members bought the Forbidden City from Charlie Low in 1962.

show, it's nothing to be ashamed of because outside of what we do for a show, we don't do anything else to shame. We earn our honest money, let's say it that way. [*Laughs*]

Even for Coby Yee, people say, "Oh, a stripper." You never see Coby Yee on stage, OK? She's very tiny—really, she's tiny. She has the nice figure, but she's not one of those, you know, funny-looking type or something; she look nice. And she could do it very graceful. And at the time, even strippers, they are not like nowadays, take off everything. They always have something to cover, and they always do it gracefully. Even the balloon dancer. You ever see the old-fashioned balloon dancer? They use the balloon, you not even see the body, right? But they can make it so graceful. Sort of like art.

At the time when they were looking for girl for [the movie] ***Flower Drum Song,*** they went down to Chinatown and they ask [Chinatown community leader] H. K. Wong, and H. K. Wong always think I'm beautiful, I guess—something like that. And he just send them to Forbidden City to look me up. And I think that the casting director, his name Henry something, he came in and he talk to me a few times. I remember the day; they said [producer] Ross Hunter going to come in. And so that night he came into the club and then he talked to a few girls. He did take some girls for the movie for the chorus line, you know for the nightclub scene.

COBY YEE

CHINA'S MOST
DARING
DANCING DOLL

But at the time they were looking for Mei Li [a character in the movie]. But he don't think I can make it because he said, "Oh, I think you look too elegant to be a Chinese girl." And he said, "Are you sure you are pure Chinese?" And I said, "Sure, I think so. My mother's Chinese, my father's Chinese, and I think we are pure Chinese." And he even said, "Are you sure you don't have a little French in you?" At the time, a lot of people think the Chinese not supposed to look so fair or something. I have fair skin, so they keep on thinking I'm not Chinese enough.

I don't get the part, which is good. I always think so because I don't think I can do a good job on that movie anyway because it's a big part and I have no experience. I have a dream for it, but I know I can never make it because my English is not good enough. Especially at the time, I really very rough on my English, I really cannot speak too much. When I was little girl, I always wanted to be in the movies. My father don't let me because my father say, "The movie studio in China is not good place for girl." At school I always play school plays and, you know, I was pretty famous—popular girl in school. And then one of the movie studios want to sign me up when I was about sixteen, seventeen. My father wouldn't let me. That's how I don't go into the movie.

Jack Soo came in for a job, and he's a comedian. You know, any Oriental come in for a job, anything is OK. Charlie always give them a job opportunity. Chinese shows at the time...there were not very many, especially professional, let's put it that way. So Jack Soo is from New York and he is a comedian and he sing a little. So Charlie give him a spot over there and he worked for...I guess he worked a year or so, late fifties, first part of sixties. And he left for New York or something and he come back again. Then one day casting for *Flower Drum Song* [on Broadway]—go to New York for the musical—and they want him to play Sammy Fong. They took Jack Soo, and at the time Jack Soo still had the contract with us. But Charlie said, "That's your big opportunity." Then he went to New York and had a big name, and he get into TV and all that. I still remember his wife really appreciate that Charlie let him go—you know, a contract is a contract.

When Charlie decided to sell the place I wasn't there, I was vacationing in Hong Kong. And he just called me and he said Coby [Yee] wanted to buy the place. He decided to sell it. I said, "OK, nothing wrong with that," because that's his place; if he want to sell it, that's OK with me. Was slow down for the last two years at least.

The music union was very strong; we had to pay a lot for the band boys. Seems like vacation pay you have to double up for the band boy.

JACK SOO

Mr. Soo, a Japanese-American who hails from San Francisco, has had a long and successful career in night clubs and vaudeville. He was tapped for "Flower Drum Song" while working in Charlie Low's Forbidden City, a San Francisco night spot. The comedian is the only performer in this show who actually hails from its locale. Mr. Soo was graduated from the U. of C. in Berkley; he is married to a Jugoslavian and the father of three children.

ABOVE: Comedian Jack Soo honed his skills at the Forbidden City and Chinese Sky Room before landing a featured role in *Flower Drum Song*, both on Broadway and in the film version. Pictured is Soo's biography from the Broadway program (ca. 1960).

OPPOSITE, TOP: Backstage at the Forbidden City (l–r): Anna Lea, Lily Ogawa, and Ivy Tam (1960s). BOTTOM: Founding members of the Grant Avenue Follies, a San Francisco troupe of former Chinatown nightclub performers (l–r): Pat Chin, Cynthia Fong Yee, and Ivy Tam (2012). Photo by Marlene Luke.

We start with six band boys, I think, six, yeah, including the bandleader. And Charlie try to cut down to four or five, cut down one or two, and we had to fight the union for over a year to try to cut one down. So I guess that's why he decided to close down [Forbidden City], because seems like you work just for the band.

And the second thing: at the time, people started not going to nightclubs. Broadway [Street in San Francisco] started those topless clubs; people going to topless because it's something new, you know, the new-generation stuff, and the nightclub is sort of a thing of the past. And the cover charge too high; people don't want to pay the price.

But anyway, we divorced at '63, I think. Why? I guess because the family...I think his older sister is sort of...to me it seems like she's running his life or something. But he always think that older sister is bringing him up and he respect her as the mother. She don't treat me as one of the family...I shouldn't talk about people after they passed away.

Oh, we divorced at '64, I don't remember. We get married '62, and '63 I was in Hong Kong. Our divorced finalized in '64; yes, uh-huh. I think I move out and get a divorce and that's it. We still friends. I mean, Charlie still calls me out for dinner. We never fight. He's a nice man. We always can talk.

I think I'm always thinking in some way I'm pretty independent, I guess. Because I never depend on him support my two children. I was still thinking I should support my own mother and my own children because I'm thinking that's not his children. Because I never ask him for any money or anything like that. I guess I've always been independent. ●

Jackie Mei Ling

1914–2000, Dancer

Excerpts from interviews conducted on
November 1, 1985; December 2, 1985; and September 24, 1988.

When did you start dancing?

Two hundred years ago. I can't remember.

I used to go with a group of school kids and audition and win prizes in gin mills. I didn't drink in those days, and they had clubs and they always had amateur nights, and I used to get up and putz around, dance, and I'd win prizes. It's like your own gang would sort of back you up, and I'd win a bottle of champagne.

Then I'd audition in cheap nightclubs and they hired me. I used another name when I started out in show business; I didn't want my father to know that I was working in nightclubs because nightclubs weren't exactly the place to go. It wasn't like the ballet. So in order to work in these cheap places—we got the smart money of five dollars a show—I changed my name to Jackie Lopez, thinking I was fooling everybody. And I worked in one club that whenever any Chinese people came in I wouldn't perform and the boss understood. I thought I was getting away with it, but I found out many years later they used to sneak in and catch me.

I was solo, [but then] I danced with a fat girl. And we used to do what you would call sex dancing: snakehips, pecking. It was just strictly ad lib and they liked it because we never did the same thing twice. My main specialty in those days was Hawaiian dancing. I'd do the hula, and we knew merchant seamen who'd come into town and they'd bring fresh ti leaves; they'd have skirts made out of them on the island. In those days they'd put it on ice and bring it in, and that made me different.

Yeah, I studied. But most of my dancing was my own. Oh, I did a little of everything—interpretive dancing. I studied with Walton Biggerstaff. Then I studied with the Ballet Company of San Francisco for a very brief period. I didn't like it; it was too technical. Then I studied with Theodore Kosloff, the Russian ballet [dancer]. And I didn't like all that barre work, putting your leg up in the air and stretching; I was too lazy at that time.

The only serious dancing was later when I teamed up with Jadin [Wong]. This was before Forbidden City. I was dancing at this club when Jadin heard about me. Of course she's a very persistent female, and she came and caught my act and then she invited me out for *siu-yeh* [late-night snack] after the show. So anything for a free *siu-yeh*. She offered me the deal and I thought, "My, my." And this agent that was hiring us was putting up the money for our costumes and our music and I figured

OPPOSITE: Jackie Mei Ling (late 1930s).

ABOVE, TOP: Jackie Mei Ling is interviewed by the author at his Oakland home (December 2, 1985). Photo by Arthur Dong. BOTTOM: Jackie Mei Ling photo (1940s), autographed to the author. Photo by Romaine.

ABOVE, TOP: Jadin Wong and Jackie Mei Ling (1940s). Photo by Romaine. MIDDLE: Jadin Wong and Jackie Mei Ling at a New York City party (mid-1940s). BOTTOM: Jackie Mei Ling meets Lena Horne at the Forbidden City (mid-1940s).

I had nothing to lose. If I didn't like it I could leave. Her agent had the Tai Sings and she wanted another Chinese dance team.

In those days, Veloz and Yolanda were a famous team, and Tony and Sally DeMarco were a famous team, and almost every club had a dance team—it started a phase. It was like break dancing today [in the 1980s]. "Oh, you do break dancing? We'll hire you. You don't? Sorry." We were more like Veloz and Yolanda; we were more the love-type team. We rehearsed for about three or four months in Los Angeles before we started doing club dates around LA to break it in.

We were dancing at Grace Hayes Lodge and there was two hours in between shows and we wanted to go to the Hollywood Bowl—it was Stravinsky's *Firebird*. In those days, we'd hitchhike because we made very little money; and I wore tails and she wore her gown.

She wore bangs, and the hair pulled back into a big chignon, which was [actress] Anna May Wong's trademark. And Jessie Tai Sing [of the Tai Sings] also did the same thing; that was sort of the standard-type hairdo for Oriental women. And the head usher—most Caucasians don't know the difference between black and white—he said, "Miss Wong?" She said, "Yes." "Miss Anna May Wong?"—which is Jadin's true name—"Yes." They said, "Right this way." And they took her to her box. And I said to her in Chinese, "You're kidding." She said, "Well, my real name is Anna May Wong. Why not? Let's go." They put us in this beautiful box and the ballet was so marvelous we sat there and didn't go back to the club until the end of the thing. And here we were sitting in Anna May Wong's box. And we got away with it. And then she had the nerve to sign her autograph—people asked her for autographs. She said, "I'm not lying. My name is Anna May Wong, legally, but Jadin professionally."

When we got [our act] broken in, she wired Charlie [Low], and he said, "Send them up." I had known Charlie through my family, and he knew Jadin. Now, Chinatown in those days was very close. Everyone knew one another—"That's so-and-so's son. That's so-and-so's daughter."

[For our act,] we did anything that was romantic. "Clair de Lune" was the opening number; it was very ethereal and Jadin liked that. We would caress one another and all but kiss, except when, at the very end of the number, I would lower her on the floor and kiss her and the spotlight would go off. And then for our second number we did "Begin the Beguine." We'd do it to give the people the illusion that we were very much in love—made lots of love. However, we weren't. But it was fun and we would get into very sexy positions and end up caressing one another. She was always doing little tricks like pinching me or pulling on my jacket, so I one day we would end up in a pose where I'd go down to caress her, and just as I got to her, I stuck my tongue in [her mouth]!

We were the featured stars at Forbidden City. I think that at the time when we did this, the salary for the both of us was seventy-five, eighty dollars a week...one hundred dollars a week at Forbidden City,

THE *Girl* IN THE GILDED CAGE

This dance is truly sensational, a fantastic blending of Occidental, Oriental and African rhythms.

Charlie Low started life as a rolly-polly baby, the son of a rich Chinese exporter. What he did with his early childhood we don't know but at twenty we find him entering Harvard, from which institution of learning he departed four years later with a Bachelor of Arts degree.

By this time Mr. Low Senior's importing business had grown to large proportions and he thought that it was only fitting and proper that Charlie, Jr., give him a helping hand.

Just to keep the record straight it must be reported that young Charlie worked for his father for a year. At the end of that time both father and son agreed that he, Charlie, Jr., was not cut out to be a merchant.

Just what he wanted to do with his life he didn't know. He started selling stock and bonds to his father's friends but at the end of three months gave up this polite form of blackmail in disgust.

He managed a motion picture theatre in the Chinese quarter for another two months, got tired of that, joined a circus as a pin ball operator, quit that and went back to school for another six months, then finally gave up and vagabonded around the country for a year.

Tempted by the African witch doctor, Joy Ching steals out of her gilded cage and the bizarre dance is about to begin.

SAN FRANCISCO, on the west coast, with its large Chinatown, is a city of romance and color. And it has the habit of bringing to the surface personalities just as colorful as the city itself.

At the present moment the spotlight is being turned on one—Charlie Low—affectionately referred to as San Francisco's Billy Rose. From which you may infer—and correctly—that Charlie Low is something of a personality in the West Coast show world.

As a matter of fact he is the guiding hand behind that picturesque and popular night club known as "the Forbidden City." It would be safe to say that more sensational dance routines have come out of "The Forbidden City" than out of any other night club throughout the country.

But before we elaborate on the latest dance novelty this 'all Chinese night club, let's say a few words about Charlie Low, himself.

Joy Ching tries to resist the temptation of the witch doctor but from the look in her eye she's losing out.

---

which was a lot of money in those days. But the waitresses, because it was such a popular place, they were making thirty to forty dollars a night. And they would come to work in jade rings and bracelets and mink coats and all that and orchids.

San Francisco was...well, it was the beginning of the war, you know, and everybody was frantic, everybody was hurting. They needed happiness, they wanted entertainment; the sons and husbands and lovers were going off to war. People were in a very friendly mood.

Nightclubs, in those early days, were the beginning of booze—legitimate booze. There was the Italian club, Bimbo's 365, and Joe Morello's—you know there were so many different clubs, Latin clubs. And then out in the Fillmore District there was a colored place called the Plantation where we used to always end up in at two in the morning—fried chicken and grits and what have you. So you had a variety, anything you wanted.

And they had a real famous Finocchio's with female impersonators. Finocchio's was just starting out. They were on Stockton Street near the Forbidden City. They asked me to dance and I wouldn't tell them I was Chinese. I was afraid my family would come out; I had an agreement

ABOVE: Jackie Mei Ling and Joy Ching's Forbidden City performance as African witch doctor and prey is covered by *Carnival Show* magazine (January 1942).

with them that if there were any Chinese in the audience I wouldn't dance. I didn't want them to see me at Finocchio's.

The Chinese nightclub was a novelty. Charlie started it with the Chinese Village [bar] with Larry Ching down there. So when his got going, they all of a sudden opened the Chinese Sky Room, which was a bar and restaurant in a motel, and they had a show there. Sammee Tong started at the Sky Room, but his major break came with *Bachelor Father*. He was sensational—he had a natural flair for timing. And he also emceed our show at the Shangri-La.

Nobody knew that they were going to pack clubs. We had the Forbidden City, then the Lion's Den opened, and the Kubla Khan opened, and then there was another one on Washington Street—the Club Mandalay—and then Fong Wan's cabaret club. There were just so many clubs and each one was trying to outdo one another. Then all of a sudden we were in demand.

And of course we had that marvelous bubble dancer, Noel Toy, who really shocked them all. She was a French major at UC California [Berkeley]. And Jadin taught her the routine to lift the bubble—as if that was much work! They [the local Chinese] didn't approve of some of the girls being in the chorus, especially Noel Toy doing the bubble dancing with no clothes on. Even the cooks found it racy; she was rehearsing and they'd all stop cooking to peek.

But I got a better story. When we were at Fong Wan's [Shanghai] Terrace Bowl there was a shortage of bubble dancers. And I can't remember the girl's real name now, but she came to Fong Wan, a Chinese man, and said, "I'd like to be the bubble dancer." He said, "No can use. I need Chinese girl." She said, "Chinese girl you want—I get you."

So she went and put body makeup all over herself—you know, suntan—and she dyed her hair black and cut bangs and she got this guy to come in to say she don't speak English. And she slanted her eyes and he saw her nude. And he went crazy and hired her. And she was as Irish as Patty Spade, and she passed as a Chinese bubble dancer!

Forbidden City opened up a...in those days they called it a cafe society [for the Chinese]. The Chinese people who were very shy and didn't

Andy Wong's "Chinese Vanities of 1954." Top to bottom: Sheryl Lee, Julianne Lew, Mae Lacsamana, Pat Chin, Jeannie Chang, and Jackie Mei Ling. L-R: Hana Abe, Lily Pon, and Dinky Lee.

OPPOSITE, TOP: Jackie Mei Ling in costume for his Shangri-La performance as "The World's Greatest Female Impersonator" (1942). Photo by Romaine.
BOTTOM: The Mei Lings: Jade Ling and Jackie Mei Ling, at the Forbidden City (ca. 1947).

ABOVE, TOP: Ad for the "Celestial Scandals" show in Honolulu (November 11, 1947). BOTTOM: The Mei Lings, Jackie Mei Ling and Jade Ling (mid-1940s). Photo by Bruno of Hollywood.

OPPOSITE: Jackie Mei Ling with dance partners (top to bottom) Mary "Butchie" Ong (ca. 1941), Mai Tai Sing (photo by Bill Cogan, late 1950s), and Kim Wong (photo by Romaine, ca. 1942).

drink very much sort of came out of their shell to go to the nightclubs. Because it was a Chinese show, they were curious. [It wasn't like] going to the Bal Tavern, which was then the big club, or the Top of the Mark, and the 365—they were strictly American clubs.

Oh, Chinatown! The things that Chinese people enjoy the most is eating and gambling and socializing. And we would always go after the show, two o'clock in the morning. And in those days you could sit down, the eight of us, and have Chinese dinner for five, six dollars. And it was always cheaper in Chinatown than it was in American restaurants. However, we used to know an American owner, at Bob's Steakhouse. He was always inviting us over after the show, and we could have filet mignon, New York cuts, whatever we wanted.

You can't get two Chinamen together that they don't gamble—it's a natural instinct. *Mah jong*, you name it, and they gamble. *Paai-gau, dou-bohk*. Like Larry Ching and his wife, Vicky [Lee], liked to gamble. Toy Yat Mar liked to gamble. And they came to my house, we'd play cards, or if not there we'd go to Larry and Vicky's house. But we only played for small amounts; none of us were making that much money. Sammee Tong, who became a marvelous comedian on *Bachelor Father*, he made so much money on that series he bought a beautiful home in Beverly Hills and he went out one night and lost it. And then Vegas—he owed so much money.

There wasn't too much gambling backstage because in Chinatown they had the thirteen basement gambling places. And that was when the police was saying there was no gambling in Chinatown! And every night we'd go, but it was strictly for the Oriental people; and it was *saph-jeung*, ten cards. We used to go all the time, every night after work. And if the gamblers, if they were lucky, they would give *chaan-ji*. And *chaan-ji* was lucky money they'd give you. Five, ten dollars. Of course the girls liked it; they would all smile pretty to get that lucky money. It was almost like Chinese New Year when they give you the *leih-sih* [lucky money in red envelopes].

Then we went off to New York. Jadin and I worked all over New York, all the Jewish Alps. In the Waldorf we dressed in the kitchen over an ice bucket. Here we were featured, and here she came out in a beautiful Chinese dress with sequins and stuff, [out] from the kitchen. That's what happens in most of the theater work—you dress over garbage cans. At the 5th Avenue Theater down in the Village, we had a terrible room. They don't care for performers, as long as you look good outside. When you're in the business, in theater, you're always striving, hoping for that one break.

We were in Havana, Cuba. We had to march in one of those parades, Fidel Castro's parade. And of course they have a big Chinese population there that's intermarried with the Cubans. They all thought they'd go into Havana [to get] into the United States. When they couldn't get in, they intermarried. They're very beautiful people. We had to dance in an un-air conditioned place. The perspiration running down our face… the humidity in Havana is tremendous. We were doing the conga; they thought it was so funny—Orientals doing their native dance. Then we danced at the Club Bamboo. The mosquitoes were terrible; they would bite through your pants. The owner had the hots for Jadin.

We danced in a club called Lobby #2—it was the best club in Juarez and she [Jadin] really fixed me. She got there ahead of me: she flew, I drove. So she checked into the hotel and she told the desk clerk, the bellboys, and the maid not to speak any English. And I went crazy because I didn't speak any Spanish. And I bought a bottle of booze to have a drink, you know, not knowing whether I liked tequila or not. So I got to the hotel and I asked them for some ice. And they said, *"Si, con hielo."* I said, "No, no! Yellow your butt! I want ice, ice, ice—*frio, frio, frio*!" And they said, *"Si, con hielo."* I said, "No, no *hielo*." After twenty minutes of arguing with them, they finally came in with a big bowl of ice and said, *"Con hielo."* So I learned my first bit of Spanish!

I broke with Jadin and I went into the service. When I got out of the service I was in New York. Then I met this very effervescent nineteen-year-old Jade Ling, who was very cute. She was from Boston and she was different from any Chinese girl I've known, including Jadin. She drank and she went to the best clubs in New York. And me, a little fish in a big pond…she knew how to order a bottle of booze for herself and a bottle of booze for me at the Copacabana.

We went to all the best places and then she wanted to be a dance team. She'd never danced. She was very glamorous. She'd buy all her own costumes and we'd split the money on the music and pictures. You take opportunities when you can, so we decided to try it and we joined a show called "Capriz Chinoise" and opened at the Belmont Plaza Hotel across the street from the Waldorf. That was an all-Chinese revue: we had two tall showgirls, Sue Mei Lee and Louise Leung, and then we had four little pixies, and then we had a Chinese magician and a Chinese singer. We danced at the Glass Hat in Kentucky, [in] Chicago [at] the Oriental Theater.

Traveling across the country was great fun, especially with a Chinese company because we were such a novelty, you know: acrobats, chorus girls, dance team, comedian. They didn't see anything like that; it wasn't a standard procedure.

We were traveling west and we were on our way to Chicago and we arrive in Louisville, and a group of Chinese people came and greeted us and said, "Come to the restaurant." So we asked them, "How many Chinese people are there in Louisville." And they said they were the only ones, which is about five or six of them who ran the restaurant. So they said they wouldn't be able to come opening day for the matinee.

Well, I used to do a little spiel after our number and speak in Chinese and then say, "English translation: Thank you very much." Well, this day I decided to upset the company because they were all on stage, and I

MAMMOTH FLOOR SHOW
For the Holiday Season
All-Chinese—All Star Acts

featuring

THE MEI LINGS
Versatile Chinese Trio
in Exotic Dances

THE SEN WONGS
Internationally Famous Dance Stars

**FONG WAN ALL CHINESE
ACROBATIC TROUPE**
In Feats of Grace, Skill and Daring

TOY YAT MAR
"The Chinese Pocket Edition Sophie Tucker"

SAMMEE TONG
Master of Ceremonies

GEORGE WRIGHT
Console King

MEI LAN
"Chinese Sally Rand"
Beautiful Fan and Bubble Dancer

TED THOMPSON
and His Orchestra

Consult PROF. YIP and his Sacred Birds from
China for readings on your future and success.

Early Show for Diners Tues., Wed., Thurs.
First Floor Show 8 p.m.

4 Floor Shows Fri., Sat. & Sun. Nites

Minimum Per Person: Week Days 75c; Sat.
$1.50. No Cover Charge.

Largest Dance Floor of
any Nite Club in the
Bay District.

**NEW SHANGHAI CAFE AND
TERRACE BOWL**
421 10TH STREET   GL-8838

ABOVE: Ad with the Mei Lings trio (Dottie Sun, left, Jackie Mei Ling, and Mary Mammon) at the New Shanghai Cafe and Terrace Bowl in Oakland (December 11, 1941).

cussed in Chinese. And it was terrible, thinking there was no one in the audience [who could understand me. The people in the audience] don't know that I wasn't saying, "Thank you very much, ladies and gentlemen." Well, [Chinese] people had come from another town—they heard about our show—and they said, "How dare you say such terrible things!" But it was fun.

There was nothing to do in Louisville, Kentucky, and so we would lay on the grass and sunbathe. Louise would tan in nothing flat, but it took me a little longer. And then one day going to the restaurant—we had a show to do, we were dancing at the Lookout House—the maître d' wasn't in the front, [and since] I saw a table in the middle of the dining room, I said, "Come on, Louise, let's go sit down and have dinner before the show." We waited and waited and waited and finally the hostess came by and said, "I have to ask you a terribly pertinent question: Are you people black?" I said, "Black? We're yellow, but not black." She said, "That's all right, we could serve you." 'Cause that was the days when they had the johns white and black.

One day we went by one of the johns and I said to Louise in Chinese, "Well, now, we're not black and we're not white. But which one do we go into?" And she said, "Let's go into the black one." And just then some women came by and said, "You can't go in there."

In the theaters in the early days, only the blacks sat upstairs. I wanted to see what it was like because of that old expression, "nigger heaven." Whites would never sit upstairs. Went to a movie house and bought two tickets to the balcony—we were both dark from the sun. Both of us were laughing and talking in Chinese. I guess the way we spoke, the manager came upstairs. The manager came and said, "Sorry, you can't stay here." "What do you mean we can't stay up here? We paid for the tickets." "I'm very sorry, but will you please come down."

In those days blacks weren't catered in clubs—they could *perform* in clubs. Even Lena Horne had a rough time in the early days, and Cab Calloway. They weren't allowed to go into the bar or the lounge. They had a rough time. And us being Oriental—never had to go through that.

Jade and I walked in the Waldorf Astoria to see what's-his-name, the famous [Spanish] conductor—Cugat. And we walked right up to the front of the line with a twenty-dollar bill in my hand. And the maître d' said, "Your reservation?" And I shook his hand and gave him the twenty, and I said, "We're the Mei Lings." And he said, "Oh, right this way." And then there was a black couple standing there and I purposely watched them. For the longest time they never did get in. That's when blacks weren't admitted. Strange thing: Orientals were always admitted because most Orientals were good spenders. In New York when I went out with a group of kids from the China Doll to Versailles, which was a very expensive club, we never had any problem getting a table. They knew we were from China Doll.

In the musical *South Pacific*, there's a line "Children are taught to hate." And if you really think about it—[for] little Chinese kids...I remember when I was a kid: "If you're not good I'm going to get the boogie man on you." And the boogie man would be the black man. So you're taught to hate.

A lot of the Americans in those early days would say, "You Jap or Chinese?" One time Jadin and I were together, and I forget where we were, and they said, "You Red Chinese?" Meaning, were we Commies? And Jadin sat down and said, "If you happen to be in a country where you've not eaten and had no food, and someone comes along and says, 'Here's some rice to feed your family'—you don't know any difference; you're going to take the rice. That doesn't mean I'm a communist—I was hungry!"

I was hanging around New York auditioning shows when Jade got a call from Charlie Low, and that's when she went out [to San Francisco]. I rejoined her again out on the coast; we came back to Forbidden City. Then Jade decided to do a solo, and then I needed another partner. There was a little girl in the chorus and Charlie wanted me to be a team again, so I danced with Butch [Mary Ong]. And then Andy Wong wanted his wife [Doris Wong] to be in a dance team, and I wasn't working, and he was opening a club called the Shangri-La. So I teamed with his wife.

Then I met Dottie [Sun] and Mary [Mammon]. They were in the chorus of the Forbidden City and Walton Biggerstaff was the choreographer and I suggested doing a trio. I'd done all these duos and thought it'd be something different. And they were very pretty and I designed the clothes so that they both wore the same thing. And I was the one in the middle—I had to lift those two cows. [*Smiles*] But they were very young and light and we had a lot of fun. And we ended up in Fong Wan's [Shanghai] Terrace Bowl, and then Charlie hired us back into the Forbidden City, and then we worked at the Golden Gate Theater as a trio.

Shortly after that I had a rough time finding shows. I was auditioning for *Silk Stockings,* and a friend was a hairdresser on that. And in those days they paid dancers nothing, but they offered me much more money than the dancers because they were desperate for someone to do the hair—and they knew I could do it. And I didn't want it, but when they told me about the money, I was excited, you know. So then I did the hair. And from that show I did *Li'l Abner,* and then I ended up doing *Annie*—two [shows based on] comic strips. And then I did the *Merry Widow.* I did lots of shows.

I decided I didn't want to dance anymore. But it was fun—not a lot of money, but a lot of fun.

The lies I've told... ●

ABOVE, TOP (l–r): Dottie Sun, Jackie Mei Ling, and Mary Mammon as the Mei Lings trio (1941). BOTTOM: Forty-seven years later, the Mei Lings trio reunite at the Oakland home of Frances Chun (August 18, 1988). Photo by Zand Gee.

To
Authur

Bruno
Hollywood
nyc

Best Wishes
Jade
Rhue
195_

Jade Ling

b. 1924, Dancer

Excerpts from interviews conducted on
November 28, 1985, and September 29, 1988.

The garbage cans in my life? Honey, there's plenty of garbage cans! Which one do you want? When I was a kid? That was my dad's club; it's called Lido, in Massachusetts. It's a big club and they had about sixteen or twenty-four chorus girls. I was a little kid and I wanted to dance so badly, and here's this show going on and I make my sister go up to the balcony, "Come on, let's do it, let's practice." She landed on her back and she starts screaming, crying, and here's all the customers. So you know what happened? He [Jade's father] came up, took us back into the kitchen, threw us into the garbage can! This is the truth. He didn't mean it, but he's just so mad.

There was a big show, Lou Walters's nightclub. In fact, he was an agent for my father's nightclub in Boston, he was a partner; Lou Walters was an agent before he had a club. So he want me to join the Latin Quarter in Florida. That's...what's that Walters girl? Barbara Walters [television personality and Lou Walters's daughter]—just a few years younger than me. And they starred me there and they gave me a big start 'cause after that he put me on the Latin Quarter on Broadway. It was the biggest thing for me. That was before I really knew how to dance; I was taking lessons but, you know, not a real dancer. But they build around me, big productions.

And here all these stars would try to date me. Orson Welles—he kept sending notes back with the waiters. And I mentioned to the girls in the dressing room and the girls would say, "Are you kidding? You know who he is?" "No." "Orson Welles, the big star that made that big announcement on the radio." I said, "Oh, yeah." But he kept doing it and doing it. I said, "Well, OK, I'll go. It won't hurt you, you get publicity." So I went out with him a few times.

He wanted to take me to places to be seen. I don't like him but, you know, he was supposed to do this big thing for me—write out this act, this dancing act. If he's so brilliant, he could help me an awful lot, you know. I helped *him*; I went out with him, didn't I? I was seventeen and a half, maybe; I had no business being with him [Welles]—they could have thrown Lou Walters in jail. That was before he married Rita. The nerve of him, you know? I guess I was so innocent I didn't know anything.

I saw Jackie [Mei Ling] dancing at the Roxie and I said, "Gee, maybe I want to become a dance team. When I teamed up with him, that was a real dance team—we could have gone far. We worked in the theater.

OPPOSITE: Jade Ling photo (late 1940s), autographed to the author. Photo by Bruno of Hollywood.

ABOVE, TOP: Jade Ling at the Oakland home of Frances Chun (August 18, 1988). Photo by Zand Gee. BOTTOM: Jade Ling (late 1950s). Photo by Romaine.

We worked at the Waldorf Astoria, and that is the greatest moment I could ever remember; it's the most beautiful moment. We went up there and did one rehearsal with the music, and honey, all of a sudden, the next thing I remember we were out on the floor, everything was pitch black, except for the spotlight. It was beautiful. That is the moment I enjoy the most.

I was working at the Latin Quarter when Jadin [Wong] and Noel [Toy] came to New York City. That's the first time I heard of Forbidden City. What did I hear? Oh, you know, "It's a very big club, it's the first big Chinese nightclub in San Francisco." You know, I'm not from San Francisco, I'm from Boston, and I guess I couldn't wait to come out. So I talked to one of the dancers I worked with because she's from here, from San Francisco. "Oh, I know Charlie well; I'll be so glad to write to him for you." "Great!" So she did. I gave her a set of pictures and all that and everything was great. I got a six-month contract because I wasn't going out there without no contract, you know. So anyway, she got me a six-month contract. "Great, honey, that's a long contract—I don't even know if I want to stay out here for six months!"

ABOVE: Jade Ling (1950s).

I came out and it so happened Frances [Chun] met me at the station. She was very nice and she took me, and I was staying with Dottie Sun's sister. And, that was OK, but it's not my style, you know, I want to stay in the hotel. Charlie said, "No." I mean, it's ridiculous; I always stay in the best hotels. I don't want to stay with nobody, I want my own place. "Too expensive." I mean, what made him say that? "I can't afford it." That's because he wasn't paying me enough, that's why. The prices are different from New York, honey!

So anyway, OK, I stayed there and they're so different, I mean, they're a different type of people. [They wanted to know everything.] "What time she come home? Is she OK? Who brought her home?" Stuff like that. And maybe [it was strange] because I've never been with Chinese people before; all my life I've never been among Chinese as much as I did since I came out here. And when I came out here in 1945, oh, it felt kind of weird, you know? So anyway, Charlie went away on vacation and he let me stay in his apartment. So that was nice.

When I first came here, nobody believed I was Chinese. I mean, I really went through something. They said, "She's not Chinese." You know the pictures I sent out and everything? Well, they saw me, hired me. "She's not Chinese." Well, if I'm not, I don't know what I am, then. But I am, I'm full-blooded Chinese. I am. I may not look it, but I am. I can't help that, can I? I didn't know what side I belonged to. Not because of me, [but] because they put me that way. They said I wasn't Chinese and *I am Chinese*. I said, "What am I supposed to be? Which way do I go?" I've been taken for everything!

OK, so I went to the club and said, "Oh, my god!" It's not what I expected. I expected something more elaborate, I mean, coming from New York. I had done a lot of shows in New York City and on Broadway, so coming out here I expected the same thing, not knowing about San Francisco. It was just like another chop suey place; it wasn't elaborate like the Latin Quarter. It was kind of a small scale, but it's not small to the people here. San Francisco...they're more way behind—New York is completely different.

The [chorus] girls used to always run out to the bar. They'd all drink. I think that they weren't truly entertainers or dancers, I think a lot of them were ex-waitresses. They were chosen because they didn't have enough entertainers, to tell the truth. These girls were chosen or hired and they were just taught to do shows, whatever they could do; Walton [Biggerstaff] would teach them and that's what they would do. I don't think any one of them were really what you'd call an act.

They'd bring bottles to the dressing rooms. At the tables, they're boozing like crazy and they'd invite me to drink and I'd say, "No, maybe after the show," because you just don't drink during it. But sometimes I go to the bar and I have a drink and it amazes me how many men...how lonely they are. All they want to do is they want someone to talk to, you know? And I amaze them because I turn right around and tell them what is wrong with them.

Men just love me. I never got along with women, anyway; I always feel they hate me. But I always got along with men. They always think, "Oh, well, [she's a] showgirl and somebody in show business..." Maybe they had intention of taking me home with them and having an affair. By the time I get through talking with them, honey, they admire me. They send me gifts and stuff, flowers thanking me—not for my time but for meeting me as a person. I feel real good because I help them, you know?

ABOVE, TOP: Forbidden City cast. Top (l–r): Robert Wong, Gladys Wong, Larry Leung, Frances Chun, Jackie Mei Ling, and Dottie Sun. Bottom (l–r): Paul Wing, unidentified, Betty Wong, Charlie Low, Rose Chan, Larry Ching, and Jade Ling (1940s). BOTTOM: Jade Ling on the Fobidden City dance floor (ca. 1947).

ABOVE, TOP: Ad for the "Gershwin Revue" at the Forbidden City (ca. 1947). Left, top to bottom: Jackie Mei Ling, Jade Ling, Larry Ching, Paul Wing, Mary Mammon, and Dottie Sun. Right: Charlie Low, Rose Chan, and Diane Shinn. BOTTOM: The Mei Lings, Jade Ling and Jackie Mei Ling, at the Kubla Khan (late 1940s).

On my day off Charlie would see that I'd see the town. I wouldn't say [they were] "dates" but gatherings. Anyway, he was like a father to me, you know? Of course he always liked his young girls. We used to go out to the beach, nightclubs one after another...everything. Charlie used to take us to go eat when I was here. He would invite the whole show, and we'd go eat after the whole show and he would bring a bottle. We'd go have big dinners on Washington Street—every night.

It's not like now [when] you don't see a soul out in the street. Before, four o'clock in the morning, it's crowded like you go to Hong Kong or any foreign country; it's just crowded full of people. There were lots, lots of clubs here; the place was jumping. Sky Room, Kubla Khan—I worked them all. In fact, I was doing a single at Forbidden City and doubling at Kubla Khan; I was doing both. They worked it out for me. I was running from one show to another. They figured I would probably bring in business. I was in the Gershwin show, all Gershwin music. That was a beautiful show. Lots, lots—too many—"Begin the Beguine." "Oklahoma." That was before the fire.

Forbidden City had a fire. Burned everything I had—all my costumes, thousands and thousands of dollars. My god, I really didn't expect that. I ordered so many gowns, you know. I came out during the wartime, [when we] had to move [between] hotels. I said, "OK, it's easier to move from one place to another without all my stuff." And the dressing room is so small, but I crammed it in, including all my personal clothes, even my music. So when the fire happened, everything went. Everything. Charlie didn't give me a penny. I asked him. He said, "Who asked you to bring all those costumes?" Could you imagine that?

And I stayed on and on and on. Off and on until the sixties...'61. We'd go away and we'd work in different places. After Jackie and I broke up I went solo. Then we got back together again and went to Kubla Khan [and] Hawaii. We would get booked as an act in nightclubs and theaters. I went to perform in Cuba with Jadin and Jackie. I had a show with Toy Yat Mar and went traveling with it.

I started hairdressing around 1959 while I was dancing at Forbidden City. I know I can't dance forever, and already I had so many injuries then. So I said, "I better take up something." I was studying at day and dancing at night. I'd lay back in the dressing room and sleep. I got to the point, honey, that my voice was hoarse and everybody said I should see a doctor; everybody thought I was getting cancer, you know. I was getting to school, what...eight o'clock in the morning, and then work at night until two or three o'clock. Well, you get so tired, you can't sleep.

I got another job right downstairs from Forbidden City. I was working downstairs, then I went upstairs to do the show, then go back downstairs, and sometimes I'm late and that's when Ivy [Tam] fired me. "Could do without you! Honey, you can't even lift your left foot!" So, anyway, I said, "Fine." I got my own shop after that. It was offered to me

ABOVE: Forbidden City performers (l–r): Haruyo Kanada, Yuki Cho, Mary Mammon, Jade Ling, Lily Ogawa, and Ivy Tam (early 1960s). Photo by Moulin Studios.

and I had nothing but business. But I always had this luck; some kind of luck for me.

I'm just sorry that I didn't plan it further ahead. All my life I dreamed I'd come here [San Francisco] and go to Hollywood and become a star. That's what I thought. I guess I just overstayed; I stayed too long. I let different things happen in my private life, which I shouldn't have: falling in love and having boyfriends. You can't have boyfriends. You can't do that and have a career. You think you're in love with a guy and you let everything go because he doesn't want you to go any further. So that's when I had to stop—I didn't have to stop, but I did. And yet, if I stop and think, "Well, gee, that's what I was aiming for—what *I* want to be, not what he wants me to be." Right?

Why do I dance? Because I love it; it's part of me. It's life. Dancing is life itself, you know. When you know you do the best, you don't even think, it just happens. When you hit that point, you don't see anything. I can't even describe it to you how beautiful it is. Oh, it's beautiful, it's just beautiful. You only get very few moments. But when you enjoy yourself, you know everything is perfect! I mean, there's always moments when you know that it's tops, it's just tops. Just like me talking to you. When you think it's perfect, you come and hug me and I hug you too, honey! ●

Jadin Wong

1913–2010, Dancer

Excerpts from interviews conducted from
October 31 to November 4, 1985, and on September 5, 1988.

In show business you try to be distinctive. I did it by being Chinese. I'm Chinese and I'm very proud of my Chinese heritage. I have a Chinese heart and an American point of view. I am very, very Chinese in my thinking; I am American in the way of business.

An artist has to make things that people are going to buy. We're Chinese, we love snails, but if you're going to open a Chinese restaurant, you better sell chow mein, chop suey, sweet and sour. If you want to sell snails, no one's going to buy it. You're selling to an American public—they want chop suey. How can they eat chop suey? I wouldn't be caught dead with it!

When I started I was very American, you know: sweater, skirt. When you're a kid, and being the only Chinese in the classroom, it's strange and you wanted to be very American like everyone else. Even as a child you want to belong to a clique.

When I came to New York, I met the columnists Lee Mortimer and Walter Winchell, who took me to the Stork Room, and I met George Jean Nathan—he's supposed to be one of the best critics in American theater. He said, "I'm going to take you to an opening. You ever been to one?" I said, "No." He said, "You can't dress like that!" I had hayseeds in my bangs, OK? A little blouse, a little skirt.

So he taught me to dress with the Chinese collar like the way I'm dressed now: very traditional, long cigarette holder. I said, "But I don't smoke." He said, "You will hold it." And [he gave me a] long fox stole, and I said, "Here?" He said, "No, you will drag it." So I went to the openings and had all kind of attention for him. I have great press because I look different.

I realized that I had to be more traditional, and the Chinese gown has a certain mystique. What's the ugliest part of a woman? The knees and the neck, especially when the woman's growing older, and the Chinese collar has this high, stiff collar. The knees are very bony, and the Chinese gown hides that and shows the side. And they're very flattering if you have the body for it. I love Chinese clothes because they look great on me. Also, it was cheaper than a gown, and all the openings...the stars would spend two, three thousand dollars for a gown. I'm a dancer; I don't have money. When you're traveling you can carry plenty of Chinese gowns in very little space—they just fold over. Effectiveness.

OPPOSITE: Jadin Wong (1940s).
Photo by Romaine.

ABOVE, TOP: Jadin Wong at her New York City apartment (November 1985). Photo by Arthur Dong. BOTTOM: Jadin Wong and unidentified male (late 1930s). Photo by Romaine.

ABOVE: Jadin Wong in *Mr. Moto Takes a Vacation* (20th Century Fox, 1939).

I was born in Marysville but raised in Stockton [California], which is a very boring provincial town, where the people are extremely square and biased. When I started to dance, everybody in the town thought I was absolutely gone to the dogs and my family [was] insane. The prejudice I felt was from the Chinese people, not the whites. Because we were poor and my father was a cook in a restaurant, they thought the dance lessons were very frivolous and not very practical. I used to skip lunches so I could study dancing and study singing. The average Chinese family would [say], "What are you going to do with it after you've learned? Are you going to make money with it?" And when I was growing up, all the Chinese girls were flat-chested, but I wasn't. Having big boobs is not a thing of beauty for the Chinese—it's not acceptable.

Leaving the city was easy. Our father passed away many years ago; if he was alive it would have been difficult because he's from the old school. But my mother's family, her side, was very musical. [My mother] always sang and danced around the house and I'd try to imitate her. When I was a young girl I was very limber; I would do splits and backbends and I got stage-struck.

A company called Long Tak Sam, they came to Stockton, and I went every day. And that's when I planned to go away and join my first show: the A. B. Marcus Show, which Danny Kaye was the star of. So I planned, and the night I was running away from home, I had to climb out of a window—can't get through the front door. And I thought nobody knew, especially my mom. So I was climbing out of the window, and I had a cardboard suitcase and a red hatbox. She reaches into her jacket and she gave me forty dollars, which was a lot of money in those days. She said, "You may need this. Just be careful." That really shook me up.

I went to Hollywood. I was very young, very dumb, and no money. Didn't know anything about living, paying the rent—nothing. All I had were my tap shoes, so I had to wear them for street shoes. We were walking along the street: gray slacks, black and gray sweater, bangs—China doll, you know. I used to stop traffic on the street because I was very long-legged and breasty for an Asian girl. So this fellow comes up to me. He said, "You're a dancer?"

"How can you not tell?" I was going *clunk, clunk, clunk* [with my tap shoes]!

"Would you like to work in the movies?"

"Yes," but in my mind, "*Faan gwai* [white demon], be careful, be careful!"

"Well, come up to my apartment tonight and we'll talk about it."

So I took my girlfriend; I figured with two of us it would be safer. So I went over there and he opened the door and said, "This is my wife, Claudette." It turned out to be Claudette Colbert. We've seen movies; we knew who she was. And his name was Norman Foster—produced all the Mr. Moto pictures. Of course I didn't know who he was at the time, so as long as we saw a woman there and she was a movie star, we figured it was all right.

He asked if we wanted something to eat; I guess he knew we were hungry too. That was the first time we ever saw room service. We ate every piece of cracker there was; there was nothing left anyplace. So then I went to work for quite a few Mr. Moto pictures. I was dancing in *Mr. Moto Takes a Vacation*.

Another time that I was walking down the street, Universal Studios hired me to dance in a short, *International Rebels*. They used to make shorts with singers, dancers, music. I'll never forget that. I had a long train, so I couldn't sit, and they had one of these things that you lean against to rest in between [shots]. When I think back, I should have been scared to death. But I wasn't, didn't have sense enough to. I didn't know how to go get work; the work I had just happened.

I had a scholarship at Michio Ito's school of dance. He was the most famous Japanese dancer, with his own technique: a combination of modern ballet and Oriental. Michio went to San Francisco—there I lived and went to classes eight hours a day, every type of dance, including fencing. I had an elegant English lady manager, Mrs. Goldville, who taught me much about performance. She would dress me up in yards and yards of silk and chiffon, and yet I looked aesthetically lovely and almost nude. I studied at McLaine Studio on Market Street in San Francisco. We were all very young, and Ann Miller was one of the girls in class with me. McLaine was the best tap dancing teacher at that time; he was a student of Bill Robinson's.

Charlie Low and his wife [Li Tei Ming] came to see me at Michio Ito's school of dance. She was a very attractive lady and she sang very well. She was actually the brains behind Forbidden City. At first I wasn't too interested because I was trained for concerts; I didn't feel that I should go into nightclubs. Michio Ito was a very astute man, and he said, "Why don't you try it? You could always leave if you don't like it." So I did, and that was the beginning of my nightclub career as a concert dancer. I opened the club—it was a classical number, I called it the "Dance of the Moon Goddess"—and for some reason it worked, which surprised me and everybody else.

Opening night we had mostly Caucasians because the Chinese were not ready for our nightclub; the only Chinese that were there were friends. When you open a business, you don't care who would come, just as long as people would come and spend money. They were curious because they had never ever seen a Chinese chorus line, or a Chinese

ABOVE: Jadin Wong (late 1930s). Both photos by Romaine.

dancer, or ballroom team, or singer. It was a great novelty, and it was a plus and a minus. The plus is you're unusual—people will see you out of curiosity. The minus is that you feel like you're odd or they'll only use you because you're different, not because you have talent.

We weren't a great big success, but we did pretty well for people who had never been on the stage before. There were a lot of nervous people; we were very young and weren't that great at that time. They had a line of girls, which opened and closed the show. They had a magician, a dance team, and me. And most of the chorus girls hadn't danced before; they were waitresses, elevator operators.

Of course, chorus girls don't do any great dancing—they can't even find their way out on the stage! They wear pretty costumes and had good figures. They look around, do a few turns. But the American public loved it because they were very honest and very fresh. See, if you're a pro they could roast you alive, but if you're fresh...And we had a choreographer named Walton Biggerstaff and he taught them very simple routines, dressed them beautifully, and that made up for a multitude of sins. I knew what I was going to do—I've danced before—and I knew my costume was beautiful. I danced there on and off for three to four years. We did strictly American, with a Chinese feel.

Noel Toy was a nude camera model in the World's Fair [the Golden Gate International Exposition], and Charlie Low hired her to do a bubble dance and a fan dance. She had a nice body, but the poor girl never danced. She walked around for three choruses—which is a long time in music—holding a bubble or holding a pair of fans, and the people were laughing and hysterical at her because it's a very long time. I couldn't stand it so I said, "Oh, Charlie, how could you do this to her? I'm going to teach her how to dance; she can't go out and make a fool of herself!" So I called her and said, "You're going to come with me and we're going to work three or four hours a day." She said, "I know, everybody's making fun and laughing at me."

So I taught her to move the fans around and do backbends, and she did fine. She's a good student, not afraid of pain; I had her do backbends and she was screaming with pain. Only thing: when it comes to turns, she would lose her balance—and it was hard, two twenty-five-pound fans—and she would fall on the tables and put her fingers in people's chow mein and say, "Excuse me!" "It's OK, help yourself."

And Charlie said to me—he called everybody Suzy—"Suzy, you've got to stop that—I mean, she's falling all over the table." "She'll learn, she'll learn." That's how it started. And I taught her the bubble; the bubble was not bad, it was popular. Anybody who's nude was popular.

We used to get lots of mail at the Forbidden City—proposals, mostly from Caucasians—but in the beginning some from the Chinese: "Aren't you ashamed of yourself, showing your legs and your body? Why don't you get a decent job and be an honorable person instead of a shame to the community?"

OPPOSITE: Jadin Wong (1940s). Photo by Boris Bakchy.

Well, the thirties and forties, the Chinese people are very closed-minded; they're sure that anyone in show business had to be absolutely insane, immoral, and everything else that's bad. But little do they know that in our business we spend so much time perfecting our art we haven't got time to be bad or immoral. And they looked upon us as loose characters and whores. Now, if we were whores, we wouldn't have to work that hard to get very little money from Charlie Low! They really ostracized us; they used to practically cross the street or spit at us.

But once they started coming to the club after a lot of publicity, they loved it. The waiters are Chinese, the food is good, the show is Chinese. They found it's a place to go; they had a wonderful time and they'd tell their friends and everybody started coming. Forbidden City got the Chinese people out of their houses into nightclubs for the first time in their lives. The bitches from Stockton used to come out and see me do all this gorgeous stuff [and say], "Tell me, how do you stay so beautiful while we get so old?" I say, "Because I'm beautiful inside; I'm not a bitch!"

Those were the days of the very plush Chinese gambling places. When you say gambling, it's not a joint, it's not Vegas—it's anything you want you can get there. I remember one, I can't remember the name,

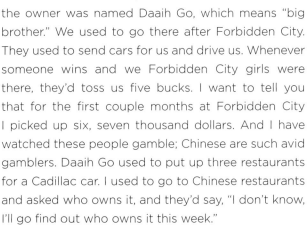

the owner was named Daaih Go, which means "big brother." We used to go there after Forbidden City. They used to send cars for us and drive us. Whenever someone wins and we Forbidden City girls were there, they'd toss us five bucks. I want to tell you that for the first couple months at Forbidden City I picked up six, seven thousand dollars. And I have watched these people gamble; Chinese are such avid gamblers. Daaih Go used to put up three restaurants for a Cadillac car. I used to go to Chinese restaurants and asked who owns it, and they'd say, "I don't know, I'll go find out who owns it this week."

People got together; we went to games, dances...we had banquets. It was just an awful, awful lot of fun, which you don't have today. Today you're afraid to go to places. We used to stay out all night at Forbidden City and in New York. We used to have a contest amongst all the show people to see who could stay out the longest. It was a dumb reason, but we did it. Jackie [Mei Ling] and I stayed up for four days and four nights one time. When you're young you could do it; they don't make us today like they did. We did three shows: 8:30, 10:30, and 2:00. Clubs were open till 4:00 in New York. We used to go out and eat, gorge, get bicycles and go bicycle riding—just to see how long we could stay up. We used to go roller-skating, go bowling. It was always a lot of laughs. Those were the days—gone.

We had just finished at Forbidden City. It was about 1944 and a fellow came from Hawaii—and the Chinese were very hot now—and he said, "How would you and your partner like to dance for us at the Club Blue Lei?" I said, "I've never been to Hawaii. I would love it."

Told the kids I was going to Hawaii. Coby [Yee] happened to have a fight with her boyfriend, who was a singer at the [Chinese] Sky Room. Coby said, "Oh, I heard you're going to Hawaii. I just broke up with my boyfriend and I'm so depressed. Can I go with you?"

So I called up Ted Lewis and said, "I have a girl that can tap dance." He said, "OK." Contract. Then four days later, "I made up with my boyfriend, Sonny [Sun Lowe]. He wants to go." I didn't know whether I could do that or not—I mean, it just started with me. So I called him [Ted Lewis]. "Little girl tap dancer, remember? She made up with her boyfriend. Do you want a male singer?" "OK."

Then there was Roberta [Robin] Wing, working with her boyfriend at the Sky Room. She said to me, "Oh, I heard you were going to Hawaii, I want to go. Oh, gee, I want to go. Can I go?" I called him again, "Hey, I got a Filipino girl singer, she's very good." He said, "Why don't you get a revue? You've got more than half of one." So I got a revue together. Prince Gum Loew—plays Chinese instruments, he's fat and chubby...I got this idea to tie this ribbon around his belly and then I shoved him on the floor to unwind and made him a comedian.

Spent four months in Hawaii, where there was love and romance. People wined and dined us; the mayor came to see us. It was the Club Blue Lei. I'll never forget it: every night somebody sent me a blue lei. And my little girl tap dancer, Coby, got married to the singer, Sonny. And I was dancing with that no-good partner of mine, Li-Sun, who was laying everybody in town. Then I got involved with two of the best-looking guys in the island; one of them was a football player. Then he [Li-Sun] came to me with his feelings hurt, "Oh, you embarrass me; you're going out with these beautiful guys." I said, "You rather me go out with short, ugly guys?!"

So here at this beautiful wedding [for Coby and Sonny], everybody was there except for this guy that I liked. So then Coby asked me to take her to the ladies room, and this guy I liked was waiting at the garden. Li-Sun had followed us and when he saw this guy they started to fight. The whole wedding went to chaos and I ended up in the hospital with a cut lip. That was a scandal. Imagine, a big, beautiful wedding with

OPPOSITE: Jadin Wong appeared in at least two movies produced by Grandview Films, a Chinese American company headquartered in San Francisco's Chinatown during the 1930s and '40s. TOP: Actors from Grandview (l–r): Leung Bik Yuk, Wong Hock Sing, Jadin Wong, Li-Sun, and Lai Yee (late 1940s). MIDDLE: Scene from the Grandview film *A Strong Wind Banishes the Swallow* with (l–r) Jadin Wong, Lai Yee, and Li-Sun (1946). BOTTOM: Jadin Wong (late 1930s). Photo by Romaine.

ABOVE: Jadin Wong organized a tour to Honolulu after her stint at the Forbidden City. TOP: Performers receive an Aloha reception at the airport (l–r): Coby Yee, Sun Lowe, Jadin Wong, Li-Sun, Roberta (Robin) Wing, and Prince Gum Lo (Loew) (ca. 1944). BOTTOM: Ad for the "Chinese Follies" show at the Club Blue Lei (ca. 1944).

everybody in a mass fight; everybody was taking sides. The police came and I had to take everybody to the hospital!

Then we came back and somebody called me to take a show to Mexico City. That was my first time in producing: fan dancer, dance team, I danced, magician, Chinese Bing Crosby [Larry Chan], and a line of eight girls. Never produced before, so when I got to the studio I said, "Oh, god!" I choreographed it. I designed the costumes.

We were dancing at the Lyrical Theater and then the El Patio [Nightclub] in Mexico City. It was famous. It had an orchestra on both sides. It was a round thing, [and one orchestra] plays for an hour and then it swings around and another orchestra swings around and plays. I thought that was fascinating. Without losing a beat, the transition was very smooth. The owner—I'll never forget that place—was an old guy: Armando. We were doubling and also working at the Teatro Cine Royal. We were working both jobs: three shows a night at the theater, and at about eight, nine o'clock we'd go to the nightclub. Dressing rooms were terrible; big rats running around.

The last three weeks the Mexicans had a strike—actors and musicians strike—so we couldn't go on at the El Patio. Now I had twelve people there that needed to be paid and I couldn't pay them unless I got paid. The Mexicans are very religious, so I feel that it was an act of God or whatever it is, and I said to Armando, "You must pay my girls. They're here and they need the money to pay the rent." So I pointed to a religious statue and said, "You must pay or I'll put a curse on you." And a month later he died and everybody thought I did it. Only twice did I curse somebody and they died; I feel like a witch! That's Mexico. But it was fun—except I got Montezuma's revenge.

We were playing at a club in Juarez, a lovely club. And I'm sort of a homebody;

after the show I just wanted to go home. I'm not a drinker. "I don't really want to meet anybody, I just want to go home." [But my friend said,] "Aw c'mon, let's go have a drink." So I met this gorgeous blonde guy and I got stuck on the guy. And being very stupid, I became pregnant.

When I came to New York I realized I was pregnant, and it's always the stupid girls that get pregnant, not the bright ones. We [Jadin and partner Jackie Mei Ling] opened at the China Doll, so we're opening, we're dancing, three shows a night: eight, twelve, and three. So we decided to get an abortion—which is an ugly word at any time—but there was no other way.

I had the abortion at ten o'clock; I came back and I rested. I think [dancer] Lily Pon came to see me. And at six o'clock I got dressed and got ready and went to the China Doll and did three shows with the aerial lifts, spins in the air. Three shows. I didn't know I was not supposed to feel good because no one told me. Jackie was like a mother hen. He took very good care of me; he was very good.

Jackie was my first partner. He was a very important part of my life. We were so beautiful: Jackie was very handsome and I was gorgeous. We were two of the most gorgeous people. People would stare at us when we walked the streets. I told him, "The first time I met you, you were wearing a black hula skirt with gardenias in your hair in Finocchio's" [the San Francisco nightclub featuring female impersonators]. He was the only Asian. They had beautiful shows. I saw him and he was so exquisitely beautiful—but I had the tits!

People thought Jackie and I were madly in love, but sometimes we would just hate each other. He is a real imp; he would do anything at any time to get a rise out of someone. We did this ethereal "Clair de Lune" by Debussy [*hums a bar*]...so elegant. In the end, I'd lay across his knees and he'd bend over and he'd kiss my cheek. And the dull nights, or when we'd have a fight, he'd lean over and stick his tongue in my mouth, and here I'm trying to be very elegant. I'd be going "Ugh, ughhh, ugh." That was his kicks. It would infuriate me. He'd tell you he did it!

You know, Jackie is gay. Although I was much younger and I didn't quite understand...I was staying in his home and his dad was this tiny guy, the most beautiful human being. Pop raised him; his mom died when he was young. Pop was "Pop" to all of us girls. He used to come to the club—little Pop. I loved him. We were staying with him and of course we were young and hot-headed. One day, during a quiet moment, he said—he didn't know that Jackie was gay, and Jackie would never dream that he knew, but parents know a lot—he said, "Jackie is a little bit different from most people. He is my only son and I love him very much. So please be kind because you're his only friend, and maybe he loves you. I don't want you young people to be fighting all the time. He's different, he's special." I'll always remember being touched. Jackie doesn't know I had this conversation. One day Jackie says, "Pop didn't know I was gay; he never told me." "He didn't say you were gay. He

OPPOSITE: Handbill from the Teatro Cine Royal in Mexico for the "Chinese Follies" (mid-1940s).

ABOVE, TOP: Jadin Wong and Jackie Mei Ling (1940s). Photo by Romaine. BOTTOM: Jadin Wong and Li-Sun (mid-1940s). Photo by James Kollar Studios.

please to present

Jadin Wong

with her

New slant

on COMEDY

said you were special, you were different." He was surprised. They [parents] know. It didn't matter. [Pop] loved him.

One time we were in between shows at the China Doll. We finished and we went to some eastside boat to have dinner. I met a girl, Gypsy Markoff [an accordionist and dancer], who was quite well known because she was in the plane that fell in Lisbon, and she said, "I'm going to Europe next week with Jeanette MacDonald, Gene Raymond, Slapsy Maxie, a whole slew of celebrities. Would you like to go?" I've never been to Europe and I said, "Sure, I'd love to go." So I said, "Jackie, I have an offer to go to Europe." He said, "Oh, you're crazy. It's Christmas. You don't know these people, and how do you know it's true?" I said, "Jackie, let's go." "I'm not going." I said, "Yes, you are." So finally by morning, "OK, I'll go." Later he told me it was the best time of his life.

Then I became a comedian when I came back from Europe. No more nightclubs; they had little tiny rooms, so I wasn't getting any work. They say, "Oh, you're Chinese and you're a woman," and "What do you want to become a comedian for?" I said, "No more nightclubs. I want to become a comedian—I have to be." They said, "Oh, we'll use you on Chinese New Year." "Now, that's once a year. Do you use Italians on Italian New Year? And Jewish people on Jewish New Year? Now come on, I'd get awfully hungry."

So, the first act I wore a headdress and black leotards. I'd go on and tell jokes and all the men would say, "Bring on the girls." I said, "OK." And I take off my headdress and then they think, "Oh, she's going to do it." Then I take off the robe. Then when I get their attention I tell them a joke. It's tough because they don't want to hear me.

I got my training in the Borscht Belt, and that's tough. And then I started to work all the hotels. I used to work at the

Village Bar and this drunk was heckling me all night long. Every time I told a joke he said, "*Ah so.*" I said, "'*Ah so* in Japanese means 'How nice.' I want you people to know he is the biggest *ah so* I've ever met in my whole life!" Usually, when the show's over they'd always come over and offer a drink and say, "Gee, I didn't know there were Chinese people like you." Their old model is the old chop suey joint where the waiter comes up: "What you likee eat tonight? Pork fly lice?"

I use my humor all the time. Mishawaka, Indiana—you wouldn't believe the name. I walked into town, the people followed me for blocks; my producer thought there was a parade! [*Laughs*] At that time my hair was black with bangs—the China doll and the chopsticks [*indicates that the chopsticks were ornaments in her hair*]. People would stop me in the streets and say, "You speakee Engleesh?" I said, "No. Not a damn word. What do you wanna know?!"

I got into the management/agency business by accident. My agent Tony Rivers's office burnt down; he asked me to take over until he rebuilt. It took a month. In the meantime, casting people called and said, "I need this." I said, "I'm only answering the phone." "Oh, please, you gotta help us; you must know some people." I started to book, and the business improved like 200 percent.

Tony came back. I said, "Take your cockamamie office, I want no part of it. It's giving me gray hair; it wasn't gray when I started! I want to go home and do my own thing. I don't need this." Two months later he came down and said, "You've ruined my life." I said, "What do you mean, ruined your life? Your business was dying, now I improved it; you're making all this money." He said he "used to be able to go out for walks with my doggie. I used to have lunch; now I can't even go to the bathroom. I don't want the business—I quit!" And then he left.

So I started this [agency] so I can specialize in Asians and ethnics because no one understands the mystique of an Asian actor. Most Caucasian agents can't tell the difference between Chinese, Japanese, Koreans. All my experience and what I've learned, now I try to give to the Asian American actors that are coming into this business—to help them and nurture them so they can have a future in this business with less heartaches than I had when I first started. I baby my people and encourage them, scold them, and they do very well. I mean, they're a real pain sometimes, but they are different. Asians are more sensitive; they lose face. If they go three, four times on a job and they don't get it, they're destroyed. Except the dynamo actors—they'd go a hundred times.

Three years ago, Joanna Merlin, a casting lady, had this nontraditional casting at the Shubert Theater. Because of nontraditional, Asians are now doing Shakespeare, they're doing things that were never open to them before, and I think that's a big step forward for Asians. The casting of Asians has improved like 100 percent. ●

OPPOSITE: Marketing brochure for Jadin Wong's comedy act (1960s).

ABOVE, TOP: Jadin Wong at her home office in New York City (November 1985). Photo by Arthur Dong. BOTTOM: Jadin Wong flies out for another engagement in this publicity photo distributed by American Airlines (April 1955). Photo by Kostin.

Larry Ching

1920–2003, Singer

Excerpts from interviews conducted on
August 25, 1988; September 22, 1988; and August 1, 1989.

I'm really from Hawaii; I was born and raised in Hawaii until I was about eighteen. Then I had to leave town and, well…I wasn't a good boy then. You know, I was pretty bad, I did bad things, they were lookin' for me. I had a friend that was a deputy sheriff…He came and told me, "You better leave town, you know, because they're gonna pick you up." So that's one of the reasons why I left Hawaii.

When I came here [to San Francisco], we'd go out with the boys and we'd go out to the bars and have a few drinks, and then they'd say, "Well, why don't you go up and sing a song?" And I'd say, "Naw, naw, I don't want to sing a song." And they'd say, "Yeah, sing." "No, I don't want to sing." "If I buy you five drinks would you—" "You got it, brother!" For five drinks I could sing all night, you know. So I'd go up and sing a song, and then I'd sing a couple more, and then, you know, we'd get feeling good, we'd all go home, and then the next day, we'd all go someplace else, you know?

You know, like Jade Palace: I would go in and there was a Chinese fellow playing the Hawaiian steel guitar and his name was Prince Wan, I think, and he played Hawaiian music. And then someone heard me down at the Jade Palace and she used to work at the Chinese Village— she was a cocktail waitress. So she said, "Say, why don't you go and try? They have a piano player." So I said, "OK."

It was Charlie's [Low] originally—he and Dr. Margaret Chung and Dr. Collin Dong owned it; that was the first bar that opened in Chinatown. Ban Lee was the owner at that time and then he asked me, "You wanna be a singin' bartender?" I says, "Singing bartender? What do I do?" He says, "Well, we get a mic for you in the back and you just roam around in the back of the bar. And whenever people want you to sing, you sing." "All I can drink? OK, I'll take the job!" And it was only thirty dollars a week and I made tips.

And I says, "Well, I gotta learn all this stuff." I was always inspired by Frank Sinatra, you know, 'cause the songs I sang when I first came over here were mostly Hawaiian songs and not very many of the popular songs. But when I heard him sing, I wanted to sing like him. I don't read music, so I would buy the music, you know, and I'd buy the record and play it and listen to it. Remember they used to have song sheets with all the songs on it? Well, I would cut the ones that I know, put it in a book, so when you asked I would try and look up the page.

OPPOSITE: Larry Ching (1940s). Photo by Romaine.

ABOVE, TOP: Larry Ching is interviewed by the author at his San Francisco home (August 25, 1988). Photo by Arthur Dong. BOTTOM: Larry Ching photo (1950s), autographed to the author.

Now, we had a piano player in the back; he plays and I sing at the bar. And at the end of the night, he and I would split whatever tip there was. My tips were better than my salary. So I worked there and then my friends would come and we'd get loaded all the time.

One night a fella came down, he says, "Hey, why don't you try that amateur show in San Francisco?" And that amateur show was called "Homestead Bread Instead." It was a bread company, and that's why it was called "Homestead Bread Instead." And I says, "No, no, I wouldn't have a chance, me being Oriental, you know." So the guy called my bluff and said, "You haven't got the guts." I said, "Well, what is it worth?" He said, "Tell you what: you go, you sing. When you sing you can drink all you want." So I took his bluff. I didn't win; I came in second. The girl that did win, she went to…I don't know, one of the high schools here. And being that, you know, all her friends in the high school voted for her—it's by ballot—she won.

Word went around and somebody went over to Forbidden City and told Charlie, "Hey, there's a young Chinese boy singing down at the Chinese Village. Why don't you go down and take a look?" So he sent his wife [Li Tei Ming] down. And she came in and she listened to me sing and she thought, "Pretty good." So she asked me if I wanted to work in a nightclub. I said, "No, I like it here. I got my tips, I got my booze…I enjoy it here."

In the meantime, Andy Wong—the guy that operated the Chinese Sky Room—he says, "You want to work for me?" I said, "If I work for you, how much are you going to pay me?" Well, the scale then was $32.50 a week; that was way back in the early forties. That was before the war. He said, "Well, tell you what. I'm going to open a new club called the Shangri-La"—and that was on Bush Street—"I'll give you fifty dollars." "OK!" So I signed the contract with him. The place was supposed to open and I think three months later it never opened; I guess they probably had [canceled] the license of the place. [The Shangri-La operated from June to August 1942.] So Charlie came over to ask me to work for him. Finally, I signed a contract to work down at Forbidden City and that's how it all started. And I worked for him for quite a few years, off and on.

The first night was tough—it was really tough; I've never been in front of an audience. And Charlie says, "You got to put makeup; you have to buy a tuxedo, you have to wear a stiff shirt and a bow tie." I says, "That's out. I don't want that. If I'm going to sing I'm gonna go the way I am." He says, "No, you can't. It's a nightclub. Everybody has to dress like that." And I says, "A monkey suit? You're crazy. I don't ever

CHINATOWN'S MINSTREL BOY—This is Larry Ching, who pours out liquid cheer and liquid notes at the same time, behind the bar at Ban Lee's Chinese Village. He's adept at Mandarins and other Village potencies, and a wiz at everybody's favorite songs, with emphasis on Hawaiian numbers. Occasionally he pauses (in the vocal work, only) to let the song-making, piano-beating combination, Frank and Lee, have an inning at your attention.

OCTOBER, 1941

work in a monkey suit!" But then friends of mine said, "Give it a try." I says, "OK."

I had to put a monkey suit on, and going out and seeing all those people sitting out there and then have to sing a song...that was...I don't know...I wanted to get off. Right after my first song I wanted to quit. I opened with "This Love of Mine"—Sinatra sang that. I know one of the songs was "I Don't Want to Set the World on Fire" and "Begin the Beguine." I did pretty well, considering.

They called me the "Chinese Frank Sinatra." Like Larry Chan: they called him the "Chinese Bing Crosby." And they wanted to give me something, you know...thought they would attract more people. The fella that gave me that, he was writing for the [San Francisco] *Examiner*—what's called, I think, the "Nightlife"—and his name was Frank Funge, but he used another name, but Frank Funge was his real name. He had a weekly nightlife column; at that time we had a lot of clubs in San Francisco. He was the one that gave me that name and I didn't like it. Every time I went out and they would call me the "Chinese Frank Sinatra" I just—aaahh, I wish they wouldn't say that 'cause I didn't sound like him; I couldn't sing like him. I wanted to be myself, but then I got stuck with that.

The backup band at that time was Wally Holcomb. They had a drummer, piano player, saxophone, and a trumpet. When we started I think it was only four; the accordion came afterwards with a different band. When Hal Wallace came in he had an accordion playing, he had a bass player, and he played the violin, and he had a trumpet player. So they had six; it wasn't a big band.

We used to do the "Gay '90s" show. We fooled around, we played around a lot. There was a trio that we did: it was Charlie, [Wilbur] Tai Sing, and I, and we sang the old Gay '90s songs—"Are You From Dixie?" and "I Want a Gal." We used to have a lot of fun with Charlie because he doesn't like to be goosed. Charlie couldn't sing, and in order to get him started, I would have to start the song and then he would come in. Well, before that, we'd goose him a little bit and he would jump up. We'd stick our finger and he'd go, "Oop!" We'd make a little comedy out of it.

There were times when he [Charlie Low] would ask us, "Well, the USO navy show—they asked if we would do a show for them," and I'd say, "OK." I would go and it would usually be on Mason Street. Usually you don't have time to rehearse, so they'd ask what kind of tempo. "Whatever feels good to you, do it." Whatever tempo they played in I'd take it and I'd sing it 'cause I don't know music, I don't read music, everything is by ear. And we did shows in Hamilton [Air Force] Field, you know, where everyone did shows and it was all gratis. But for some of the shows we did, the union wouldn't let 'em get away with it, they have to pay us. So what we did is we took the check, we signed the check, and we'd give it to whatever charity we were doing it for, like the Chung Mei Home [for boys]. For about four or five years, I think, we did shows for them.

OPPOSITE, TOP: The Chinese Village bar, where Larry Ching earned tips as a singing bartender in 1941. Ching worked under owner Ban Lee, who bought the business from Charlie Low. Tending the bar in this earlier 1936 photo is Hubert Wong. To the right of Wong is Charlie Low, Mrs. Hayne Hall, and, in glasses, Dr. Collin Dong (Wide World Photos). BOTTOM: Chinese Village ad featuring Larry Ching (October 1941).

ABOVE: Pages from a Forbidden City program (ca. 1942). TOP (clockwise): Larry Ching, Mary Mammon, Larry Chan, and Jadin Wong. BOTTOM: Wally Holcomb and his band.

ABOVE, TOP: Forbidden City postcard (1940s). BOTTOM: Larry Ching and a Forbidden City customer during the "Gay '90s" show (1940s).

You know, being in show business you don't have to be good-looking—as long as you're in show business you can get anything. What I mean by anything is the girls. It's very easy! Oh, talking about offers—boy, did we get it! [*Laughs*] The offers are good. The girls would come and sometimes I would take them to the dressing room and have a piece or two in between shows... take a hike and come back and things like that. And other times in between shows, we would go to the other clubs. We had three Chinese clubs at that time. A lot of the girls...the dancers, you get to know the dancers, and you take them out and after work you get together. Do a lot of drinking, a lot of fooling around. [*Laughs*] A lot of beds!

When Duke Ellington come into town, the first time he played at the Veterans Memorial, he had a concert and he loves Chinese food. He came over to Forbidden City and everybody knows who he is—so did Charlie. So Charlie set a table right in the middle of the floor—dance floor—and fed him. Took the check and then he asked Duke if Duke would play a song, and he got up and played a few tunes for us. That was terrific! What a man—nice guy. And Lena Horne was there and she got up and she sang a couple of songs. She generally doesn't do that, she don't go to clubs and sing.

Charlie as a boss and host...he's really a terrific guy. When the janitor [at Forbidden City] was sick, I would go out and do the job of janitorial work for him. I used to clean up the joint after everybody was gone, and people used to see me and say, "Are you the singer?" I says, "No, that's somebody else. I'm the janitor here." It's kind of embarrassing to tell the guy. And the guy says, "You're Larry, aren't you?" I says, "Yeah." I didn't mind doing those things. When I worked for Charlie at Forbidden City I did all that. He had a ranch out in Pleasanton, and I would go out twice a week and get the eggs and deliver the eggs for him. And I would leave the fresh eggs and take the old eggs and [sell them]. And some went into my pocket and some went to him. You got to make a little profit! [*Laughs*]

The reason why we were popular—number one—we had a good show. And we always had different shows, like we had the "Gay 90s," we had a Hawaiian show, we had a Chinese show. A lot of the Chinese came to the club, they enjoyed it. People our age would come. A lot of older folks would come because they enjoyed our show—our show was clean, there was nothing dirty. We had dancing. It was a complete show:

everything was put together, it was synchronized, you know. It was just rolling without stopping in between.

But the reason they came up, 'cause it was true, was not to hear us sing, it was to watch the Chinese girls dance. They were more, you know, interested in the girls than they were with us. Usually, you know, after the show they would call the girls; all the girls would sit down and have a drink and have something to eat. They wouldn't call us to go sit down and have something to eat, you know.

A lot of the parents were against the daughters dancing like that—it was something new—it was here in Chinatown it was against the rule. A lot of them were good girls, a lot came from good homes, a lot of them were married—husbands would pick them up after work.

Sometimes you didn't have enough girls to dance. You want six in a chorus, you'd only have four. And when you did get those that wanted to dance, they couldn't dance. A lot of the girls...I noticed when they dance they couldn't dance by the music, they'd dance by count: one, two, three, four, one, two, three, kick. That's how they learned. But there were a few that could dance to music.

Orientals were just novelties because they'd never seen an Oriental do this type of singing and dancing. This was something new to everybody—even for ourselves it was new. We couldn't get jobs like the other [white] stars were getting and the kind of money they were getting. We weren't getting that kind of money because the talent at that time wasn't what you'd call great talent like we have today.

We're not known as entertainers as far as the American type of entertainers—dancing, singing—we're not known for that. If you're black, fine, because they know they have rhythm and everything, right? They were used to watching [black people]. They would go to Bimbo's or the American clubs or the Mexican clubs and see them perform. And you know, when you go to see them perform, they perform a lot better than we do.

My own thing was I could never compare with these people. I went to a white club and I'd just be someone to fill up a slot. Yeah, there was talent, [but] they would only recognize it if you were in a Chinese nightclub, and that's where you belong and that's fine. The American clubs wouldn't hire us. For myself, I think I was a little timid 'cause when I'd go out I'd be nervous; I'd have butterflies and it would take me maybe about sixteen bars before I can really break loose. I was just afraid of what people would think or what people would say.

When I sing I would never open my eyes; I'd sing through the whole number with my eyes closed. As long as I can't see the people staring at me I could sing, otherwise I couldn't sing. I learned from a girl—I was going to take singing lessons from her—and she taught me one thing: "When you sing, don't look at the people. Your problem is you look at the people and you get scared. Just look above them." Sometimes I'd be singing and I'm closing my eyes and I'd bang the mic. She said, "Just look above them." So that's one of the techniques I learned.

ABOVE: Larry Ching at the Forbidden City. Behind him are Fritz Jensen, left, and bandleader Harry Abramson (ca. 1946).

You work in a nightclub, you're right in the middle of it: people sitting on your left and on your right and up front. But what irritates me are the people sitting right alongside of me and they know you're trying to perform, and they're all talking and banging their glasses. Especially that was during the war and some of them took us for Japanese instead of Chinese. You know, these Haoles, these white people that come in, and they would call us like they'd always do: "yellow-belly" and all that kind of stuff. "Oh, a bunch of Japs." "That chink can't sing." "That Chinaman." "That slant-eye."

Being in the business, we had to take some of that. We're supposed to take some of that—but we don't. I wouldn't take any of that crap when I was working up front. I think I was the only one that wouldn't take any of that crap they were dishing out. I had a bad reputation. After the show I would go and tell the guy what I thought. And if they didn't like it, I would ask him to go outside. I'd tell them what I thought. I'd come out—I have a bad mouth—like, "You asshole! Hey, let's go outside and settle this thing." I didn't care how big they were, that was my problem.

The biggest mistake I made was when this guy came in and he said something to Vicky [Lee, Larry's wife]: "Oh, she's just a Chinese whore," or something like that. Charlie had this reputation that if you come in with a group of men, he would tell the girls to sit down there 'cause they want the girls. But this guy just had a big fat mouth. He was sitting with four or five other guys. I said, "Hey, what you said to my wife—you'd better apologize." You know how *louh-faans* [white people] are: "Who the hell do you think you are?" and stuff like that. You know: "You little shit!" I said, "Come on, I want to talk with you." And like a dummy, he came backstage. And he was big, he was about at least six feet. How the heck was I going to get this guy?

We took the stairs going up to the dressing rooms—we had dressing rooms on each side and you go up the stairs—took about two steps, just right for me, so I—boy, I just smashed him! Oh! Then I took him upstairs to the dressing room. I gave him some more: had him down on the floor. I keep pounding him. The wife was in there and Tony Wing, one of the acts, was in there. I closed the door and I let him have it. Oh boy, did I bust him, I really smashed him. He was a little drunk, but it was to my advantage because a big guy like that, he would have killed me. But I think I caught him by surprise. I know I did some kind of damage.

So when he left, I took off. When they called the cops, they were looking all over for me, but I wasn't there because I left. I took a hike. And the doorman—I know the doorman...I says, "How's everything?" He says, "Fine." So I went back upstairs and did my last show and went home. Fixed him up good.

After that Charlie had a suit; [that man] sued Charlie and myself. When I went to see his attorney, I said, "Look, I only weigh 130 pounds. How can I do this to a big man like him? It's impossible. Somebody else probably busted him up, not me." The problem was I did it in the club; I should have taken him outside. We lost.

After the war, the club started going down. People didn't have money to spend 'cause during the war everybody had money to spend and that's when things were booming. We had the shipyards and all that, and we had these service people, the sailors and everybody, and there was money to be spent. Right after that the boom was gone, everything started to hit rock, rock bottom. [Charlie] would take off and he'd say, "Will you emcee the show? I'm going to Bimbo's," or "I'm going to this club to see how're they're doing." Even those clubs weren't doing good. That's why Charlie got out; he sold his club 'cause he couldn't make it. For a fellow with a nightclub, the overhead was too high.

ABOVE: Larry Ching performs at the world premiere of the documentary *Forbidden City, USA,* Palace of Fine Arts, San Francisco (November 15, 1989). Photo by Bob Hsiang.

I quit singing because of fooling around: married, dad, two kids—and fooling around. I would take the offers and have a good time and forget about the wife and kids. That's where all my problems started. I came to the point [that my wife] would come out and say, "Well, it'll either be this or that." So I took this, and I gave up singing.

I was drinking a little too much. If I got away from show business, I wouldn't drink as much; it was an every-night thing. You'd come in and say, "Hey, you want to have a drink?" So I'd have a lot of drinks. I used to sign a lot of slips; I would put it on my tab because I worked there. At the end of the night it'd go to Charlie, so when I got paid Charlie takes out what I owe. So that's when I quit.

Then I owned a service station and that didn't work out. And then I worked for a painter and contractor in Chinatown. I worked for the [San Francisco] *Examiner*; I drove trucks for the *Examiner* for twenty-eight years and now I'm retired.

I didn't have a goal [for my showbiz career]—it's just that I enjoyed doin' it. One thing I'm glad about is that we were breakin' the ice for all the people, you know. We gave 'em a good start. So I mean, now it's a lot better for them. We showed 'em that we had a little talent—and we had some talent.

Today I know a little more and I sing better and my style has changed. And I think I would have gone on and learned how to read music and play something like the piano. But I sing a little bit at home—not too much. Once in a while I'll sing for friends when the kids are getting married. I'd do the "Hawaiian Wedding Song" for them, and that's about the only singing I do.

It was a good life. I liked it, I enjoyed it. [*Laughs*] That was the life, let me tell you. I wish I can do it again, but I guess I'm too old to do it, that stuff. What do you think? No?! Oh boy! ●

Mary Mammon (Amo)

1918–2002, Dancer

Excerpts from interviews conducted on
December 2, 1985; September 25, 1988; and June 11, 1989.

I left Arizona in 1935; I was sixteen. When we got to San Francisco, strangely enough to say, the first thing I thought was, "Oh, look at all the Chinese faces. They look like us!" It was sort of a shock, I mean, not forbidding or anything, and certainly not strange or anything, but just, "Wheee! So many of them!" You know?

I was born in a small town in Arizona—Clifton, Arizona. There were only two Chinese families and a few single men working the mines and ranches and what not. We had to mingle with all the other population, which mostly were whites. We had to grow up with ideas that were theirs, as they were the only people that we could mingle with. Our traditions were the American traditions—this is what we learned in school. The culture that we learned of the Chinese was learned secondhand from our parents. I think that a lot of the culture is great, and I wouldn't give it up, but what we grew up with is also great: we grew up as Americans.

The name Mammon is something that my dad picked up. He was working at the time with a German family and they couldn't say his Chinese name. So he said, "Well, all right, if I'm in the United States learning to speak English and being an American and an American citizen, I may as well have an American name that American people can pronounce." He's a "Ma," but everybody thinks that his name was "Ma-mon." The German suggested "Mennor." Dad didn't write English very well, but he learned to copy it, but in his copy he slurred or ran it together and they read it as "Mammon."

My dad was a very outgoing person. He married late—he didn't get married until he was forty. My dad began to look around and all his friends were getting married and he began to find himself alone. He said, "I'll go find myself a nice, young wife so I'll have someone to take care of me when I grow old." He came to San Francisco and found my mother. Mother was a very enterprising lady, having been the oldest daughter and having to take care of the younger ones. She didn't have any schooling herself.

When she married my dad she was seventeen years old and he immediately took her to Arizona and she started raising a family. I was the sixth child; there were seven altogether. Not knowing any English, she took the six of us back to San Francisco on a train because her mother was sick. My father stayed in Arizona because of the business.

In Chinatown they only spoke Chinese. I was amazed at the broken

OPPOSITE: Mary Mammon photo (ca. 1944), autographed to the author. Photo by Bruce Chin.

ABOVE, TOP: Mary Mammon is interviewed by the author at her Oakland home (December 2, 1985). Photo by Arthur Dong. MIDDLE: Mary Mammon's parents (1910s). BOTTOM: Mary Mammon, second from right, and siblings (1920s).

ABOVE: Mary Mammon, left, and Dottie Sun (ca. 1944).

English that I heard from kids and my uncles; they spoke broken English with an accent. I attribute that to the fact that they would go to school, come home, and then go to Chinese school. At home they never got away from it—their accent and their way of speaking.

We'd read the stories about the discrimination and the bias, about renting out of Chinatown and places where Chinese weren't allowed to eat. People had told us stories about what happened: they were not allowed into Topsy's [a restaurant and nightclub]; a lot of them were not allowed to go to the Sutro Baths; they were discouraged from buying property outside of Chinatown.

When I worked in one of the cocktail lounges in Chinatown, I met an Italian fellow who owned a couple of buildings up on Mason Street, which is more the outskirts of Chinatown. He said, "I like the Chinese people, I'd rent to them in a minute, but if I do, all the other tenants would move out." And the big thing was when Dr. Margaret Chung wanted to buy a home in the Marina [District] and she had to pay an awful lot to the guy who sold it to her—and she was a prominent doctor.

At one time the boundary line was Broadway, and the Italians didn't cross over to the Chinese side, and the Chinese didn't cross over to that side without causing some sort of fracas. North Beach was for them, and the Chinese had to stay here. But most of those [barriers] broke down after the war. I don't know if you know about it, but one time the parks had signs that said "No Chinese or Dogs Allowed."

When we got to San Francisco, the first thing we had to do was to look for a job. I tried to look for the traditional jobs: stenography, typing, shorthand and such—couldn't get that being Oriental. Then I tried for modeling but not only was I too short, I was Chinese, and they just weren't used to a lot of Chinese girls modeling at that time.

There were bars opening up in Chinatown—different things coming along. I started as a cocktail waitress in a bar—I think I was seventeen at the time or eighteen—in the Chinese bar called the Chinese Pagoda. I asked him [Father] if he minded. He said, "You're old enough to go out and get a job and earn a living. I know that I brought you up properly; you can do what you think." Mom said, "You should know what was right and what was wrong." And then of course my brother went to work for the same place, so he was kind of watching over me.

The vogue then was singing waitresses and singing bartenders and such. I worked with a piano player that knew all the old songs and all the latest ones, and one of the songs that the customers liked that she taught me was "A Tisket, A Tasket." One night Mr. Herb Caen [a *San Francisco Chronicle* newspaper columnist] must have been in the audience because in a couple of days I read in his column that he had gone into a Chinese bar and heard a Chinese girl singing, and he was a little surprised to find a Chinese girl, a very petite and dainty Chinese girl, singing a song such as "A Tisket, A Tasket." He thought that she should be singing something very Oriental, in the Oriental language. I got a laugh out of it. I think it must have been me because I was the only Chinese girl working there at the time. I think that this happened because Chinese performers, they were just seen in the Chinese operas.

Let's go back to Forbidden City days when it opened up in December '38. It more or less gave us all a chance to get into the business. All of us who were interested in this sort of thing, and the ones that were already singing in the different little bars and lounges—it gave them a chance to perfect their act or get an act together and go on from there. If it had not been for that, I doubt we could've gotten into a white club being that most of us were untrained. We had no act that we could present; we couldn't have gotten up there and said, "We're chorus girls." We weren't! We were trained on the spot and we were given our chance there.

When Charlie [Low] bought the Forbidden City for Li Tei Ming [Low's second wife], he and his wife were both sold on the idea of presenting entertainers. A call came for chorus girls. We went to look to interview, and it wasn't hard. The Chinese families in San Francisco looked down on such things. "Show your legs out there for people to see?" It was unheard of! Girls were taught to grow up and keep house, and we were supposed to get married at a certain time, and we were supposed to know how to take care of a house, and take care of the children, and take care of your husband. We didn't have ballet lessons, we didn't have piano lessons when we were kids. This was just not part of the Chinese culture.

I didn't care because my mom and dad didn't; I had their love and respect. He said, "I know you wouldn't do anything to shame yourself or the family." And that was it, that's all that mattered to me. My brother thought it was great. I suppose being more Americanized, our thoughts might have been a little bit different, our goals might have been a little bit different. I always liked show business. I liked dancing and singing, school plays, that sort of thing. From the time I was in the second grade—we had a small school, and every year we'd have pageants—it was just something that I gravitated to. So I went in and tried it out.

I got it—it was no competition. When they wanted dancers, if you could move both feet in time, why, you were in! [*Laughs*] We were all from out of town, none of us were from San Francisco: Mel [Got] was

Everyday life at the Forbidden City is captured by *Laff* magazine: "...boogie-woogie with an oriental beat..." (June 1948). TOP (l–r): Lily Pon, Fay Ying, Ethel Lau, Dottie Sun, Toy Yat Mar, Mary Mammon, and Rose Chan. BOTTOM (l–r): Lily Pon, Mary Mammon, and Dottie Sun.

from Visalia, Lily [Pon] was from Sacramento, I was from Arizona, and the other girl was from Honolulu—she was Chinese Hawaiian. Dottie [Sun] was from Sacramento and Butch [Mary Ong] was from Arizona.

We started with five girls, I believe. He had Li Tei Ming as the girl singer and some other act—I don't remember who it was, probably a magician. I think Gale Fischer—I can't remember her first name...Genny Fischer, was the choreographer. And she gave us very simple interpretive numbers. We danced in a group. We had to rent the costumes, we didn't make them. We did three numbers for each show: one to open the show, one in the middle, and one to close.

ABOVE: GIs meet Forbidden City women (l–r): Hazel Jay, Mary Mammon, Dottie Sun, and Frances Chun (ca. 1944).

And things were not really great. I mean, the country was just coming out of a slump. There were faint traces of military build-up at the time, but it really wasn't enough to affect business that much, and times got a little hard. And even though we were receiving...I think it was twenty-two dollars a week—somewhere there, twenty or twenty-two dollars a week as chorus girls—we had to sometimes stand in line and wait for that pay 'cause there just wasn't money coming in. So it was kind of a struggle for Charlie at the time, and he was trying to keep his show together.

I think Miss Fischer left us after the first show. We had another woman come in, and then I think [Walton] Biggerstaff started. When Biggerstaff started with us we all started to take lessons from him. I don't know what Biggie thought of Oriental dancers [but] he got a bunch of untrained girls and he did a tremendous job. And a lot of the waitresses did turn their hand to dancing for a short time. I think he discovered that we were interested and we worked at it and he went ahead and did it. He had a studio down on Jackson Street, and then Tony Wing started with us. We just grabbed some training here and there.

The war made everything possible. The time he [Charlie Low] was just about hitting the bottom of the barrel, as it were, there were more servicemen being sent out. You could see them: the navy was sending ships in, the draftees were being sent over for training at Fort Ord. There were several very good clubs in town and they were all patronized by the servicemen. And of course, nightclubbing was the thing. I think they came to the Forbidden City because we were different.

But I believe the magazines really gave it the shot in the arm. It drew the attention of the country to the fact that there was a Chinese nightclub with a chorus line of Chinese girls. They were not only surprised that we could dance and sing, but most of them were surprised that we could speak English. It was something they had never heard of—not only for the American audience but we were something new for the Chinese people. The Chinese line was a novelty, so business picked up and we started a boom!

We did the Gay '90s, the Roaring '20s…we picked up on all those American dances. We did Western numbers, we did comedy numbers. The Oriental dances we did were the Chinese sleeve dance and the ribbon thing. You're not going to throw away your culture; you will embrace a new culture, but you don't have to discard your old one.

We used to wander until four o'clock in the morning through Chinatown and nobody would bother us. We used to go to the Fox Theater downtown after the show. We used to bowl until three o'clock in the morning and walk all the way to Coit Tower, come back down on Grant Avenue, and buy French bread to eat and walk home. Three or four girls. A lot of times it would be Frances [Chun], Toy [Yat Mar], Dottie [Sun], and I and Hazel [Jay]. We were never bothered.

A lot of the boys expected… well, they might have expected every Oriental girl to be very exotic and very mysterious and hard to know and whatnot. They thought we were so cute and so dainty, and as one guy put it, they thought if they touched us we would break. In other words, we were little China dolls—cute little Chinese dolls! Oh yes, we were told by the servicemen, they all wanted dates and whatnot, you

know, or we'd sit outside with them between shows and have our little sodas or sometimes we'd have a bite to eat. We were just like ordinary people. What they thought amused me more than anything else because I thought of myself as an American.

The stereotype is not made by us—we weren't trying to make ourselves exotic or mysterious in any way. And we certainly didn't want to set up this sort of image. We were just kids doing what we liked: we liked to sing, we liked to dance. Here was an opportunity to do it and we did it. And a bunch of us tried to do it to the best of our abilities. We didn't profess to be exotic and mysterious. This is your idea of us: you haven't looked beyond the fact that we are people. We could be anything we want.

TOP: "We used to bowl until three o'clock in the morning," remembers Mary Mammon. L–R: Mary Mammon, unidentified, Toy Yat Mar, Hazel Jay, and Rose Chan. BOTTOM: On stage at the Forbidden City (l–r): Lily Pon, Hazel Jay, Dottie Sun, Mary Mammon, Rose Chan, Mae Dong, Fay Ying, unidentified (both photos 1940s).

FEBRUARY 1, 1941

10¢

Spotlite

THE MAGAZINE OF SAN FRANCISCO'S
after dark Pleasures and Places to Play...

THE THREE LOVELIES *of the Lion's Den*

REMBRANDT

LEFT: *Spotlite* magazine highlights the engagement of (l–r) Lily Pon, Mary Mammon, and Dottie Sun at the Lion's Den nightclub (February 1, 1941).

OPPOSITE, TOP: Mary Mammon, left, and Hazel Jay are pictured on a handbill for their appearance at Papiano in Salt Lake City, Utah (December 13, 1943). BOTTOM: The "Chinese Follies" on tour with the USO. Front row (l–r): Dottie Sun, Toy Yat Mar, unidentified, and Mary Mammon. Others unidentified (ca. 1945).

At one point I remember hearing people say, "Chinese, dance? They don't have any rhythm. And their legs: they're terrible, they've got terrible legs—I think they're bow-legged and short and squat." And that seemed to be the popular conception of the Orientals—that none of us had any rhythm, that we couldn't keep a beat or stay on time if we had to.

They were just not educated to the fact that we had any talent in any other field than, I suppose, cook or laundry boy or houseboy. Those were the stereotypes at that time, I believe: a good houseboy or a good cook, that was fine. They thought that John—I think most people called Chinese people "John" at the time—"John was a great cook" or "John was a good houseboy and he had everything all cleaned and nice for everybody," and that was it. They were well liked, but as far as being intellectually equal to them, they just didn't think this. Anything Americanized was a bit of a shock to them.

Two other clubs sprang up and, well, we could have gone anyplace to dance at that time. We decided after working at Charlie's for a while that we were experienced enough to try to put some acts together. We [Dottie Sun and Mel Got] first left and went to the Lion's Den. And then Jackie [Mei Ling] and Dottie and I formed a team: picked a teacher, got ourselves some publicity pictures, threw together three routines, and we got out to the Shanghai Terrace Bowl, which was over in Oakland.

Oh, it was fun. It was more of a learning process for us and more exposure to the public. We did a stint at the Golden Gate Theater, and if you don't think that added to our experience! The bandleader decided that his tempo was better than ours, but it was about three times as fast as we wanted to dance to, but we managed to get through it.

From there, we were interested in branching out our horizons. We got ourselves an agent and we booked ourselves; we got a little show together. We met this fellow, Ken Walker, and he got some things together and took the show on the road. It was a complete Chinese show, about a forty-five-minute show. So we booked ourselves across

country: up to the northwest, and down into Idaho, and on into Chicago.

And we heard of the USO, and the army, navy, and whatnot getting people together. And so we tried out for it. We went to New York and they put together a show which they called "Allies on Parade," which consisted of Mexicans—two Mexicans—a Russian girl, Chinese, a Scotch (I think he was a juggler), and I think a magician. So we went on a USO tour.

When we arrived at some of the small towns, they were even more surprised. I mean, they liked the Chinese people, it seemed, but they pictured them in just certain types of occupations, and a lot of them just were very amazed that we could sing and dance and keep on time, count the music. [*Laughs*] And they didn't know too much the difference between Chinese and Japanese. I think we were good ambassadors. I think that we educated the American public to what another race could be. We gave them an insight to our race and our culture.

I came back to Forbidden City in '49...was out of there for about five years. Then I just wasn't working at all for a while. When my husband's car business got kind of bad and we needed an extra salary in the house, I went back to work. But it did slump, business slacked off some, but not an awful lot. It was still a spot where people wanted to be seen; people who were visiting San Francisco...that was the spot to go to. It was still a nice supper club. The Gray Lines took the tour groups up there—that helped. They would bring in, I would say, twenty, thirty, forty people each night.

The club business did sort of take a nosedive. Things got a little quieter. I guess there were just too many of them and they did not have enough entertainers that wanted to stay. People were beginning to get tired of that life. We had to more or less compete with the clubs that were springing up at that time: the discos and the topless bars. Now I'm taking you into the sixties: the little go-go dancers and the big Las Vegas shows—the big spectaculars that they were putting on attracting so many people. And our shows just couldn't compete with these, so this was, as far as I was concerned, the end of an era of show business.

I left in '63. You can't dance for the rest of your life, so there has to be a time, unless you can go into another phase of show business, which was still difficult for Chinese people. There just weren't that many roles in Hollywood for Chinese people, and they were still reluctant to have love stories [with] mingling [between races]. Of course, by the sixties we were all getting along in age too, so you just have to know when to

ABOVE, TOP: The Forbidden City lineup ca. 1961 (l–r): Haruyo Kanada, Anna Lea, Yuki Cho, Mary Mammon, Lily Ogawa, and Ivy Tam. MIDDLE: Tony Wing and Mary Mammon prep for their next performance (1940s). BOTTOM: Tony Wing and Mary Mammon at the world premiere of the documentary *Forbidden City, USA,* Palace of Fine Arts, San Francisco (November 15, 1989). Photo by Bob Hsiang.

ABOVE: Mary Mammon (1940s).

call it quits and go into something else. So as far as the entertainment was concerned, it boiled down to just a few that were staying around. It seemed like I was in at the beginning and it seemed like I was there at the very end of this era of show business.

After I got married and had the kids, I figured I'd better get a job in the daytime so I'd be home with the kids at night, at least. I applied for a position with Safeway—worked there for the next nineteen years. It was a good-paying job; it was good for the children—I had two sons to bring up by myself. And again it was working with the public, which is what I like to do.

It was a wonderful experience and I'm glad that I did it—wouldn't have given it up for anything in the world. It's hard to say whether I accomplished a goal or not. I don't know what my goal actually was as far as that goes. I was always interested in show business; I was always interested in singing and dancing. I did what I liked doing, so I feel that my accomplishment there was good. As far as the glamour goes, you can still get yourself all dolled up and go out. I mean, what is glamour? ●

To Arthur –
A great showman.
All my love –
Noël Toy

Noel Toy

1918–2003, Dancer

Excerpts from interviews conducted on
December 13, 1985, and June 18, 1989.

When I first started out I was an oddity, I was a draw. At that time there weren't many Orientals around—in show business or in the public eye—and they all wanted to see who and what I was. I wanted to be in show business and I said, "Well, at least this is one way of getting into it." I knew that in order to get the most mileage out of anything was to be as Chinese as possible. I even wore Chinese clothes exclusively.

I was pretty wild. I always tried to titillate them. I had long fingernails and I painted them green. At that time people smoked cigarettes. I'm not gonna smoke just a plain old cigarette—I had a long cigarette holder, an ivory cigarette holder that broke into three sections. And so I had the longest cigarette holder in the world! I was very publicity-minded.

I was born in San Francisco, right past the Stockton Tunnel in Chinatown, although I never lived in San Francisco. As a child, we moved to Vallejo. Then from there we moved to a small town in Marin County called Inverness, where we were the only Chinese family. Consequently, I grew up not knowing too much about Chinese things except what was spoken and taught at home.

All my playmates were Caucasians and all my friends were Caucasians. I knew about Chinese New Years because we always went to San Francisco and came back with all sorts of goodies that then we would package and hand out to all our friends, our Caucasian friends. They looked forward to Chinese New Years also!

I went to a high school that was called Tomales Joint Union High School. Let's see, I went to Marin Junior College. I had a scholarship to there and it wasn't until I went to junior college that I looked and I saw— "Ah! An Oriental!" And I looked and I said, "Gosh! There's an Oriental over there!" I never thought of myself as one!

We were always drilled that we had to excel scholastically. Consequently, I studied; fortunately, it came easy to me. I graduated from Marin Junior College and I had a scholarship to go to the University of California at Berkeley. I still had to work because my family was very poor; I think I was working as a waitress in a tearoom.

And then the World's Fair [the Golden Gate International Exposition] came along and someone said, "Well, gee, they're paying good money at the fair." So I said, "Well, great. Let me see what I can get into there." I don't know how, but somehow I wound up in a place called Candid Camera. They were looking for an artist's model, totally nude. I

OPPOSITE: Noel Toy photo (1940s), autographed to the author. Photo by Romaine.

ABOVE, TOP: Noel Toy is interviewed by the author at her Los Angeles realty office (December 13, 1985). Photo by Arthur Dong. BOTTOM: Noel Toy (1940s). Photo by Murray Korman.

thought, "Gee, how much is it?" At that time it was thirty-five dollars a week—that was big money at that time, of course. So I said, "Well, I'll do it in the summer."

They had a stage, they closed the curtain, we assumed a pose. There were about three or four of us—they were all women, posing—and then the curtain would open. It was Candid Camera, so people could take photographs. The thing is you could not move, so you can't look around at the audience. That was the main thing: we were statues, we were a tableau. We were on stage and they were in the dark; we couldn't see them. Then they'd close the curtains and we'd assume a different pose. We'd hold the pose of thirty seconds or whatever, and then they'd close the curtains and we'd change poses. We had four or five poses. We were doing artistic poses. They had to pay to come in. If they wanted to take pictures, fine. If they didn't, that's OK. There are a million photographs of me around!

At first it was a temporary thing, working at the World's Fair, but then I stayed on. By the time the fair was over it was in the middle of the semester, so I said, "Oh, well. I'll wait until next semester." I think I need about a couple of semesters and I would graduate, you know, something like that. But one thing led to another so I just never went back to school. I got into showbiz and that was that.

ABOVE, TOP: Noel Toy in her junior college years (ca. 1936). BOTTOM: Noel Toy and fellow models pose for the Candid Camera concession at the Golden Gate International Exposition on Treasure Island (1939).

The next year I came down to Hollywood and I did some modeling for Otis Art Institute or something like that. Then the World's Fair came back on again so I went back to work for them. And then it was at the end of that Charlie Low came to me and said, "How would you like to do a bubble dance for my club?" And I said, "I don't know how to dance." He says, "You don't have to know how, all you have to do is move around with the bubble—be the Chinese Sally Rand!" So my first thought was, "Well, how much will you pay me?" So he said, "Well, I'll pay you fifty dollars a week!" I thought, "Well, gee, that's better than thirty-five." So I said, "All right, why not?" So he said, "You've got a good figure. Maybe I can get Jadin to teach you."

So that's how I became a bubble dancer. And also too, that was when I met Jadin Wong, who was dancing at the Forbidden City. I asked her to teach me a routine because I said, "Look, this is ridiculous. I'm going out there not knowing what to do. I don't know how to dance. I should have some sort of a routine." So for some reason she took me under her wing. She gave me a routine and gave me the music and everything else. She taught me everything—she taught me how to dance, period. And evidently, I mean, I was a pretty good dancer because even though

I never had any formal education, I was pretty limber and I could catch on fast. And then we branched on to the fan dance. That was 1940.

The bubble dance consisted of this huge latex bubble, which was about five feet in diameter—it was a great big balloon! It was really big, and in order to fill it up we had to take it to a gas station to get it blown up. And then after that we'd have to bring it back to the club through the streets. I'm trying to remember how on earth I ever got it back—really! We had to walk it 'cause we couldn't get it into a cab or anything. I'd have to hang on to it. I mean, I'd have to hold it, otherwise it would just float away. How did I manage that?!

[On stage,] I was nude, but I wore a patch. [*Laughs*] In San Francisco there was a law that you had to be covered completely, so we had a moleskin patch covering, uh…your vital parts. Which was the part that people wanted to know whether it ran the same way as Caucasians! [*Laughs*] At the time that I started in show business, there was this weird concept that Oriental women were built differently. And so consequently I had a song written which said, "Is it true what they say about Chinese women?" And one of the lines was, "Do the streetcars run North and South or East and West?" My last reply would always be, "It all depends on the way you look at it." I mean, I didn't get annoyed at it, and I'd play along with it. They'd say, "Is it true what they say about Chinese girls?" And I'd say, "Oh sure, didn't you know? It's just like eating corn on the cob!" [*Laughs*]

ABOVE, TOP: Noel Toy autographed this photo to singer May Lee. Below is Toy's patch, glued onto the other side of the photo. Performers were required by law to wear a patch over their genitals in order to only *appear* nude on stage (1940s). Photo by Murray Korman.

But anyway, I would put the patch on early and I'd sit in it for a while and then naturally you'd have a crease in it. And when you appeared, you know, you couldn't be completely hidden all the time, and actually your final thing—the final thing at the end of the fan dance—was that you held the fans up and you exposed everything. That was it: that was the pièce de résistance!

When I first performed, I think I was numb. [*Laughs*] I think I was scared silly, too. I don't know how I had the nerve to do it, but I did it. I suppose I didn't know any better. It didn't happen too often, but every once in a while we'd get a drunk at ringside, some smartass would put a cigarette in the bubble and break it, and that really hurt. A big "pop!" I would then walk off the floor, of course. Nothing else I could do, I couldn't perform anymore. It happened once or twice and I was so furious. I put twenty-five dollars on that man's bill for the bubble.

I was the "Chinese Sally Rand"; she did the bubble and then she also did the fan dance. I was billed that way; they would capitalize on it. I was the biggest attraction they ever had. When I appeared at the

Broadway Breaks Even on Oriental Beauty

By LEE MORTIMER,
Popular Broadway Commentator.

The Japanese Dolls Are Vanishing, Leaving the Playful Gentlemen Who Like to Be Seen Around With Exotic, Slant-Eyed Lovelies, to Seek the Company of the Chinese, Filipino and Hawaiian Charmers

NOBODY can accuse Broadway, and the cafe society that clings to its outskirts, of not keeping abreast of the international situation.

The revolving electric news bulletins may be blacked out, but the night-blooming set is still up on its headlines.

You can tell that from the way the fashion in Oriental beauties has changed over the last few months.

Before Pearl Harbor, Japanese glamour girls were the rage. It was Broadway's way of showing that it knew something was going on in the East. Possibly, if it had known what that something meant, it would have had the jitters.

Unquestionably, people who lived umpty thousand miles from the scene of action—and besides usually missed the morning papers by not getting up till noon—deserve some credit for just being able to tell in which direction the rest of the world was looking.

Anyhow, it used to be the rare Jap maiden with anything on the ball at all who couldn't find herself a playboy. Sloe-eyed, potential Mata Haris were everywhere, stomping in floor shows, eating Sukiyaki at night club tables while the band swung "Poor Butterfly."

Then came the great awakening. Before the reverberations of bombs falling on Pearl Harbor had died away, 50 per cent of the Jap glamourettes had gone into hiding and the other 50 per cent were trying to pass themselves off as Chinese.

The weathercock of Broadway fashion, which had been pointing straight at Tokio, shifted a few degrees south, towards Hawaii, China and the Philippines.

These lands responded nobly, rushing in a shock battalion of their fairest daughters to take over the still warm seats of the disappearing banzai girls.

It was all a wonderful example of the workings of the law of supply and demand, accomplished so smoothly and quickly that sensitive playboys suffered the least possible inconvenience. It seemed as though they just said good night to a Japanese one day and the next afternoon met a Chinese substitute, for cocktails.

Any who felt uneasy about it were quickly reassured when that arbiter of elegance, George Jean Nathan, the dramatic critic, began visiting a well-known bistro to watch Noel Toy, a Chinese Sally Rand, get down to fundamentals.

Seductive Noel was no doubt one of the first to profit from the quick change because her profession of strip-teasing had made her adept at quick changes.

Originally entered as a language student at the University of California, she had received high grades in French, Spanish, Italian and German, but flunked her native tongue. This setback may have made her decide to display her body rather than her mind.

In any case, she was presently on view as a nude model at the San Francisco World's Fair. Then she switched to a night club where she panicked the customers, and probably her own illustrious ancestors, by becoming the world's first Chinese fan dancer.

After which, to reach Broadway and

Michi, Mary and Midi, sometimes known as veni, vidi, vici, offer a blackboard example of the rise and fall of Japanese glamour girls.

Michi was probably more responsible for inaugurating the playboy craze of escorting Oriental women, than anyone else in the country.

She popped into show business seven years ago when she was about 15. Mary and Midi were respectively two and three years older.

Despite the fact that their father was a Christian minister in Los Angeles' Little Tokio, the three girls went all out for the theatre, forming a sister trio known as the Taka Sisters.

They played with great success on the West Coast, were booked across country, and finally hit New York where their success in vaudeville was so great that they were rewarded with an engagement to play London and Paris, the ultimate dream of all variety acts.

Two years before, Midi had fallen in love with Raymond Johnson, a waiter in Los Angeles. During her long absence on the road she remained true to him, and they exchanged burning letters.

She could not bear to cross the ocean without seeing him once more, so she set out for California in a bus while Mary and Michi remained in New York.

posed and was accepted.

In Los Angeles, Midi was faced with the necessity of telling Johnson that she no longer loved him.

Later Johnson told police, "When I heard that I went blind with jealousy. I grabbed an ice pick and stabbed Bachand, hoping I could frighten him. Then I ran away, but I was unable to sleep all night.

"I sat in my hotel room and prayed. I had procured a butcher knife from the cafe in which I worked, and as I sharpened it on a whetstone I prayed for strength."

Next morning he entered Midi's bedroom. "Midi, what has happened?" he pleaded. "I guess New York spoiled me," she replied.

Enraged, Johnson struck her again and again on the head with a chisel and slashed her throat with the butcher knife. A few moments later she was dead. He was convicted and given a life sentence.

The two remaining Takas kept the engagement in London

and Paris, then upon their return to the States the act broke up. Mary went to Chicago to study grand opera, later married a Japanese youth and retired to California.

But Michi, cashing in on the sanguinary publicity of Midi's murder, remained in Gotham, to work in Broadway night clubs and be accepted as a member of the glamour set.

She again jumped into front page prominence when she was the unwitting cause of one of New York's funniest night club fist fights.

While she was dancing at a popular hot spot, one of her constant admirers was Jack Doyle, the Irish Thrush, whom sports writers called a singer and music critics, a pug.

Doyle had recently achieved fame as the only boxer in history to knock himself out (an accident), but on this particular night, keeping a date with Michi, he reached a new low when he was bashed on the nose by Eleanor Troy, a handsome six-foot Amazon, who claimed that he had stood her up in favor of Michi.

Thanks to that blow, the latter was lifted high on a brand-new wave of publicity.

When U. S. opinion began to crystallize against the Nipponese, Michi, though a loyal American, saw that if she wanted to

Jadin Wong, Who Rec[...] Diplomatic Roses When [...] Worked in a Washingto[...] Hot Spot.

stay in show business she'd have [...] her name and pretend to be Chi[...]

So, as Lotus Joy, she worked in [...] the best clubs in New York and Holl[...] played small bits in pictures.

But this was just postponing the [...] Today she has been evacuated to a [...] reception camp, where she is reg[...] Michiko Takaoka, her real name.

As she goes about her humble w[...] her fellow inmates realize that thi[...] daughter of the Rising Sun has ha[...] book past.

Meanwhile, in New York, two or [...] and exciting Oriental girls are [...]

Vincent Lopez, the band leader, l[...] seen with them as did Artie Shaw [...] marriage to Jerome Kern's daughter [...] who liked the slant-eyed misses w[...] artist Peter Arno. So did young [...] Benny Baker and a whole raft of [...] stage stars.

Pert Asiatics in the cafe society [...] cluded lovelies like Jadin Wong, w[...] string of broken hearts from Cali[...] Broadway, and received roses from a[...] one diplomat when she worked in the [...] Capital.

Helen Kim, a Korean in San Fran[...] known across the country for her ra[...] and when Lani Lee [...] Broadway from Hollyw[...] was the most sought [...] in town.

Lotus Ann, another [...] charmer, whose father [...] lulu is vice-president [...] Korean National A[...] fighting for freedom fro[...] came to New York [...] singing on a scholarsh[...] Juilliard School and ga[...] as a radio and cafe si[...]

Prominent in night [...] dancers Ann Jung, Ja[...] the Kim Loo sisters, [...] and Florence Thom[...]

Beatrice Fong, Oye Moore and [...] aviatrix Li Ah Ching, fashion desig[...] Tsang, burlesque star Amy Fong.

Another Korean beauty with a [...] society rating is Katherine Lee. Pret[...] town lovelies like Louise Leung, [...] Wong and June Louie are constantl[...] glamour glare.

Recently arrived in New York C[...] fornia and already tops in night [...] talented Sandra Lee, pretty singer a[...] and Helen Toy, also a warbler of n[...] sister, Dorothy, is the beaut who dan[...] Chinese team of Toy and Wing.

The Philippines, too, have contrib[...] share to the glamour market. Eliya[...] perfect Malay type, who came to t[...] from Manila in President Quezon's [...] is an example of what they can do [...] put their minds to it. She sang at [...] House reception, and over-night beca[...] priced opera and concert star.

At 23 she's famous, pretty and [...] for weeks in advance, not only profe[...]

So is petite and lovely Maria [...] young daughter of Sergio Osmena, [...] dent of the Philippines. Maria, cu[...] New York studying singing, alway[...] a stir wherever she appears.

Another stunning Filipino lass, [...] New York and Washington, is the [...] Roces, cutest Oriental in these pa[...] father owned Manila's largest news[...] fore the war. Just to show her [...] she's become an expert at skiing.

Murray Korman Photo

Noel Toy Panicked the Night Club Customers — and Her Own Ancestors — by Becoming the World's First Chinese Fan Dancer.

Michi and Midi Taka, Two Former Toasts of Broadway; Today the First Is in a Concentration Camp, the Second Murdered.

Forbidden City, it really made Charlie Low because, evidently, being the Chinese Sally Rand was a big thing and we got more publicity for the club. We made all the magazines all the time, and we made *Life* a couple of times. It brought people in.

Evidently I was pretty good. [*Laughs*] No, I was different. So they wanted to come in and see. I was unique, the one and only. I was using it—absolutely—I was capitalizing on it. It worked; it worked beautifully. And also too, I mean, I did more than just walk thanks to Jadin Wong, you know, she gave me a routine. So then consequently I fooled a lot of people; they really thought I could dance, and I guess I had enough talent that I could pass it off

I didn't perform there [at the Forbidden City] that long. I was only there for about a year. Then Andy Wong came along from the Chinese Sky Room, and he says, "How would you like to come and do a strip? You can be the Chinese Gypsy Rose Lee." And I said, "Well, how much?" And he said, "Well, how about seventy-five dollars?" And I said, "Well, great, OK!" So I learned how to strip. I think Jadin taught me that too. We worked out things: Chinese costumes, very theatrical. I really enjoyed it. Stayed there about six months.

Then I went to Leon and Eddie's in New York. It was a very known nightclub on 52nd Street. A columnist by the name of Lee Mortimer came in the Sky Room and said, "How would you like to work at Leon and Eddie's in New York?" I said, "It would be interesting. How much?" He said, "All right, when I get back to New York I'll discuss it with Leon and Eddie, the owners of the club."

I said "OK," thinking that was the last I'd hear of that. I was so shocked when I received a telegram that said, "Leon and Eddie's would like to book you for four weeks at one hundred dollars a week." That was a lot of money then. So I thought, "Well, should I do it or shouldn't I?" And everyone said, "Oh, you're crazy to go back there." I said, "Well, it's for four weeks. If nothing else, I've never been to New York." So I went back there and stayed at Leon and Eddie's for six months—my four weeks lasted six months!

That was when I started to do a lot of talking because Eddie Davis, who owned Leon and Eddie's—he's the "Eddie" of Leon and Eddie's—he also appeared and he always did a skit, so he and I did Scarlett O'Hara and Rhett Butler. I had to put on a costume and do a Southern accent and do a skit from *Gone with the Wind*! That's how I got started talking, and from that we progressed into, you know, jokes and all that.

Everybody wanted to meet me. I met George Jean Nathan [a drama critic] and he took me to a lot of Broadway openings. I went out with Lee Mortimer for a long time, and of course I got more publicity. And [columnist] Walter Winchell—at that time he was big stuff. He would kill me because I belonged to a clipping service, and every time he mentioned me, all these clippings would come in and I'd have to pay for every one of them!

OPPOSITE: *The American Weekly* reports an increased level of interest in Chinese, Filipino, and Hawaiian women over Japanese women following Japan's attack on Pearl Harbor. Pictured are (clockwise from top left): Noel Toy, Jadin Wong, Midi Taka, and Michi Taka (September 1942).

ABOVE, TOP: Ad for Noel Toy's engagement at the Chinese Sky Room, performing "her own original impression of Gypsy Rose Lee" (April 20, 1941). BOTTOM: *Slick* magazine covers Noel Toy's appearance at the Chinese Sky Room: "To defeat Japan, she works hard at her profession, sends all her money to the Chinese government. She keeps barely enough to live on" (January 11, 1941).

CHINESE GIRLS IN WEST COAST NITECLUB LIFE

ONE of the choisest items we are getting in reverse lend-lease from China is the glamorous array of Chinese nite club entertainers who are currently wowing the paying customers on the West Coast. Queen of them all in popularity is exotic Noel Toy, specialty dancer deluxe at the Kubla Khan Nite Club, exotic nighterie in San Francisco's Chinatown. Noel Toy knows exactly what her customers want and she gives with a gay abandon that has them coming back for more. Miss Toy has more than her exotic beauty to recommend her. She is an accomplished dancer and she possesses a personality that sweeps all before it. Recently, in honor of the United Nations Conference then being held in the Golden Gate City, she created a specialty dance which she called the "Dance Of The United Nations." This, it is said, helped to unite the United Nations. Miss Toy isn't the only Chinese glamor girl to carry on the work of cementing a world of peoples which threatens to come apart at the seams. Dotty Sun and Fei Ying, two almond-eyed beauties appearing nightly at the ForbiddenCity Nite Club, also have a large following. This Nite Club features a chorus of twelve China beauties, each one as lovely as a piece of Chinese jade.

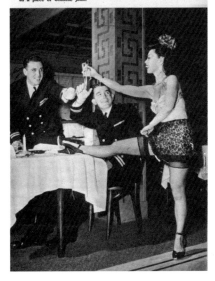

ABOVE, TOP: *Hit* magazine reports that Noel Toy created a specialty dance, the "Dance of the United Nations," in honor of the UN conference being held in San Francisco during her engagement at the Kubla Khan nightclub (December 1945). BOTTOM: Noel Toy and husband Carleton Young at the world premiere of the documentary *Forbidden City, USA,* Palace of Fine Arts, San Francisco (November 15, 1989). Photo by Bob Hsiang.

From then on I went to play different clubs around the East Coast: Philadelphia, Baltimore, wherever they booked me. I did a lot of shows for the armed services. After New York I came back to San Francisco and I was appearing at the Kubla Khan. Ed Pond was able to pay me much more money. I think by this time I was up to five hundred dollars a week, which is peanuts today. I was living at the Mark Hopkins hotel for four dollars a day. Try doing that today!

I met my husband at the Kubla Khan: Carleton Young, he's an actor. He's Caucasian, but he said I married him for his Chinese name. My husband swears that he's made me more Chinese than I was when he first met me. He was in the Air Force—intelligence. I stopped my act; he didn't like it. Before we got married he didn't mind it; after we got married he didn't like it—wanted me to become a serious actress.

Then we went into the antique business, and after that we came back to Los Angeles and I did a lot of pictures and TV in '49, the fifties. I did one with Humphrey Bogart, *Left Hand of God*. I played a madam. I didn't have a thing to say. I did one with Clark Gable, *Soldier of Fortune*. The part in *Soldier of Fortune* was a speaking part. In fact, it was playing a couple of months ago on TV—I saw it. And then I was in *How to Be Very, Very Popular*; it was a picture with Betty Grable and Sheree North. That was the only picture I ever danced in, and it was a thing where I danced and I was killed and that was the start of the picture. And the rest of the picture was trying to solve the murder. I did a regular dance.

We had a lot of fun. Actually, people in show business...they're great. I supposed some people must have been scandalized by what I did, but since I didn't know any of them and I didn't mix with any of them, it didn't affect me. I really didn't know what the old-fashioned Chinese thought because I really didn't have any contact with them. And I always say that if you're looking to be ostracized or to be discriminated against, if you look for it, you'll find it. But I never looked for it. I just said, "Look, I'm what I am and if you don't like me, well then, fine, don't. I don't need to force myself on you. I've got lots of other people who are friendly to me."

I used to talk to a lot of Chinese girls who were timid and shy and I'd say, "Well, don't be. You don't have to be. Just go out there and be yourself; you're just as good as anybody else." Actually, the only thing that I see is that the Orientals aren't out there beating their breasts and screaming, "Look, we want to be in the mainstream of everything. You've got to put us in every picture, that every chorus line should have an Oriental in it." We haven't screamed enough.

However, I think that things are coming around. It's true. And I've always said that if the blacks could get into everything, so should the Orientals. Now you could make it big on television, maybe. Now they're going to have to write some shows for Orientals—period. ●

Noel Toy (1940s).
Photo by Romaine.

*To Arthur —
Thanks for including
me in "Forbidden City"
It was wonderful
Sincerely
Tony Wing*

Tony Wing

1921–1996, Dancer

Excerpts from interviews conducted on
November 30, 1985; October 1, 1988; and August 1, 1989.

They used to ask me questions, "Well, gee, what nationality are you?"
I said, "Oh, I'm chop suey." And they go, "What do you mean chop suey?" And I say, "Well, you know, the dish is a mixture of everything. I'm Portuguese, Spanish and Filipino, and Chinese. And that was it: chop suey!"

My mother found me in a lettuce patch, that's what she always told [me]. I said, "Mom, where did I come from?" She said, "Well, when we were living in Salinas we used to live near this lettuce patch and we found you there." And for years I believe her! But I was born in Salinas and raised in Stockton and went to school there.

Any Oriental boy that went into show business—the same thing like an Oriental girl going into show business—the community thought there was something wrong with 'em. If your father was a grocer...well, when he passes, he expects you to keep running the grocery store; you follow in your father's footstep. I suppose if my father hadn't passed away and I finished school and became a pharmacist—a pill roller...you know what I mean? Oh god, I'd be bored stiff!

I had a hell of a time. First thing, they see a boy dancer they'd think he was gay. That's the first thing they would say: "Oooh, you know what he is." I said, "What's the matter with these people?" They said the same thing about Jackie [Mei Ling]. I had a guy one time sitting in the audience, and he says, "Aw, there's a three-dollar bill!" And I looked to him and said, "Yeah, it takes one to know one." And then he shut up. Jackie and I used to talk backstage and say, "Well, just consider the source. They're dumb, they're ignorant."

Later on it got me because those people who talked bad about me became my friends after they got to know me, took dance lessons from me. And then they sent all their children to take lessons from me because I taught, oh, I've been teaching thirty years at the YWCA— twenty-eight years at the Clay Street Y—which is all children, you know. And they gradually got out of it. It took a little bit of time—the Chinese are the slowest ones.

I never took dancing lessons, couldn't afford it. My dancing lessons were seeing movies of Eleanor Powell, and the one big number that I saw her do was in *Broadway Melody of 1936,* when she danced without music. And I came home and I practiced and practiced until I got the

OPPOSITE: Tony Wing at the Forbidden City, with Joe Marcellino and his band (1950s). Photo autographed to the author.

ABOVE, TOP: Tony Wing is interviewed by the author at his San Francisco apartment (November 30, 1985). Photo by Arthur Dong. BOTTOM: Tony Wing (ca. 1928).

ABOVE, TOP: Performance at the Kubla Khan nightclub (l–r): Connie Parks, Tony Wing, Helen Toy, and Eddie Pond (1940s). BOTTOM: Tony Wing at his makeup table: "I had to start hitting the Clairol bottle and dye my hair black and slanting my eyes with an eyebrow pencil [to look Chinese]" (1940s).

thing down pat. But then from then on, whenever she made a movie, that was a dancing lesson for me.

I went on the road with Jadin [Wong] and Li-Sun and Coby Yee and Roberta Wing. When I came back, Ed Pond had heard about how when I was on the road I would stop the show, so they got interested and started calling me. The Kubla Khan was bigger than Forbidden City in size: they had a big downstairs, a big lobby that you'd come into. It also had a balcony with a little dance floor up on the corner there, and there was an upstairs, which he called a recreation room, which was where his living quarters were. Actually the building still stands there, it's on the corner of Grant and Bush.

He [Ed Pond] was doing real great during the war, and even after the war. He kept thinking the money would come in all the time, and with gambling and stuff like that, he got himself into debt. When I went to work for him he was already in debt.

I went to work for Charlie [Low] in December 1945. Charlie came into the Kubla Khan, he saw me, he hired me. So I told Ed Pond that I'm going to work at the Forbidden City. Ed said, "You'll never get in there because Charlie only hires Orientals." But he didn't know that I had already signed a contract with Charlie. And that opening night he said, "I would have never believed it. You're the first non-Oriental to work there."

As I understand it, when the Forbidden City first opened they did have Caucasian acts in there. It had a mixture from the beginning; it wasn't all-Chinese at first. In fact, he was having a real rough time when he first started off. That was before the war years. When the war broke out, that's when he changed it into an all-Oriental show—and that's when it made it.

I was using my mother's maiden name; I was using Tony Costa. And then when I went to work [at Forbidden City], Charlie said he had to change my name to a Chinese name. He said, "After all, we're advertising all-Oriental revue, Chinese revue." And I says, "Can I be a Wong?" He says, "No! You gotta be a Wing. There's too many Wongs in the show now: Gladys Wong, and all these." And he's naming all these Wongs. I have to have a different name, and that's how I got the name of Tony Wing.

And then one night Bobby Chang was out on the floor and I was watching him, and all of a sudden Charlie comes out and he says, "Your hair is brown on the floor." And I says, "Naturally my hair is brown; I got brown hair. Look at Bobby, his hair is brown." And he goes, "Yeah, Bobby's the real thing." And so I had to start hitting the Clairol bottle and dye my hair black and slanting my eyes with an eyebrow pencil. And then, oh, after about two years, I started easing down on it and finally no more dyeing of the hair, and he didn't know the difference. I said, "Thank god I don't have to dye my hair anymore." It was driving me nuts.

When I first came in they all gave me a bad time because I was non-Oriental. Toy Yat Mar, all of them—who later on became my best friends—kept away from me like I had the plague. The only ones that would talk to me were the boys in the orchestra because they were all Caucasian. In other words, they had a thing going of their own, which was an all-Oriental show—they were proud of that. They didn't like an outsider like me coming in and invading their area. It was the same thing with the blacks: they had their own clubs and didn't want white acts to come in. So I saw the kids' point afterwards, but it was kind of rough. I became very, very depressed.

One day I couldn't take it anymore, so I went to Charlie and said, "I want to get out of my contract." And he said, "Why? You're doing so well here and everybody likes you and everything." And I just came out and told him, "Well, nobody ever talks to me backstage, they act like I'm an outcast." I'd come to work and sit there all night long and have nobody talk to me or anything. They're planning to do things and excluding me all the time." So I just said, "I just couldn't take it."

And man, he got on their tail—no, really, he did! So one night Toy Yat Mar said, "Well, I'm going home." I only lived about a block away; I was staying at the Court Apartments or Hotel, which is now the Stockton Street garage. She said, "Would you like to go out and have something to eat with us kids?" I said, "Gee, I'd like that very much." So they took me to Chinatown. We walked up Grant Avenue. That time of the night, it was so safe. We walked together.

We went to eat and they ordered, and they made me eat with chopsticks and I didn't know how to use them. And finally Toy Yat Mar said, "You'd better learn how to use them or you're not going to eat." And boy, I learned fast! That's how they broke the ice. And another thing too: they used me as a pigeon. They taught me how to play poker and they used to take half my wages a week. I am telling you, Toy Yat Mar is a card shark—I am telling you! At the end of the week I was paying them half my wages. "Thank you, sucker!" And that's how I learned how to play poker.

Actually, when I got in there, Walton [Biggerstaff] did only two shows, and they weren't very much. You knew exactly what he was going to do. I don't know if I should be telling you this...Like the Rockettes in New York...for years they did the [same] tap number over and over and just changed the music—so it was the same for Walton. He was using the same numbers over and over and just changing the costume and music. And no one knew the difference, except if you were a dancer, it got stale. There was nothing at that time that intrigued me as a dancer.

He made good money. He would do the choreography for a show and Ed Pond and Charlie Low would hire him to put a show in, and he would get a weekly salary as long as that show was in there. So he had three shows going on and he would get a good $125 to $150 from each club. And that's coming in each week, and back in the fifties that was good money.

ABOVE, TOP: Toy Yat Mar and Tony Wing: "I am telling you, Toy Yat Mar is a card shark—I am telling you!" BOTTOM: Singer Helen Toy, Dorothy Toy's sister, and Tony Wing (both photos mid-1940s).

ABOVE, TOP: Tony Wing entertains at Travis Air Force Base (Air Force photo, 1940s). MIDDLE: Diane Shinn and Tony Wing at the Forbidden City (1940s). BOTTOM: At the Forbidden City (l-r): Estelle Jung, Rita Adonis, Paula Ming, Tony Wing, unidentified, and Fawn Yee (1950s). Photo by Warren Straw.

He was the one who made the conversion from Caucasian acts; he was the first one to choreograph Charlie's first all-Oriental revue. There wasn't very much for him to do—he just had to teach the girls how to walk and did little things. All the other acts in the show had their own choreography already. He only had to do three numbers for the girls: [an opening number,] a middle number, and a last one with everybody in it. And usually the last one the girls would come out and do a little dance and each one of us came out for a bow—that's all. In fact, Walton didn't even hardly use anything from the swing era; I mean, he was [from] that far back. He used simple little tunes: nothing really big-band era, very simple-type numbers.

The first time I saw those girls dance, I couldn't believe what I was seeing! I'm talking about the ordinary chorus girl, who one week were waitresses and the next week they were chorus girls, you know what I mean? They just knew how to walk. You had to actually be there to see it. They walked out and just go one-two, one-two, and they're strolling with little umbrellas and they bring their little umbrellas down and up and off the floor they go, and the house just came down! And I go, "They didn't do a thing! They brought the house down!" And another time they come out in their little fans and they're fanning themselves, and it's only about two fast choruses of "Chinatown, My Chinatown," and off they go, and the house thought they were great! They just thought it was cute, a novelty—Chinese girls.

I had a write-up years ago by Herb Caen [a *San Francisco Chronicle* columnist], and he was telling about all the different acts and he praised all of us. And he said, "And the chorus girls, they all got two left feet." It got to the point that they started knocking the chorus girls down because, well, actually, you're still paying good money and you're not getting a show out of the chorus girls.

You should hear me sometimes: "Goddamn, you mother-loving chorus girls! Why don't you go and take dancing lessons? One's doing one thing and one's doing another. Shit!" I'd run upstairs and say, "One's running across that way and I'm in the middle and she's cutting across me. She doesn't know where she's going and—Jesus Christ!"

But then after the war people got tired, you know, that novelty wore off. They wanted to see the chorus girls do something, they started demanding something for their money. That's when the kids started having to do harder numbers and actually working harder. That's why when we got this choreographer, Babe Pierce, he made me dance in front of the chorus girls. They weren't strong enough to be by themselves, so [he] put me out there.

I got tired of it. I'd have to do the opening number with the girls and then turn right around and do my number. And then Larry would come out and sing, and then I'd come out and do another number with the girls again. And then I got a break before the finale when everybody would go out there. I was out there all night long. I didn't get paid more, it was a one-day salary. I used to do four numbers each show: tap numbers, solo numbers...sometimes it went to five. The show was forty-five minutes.

There was dancing before the show and after the show. It was three shows a night. During the war there was a cover charge. After the war there was a minimum charge—it was a minimum charge of two dollars per person. That meant when you sat down you had to spend at least two dollars; you could stay for all three shows. Of course, you could nurse that drink for forty-five minutes, but they'd come and ask if you'd like another one. And that's how it was—you could stay for as long as you want.

When Babe Pierce came in he started injecting more jazz dancing into it. He came in around the fifties. His dance style was different, he had started going into jazz. I had never done that sort of stuff. It was hard for me at first, but I got with it. I learned more from Babe than I did from Walton. Walton had to leave when Babe started because Charlie hired Babe. And after that I took over for him. I did the show for about four years.

ABOVE: Jimmy Jay (Borges) and Tony Wing, right, at the Forbidden City. Wing's sister, Arlene Wing, is seen above his head. Sisko Borges, Jimmy Jay's then wife, is behind Jay, to the right (ca. 1959). Photo by Bill Cogan.

Mainly what kept the Forbidden City popular was each one of the kids in the show, they had a following of people. Like, I would have certain people—maybe friends who come into town and say, "Well, let's go to the Forbidden City, we want you to see Tony. Or Toy Yat Mar." Or someone like that. That's what kept the club going: we all had a following. They'd come in, we'd reserve a table for them, and Pop [Charlie] would set them up and we'd be sociable.

Bimbo [Agostino Giuntoli, owner of Bimbo's 365 Club], in his nightclub, he'd never let his people go out—it was a no-no. Chorus girls couldn't go out and sit with the customers, acts couldn't go out and sit with the customers. It would happen in Forbidden City; Charlie was always calling the chorus girls out all the time. He didn't tell you that, did he? All the girls would get so t'd off because in between shows they had to mingle. He'd call them out with a microphone backstage: "Hey girls, come out. I want you to meet some very good friends of mine." I think he took turns—two or three at a time. And the girls used to go out and meet his friends and finally they found out he didn't even know them.

My younger sister [Arlene Wing] came to work at Forbidden City. I got her a job there when she was eighteen, nineteen years old. She was a chorus girl, dancer. She was one of the best-looking ones in the whole place. And she said to me one day, "I'm getting tired. We dance all night and in between shows we'd have to come out and sit with these dumb guys, and they're supposed to be so-called friends of Charlie. I've been checking and I'd ask the guys if they know Charlie and they'd say they never met him before and this is the first time. In other words, any guys who want girls, we'd have to go sit with them." They'd buy the girls a drink or dinner or something and Charlie's making money off of it. My sister said, "I don't like that." And so they put a stop to that; the girls got tired of it.

Hell, a lot of them liked going out anyway. There was one girl there, Connie Parks. You mention Connie Parks to any of the kids and they'll know who I mean. She was a chorus girl. Connie got fired from Charlie more times because...The only time he hired her back was because she was a good hustler for drinks, and he had to really need a chorus girl bad to hire Connie Parks back. She said to me one night...she says a couple of her friends were going to come in to see the show. And after the first show, Connie came over to me and says, "Would you like to make a hundred bucks?" And I said, "How?" "Oh, my friend that came in, they're interested in both of us." And I said, "Gee, they're going to pay me one hundred dollars to go to bed with that elderly lady?" And Connie says, "Oh, no—her husband." And I says, "No way!" And I don't think Connie took it up either. But that was a proposition we got. And

BELOW: At the Club Shanghai. Back row (l–r): Walton Biggerstaff, producer and choreographer, band members (unidentified), and owner Fong Wan at the end. Middle: Professor Lee Tai King, Choy Shin Hung, Lily Choy, Wilbur Tai Sing, unidentified, and Tony Wing. Bottom: Fawn Yee, unidentified, Gladys Wong, Barbara Yung, unidentified, and Lynne Wong (early 1950s).

there's been other types of propositions I don't want to mention. Offers? The kind of offers I got—you would have died!

One time, Larry Ching...we had to do a production number, it was a roaring '20s number: [*singing*] "Baby face, you've got the cutest little baby face..." And Larry and I were learning the words upstairs and Larry kept on singing, "Baby face, I'd like to stick it in your baby face, it's so much cleaner than the other place..." And he kept on singing it that way, you know?! Do you know that when I got out on

the floor that's what came out of me? I'd go, "Baby face..." and all of a sudden I went—and he's standing there laughing. He'd stop his voice, see, he didn't sing. And everybody started laughing. You know, I walked off—I got red in the face and I walked off and he was laughing. I said, "Larry, it's all your fault. You know I didn't know the words and I was learning them upstairs and you kept on singing them that way, and that's how it came out on the floor!"

And the worst part of all this—I sang this with four people and everybody up front told me, "Tony, you got to be on Broadway because, man, you're the Ethel Merman of Sutter Street! Your voice just carries out there and it just goes." And Helen Toy, she's spitting and cracking up. I wouldn't sing it anymore, and they finally took that damn song out. He used to always do things like that—that's Larry Ching. But he was nice. Larry was really a sweet kid. All the kids I enjoyed.

Once I got established in San Francisco I never had to worry about work. You had three big clubs: the Chinese Sky Room and the Club Shanghai and the Forbidden City. We would move between the three different clubs. They were always calling me for jobs; I never had to go and ask. I worked in quite a few American jobs too [i.e., jobs in venues not specific to Chinese Americans]. I worked Bimbo's, Italian Village. I remember the time in San Francisco [when I knew] that if I quit tonight I could work in another [club the same night]. Oriental acts were hard to get ahold of.

We'd get mad at Charlie and we'd go work for the Club Shanghai. And it seemed that at that time, Dr. Fong Wan...he didn't like Charlie, and every time that Charlie would let an act go, he'd hire them. And so when I was leaving, he [Charlie] says, "Where're you going?" I said, "I'm going to Club Shanghai." "He hired you too?" "Yes, I'm going over there." And he had the biggest show in Chinatown because he had almost all the Chinese acts working there. There was over twenty-five kids in the show and we had a ball because we all knew each other.

Every night I would go to work and I would think, "What's going to happen tonight?" And for sure, every night something new would happen. But funny...I'll never forget one night: This Lana Wong was

ABOVE, TOP: Unidentified men with Forbidden City women (l–r): Marian Gee, waitress, Connie Parks, Coby Yee, and Arlene Wing (ca. 1959). BOTTOM: At the Forbidden City (l–r): unidentified man and woman, Tony Wing, Diane Shinn, and Charlie Low (1950s).

brought over [from China] by Dr. Fong Wan to be featured in his club. Charlie hired her [because] Charlie wanted to get back at Fong Wan for taking all of his acts, and so she left the Club Shanghai. And she was a stripper and she danced on this big drum—lousy dancer. But Larry [Chan] gave her two bennies. She came in and said, "Oh, I'm so tired," and Larry said, "Oh, I've got something." He gave her two. I said, "Larry, two Benzedrines and she'll be flying." He just laughed.

She went out on that drum, and man! I and Larry, we couldn't help it—we were standing in the wing and we're cracking up because she was throwing her clothes at the customers' faces, you know, and her bra was in somebody's face and she just went wild. And she was jumping on that drum and throwing things, and the guys in the orchestra were cracking up because they've never seen her go so fast. Then later on she went back and said, "Gee, Larry, you've got to get me some of those, they made me feel so good." And I said, "You better not take any more." And Charlie came back and bawled the hell out of her. He says, "What's the idea of throwing all your clothes in the customers' faces?!"

All those clubs...gradually they faded out one at a time—like you had the Club Shanghai, the Sky Room, you had the Lion's Den, you had the Kubla Khan. I think what really ruined it was because Charlie got propositioned from the Gray Line [Tours]. You pay one lump sum and the Gray Line would take you to three different nightclubs and you'd get to see a show. And a lot of the other club owners, they said the same thing: they shouldn't accept that because they're losing out. But it was a guarantee, that's what it was.

And not only that—the unions, they required Charlie to have six people in the orchestra, and he asked if he could only have five, to cut down [on costs]. And they refused, and so he just decided he had enough and sold [the club] to Coby [Yee]. She did away with the orchestra entirely and used records. It was on account of her that I quit show business. I left overnight; it was a very funny way. Being a stripper, she could never make it as a straight act. I found that I was following a girl stripper, and there was one behind me, and the place was becoming like Broadway [Street in San Francisco]—a strip joint. And so one night I said to her—I only worked for her about a month—I said, "I quit." I got all my music and I left and I never went back to the club again.

And I left show business very abruptly. But already I was teaching. I had my own dance studio and was also teaching at the YWCA, teaching children. So I sensed it was coming on that I was going to put more time into teaching. Which I still am doing. ●

ABOVE, TOP: Tony Wing and students (ca. 1970). BOTTOM: Tony Wing performs at the world premiere of the documentary *Forbidden City, USA*, Palace of Fine Arts, San Francisco (November 15, 1989). Photo by Bob Hsiang.

OPPOSITE: Tony Wing autographed this 1946 photo to singer Dudley Lee. He signed it "Tony Costa," the stage name he used before changing it so he could be identified as a Chinese performer at the Forbidden City. Photo by Bruce Chin.

To the smallest fellow
with a very find
voice & whom I
had the greatest
pleasure of working
with— Dudley—
Sincerely
Tony Costa
10-25-46.

Bruce Chin

Dorothy Toy (Dorothy Takahashi, Dorothy Fong)

b. 1917, Dancer, Toy and Wing

Excerpts from interviews conducted on
April 29, 1989, and June 14, 1989.

My name is Takahashi, but that was kind of long, you know, so we decided to use Toy. It's three characters, right? It's much shorter. Paul [her former husband and dance partner] was Paul Jew, and it didn't sound good for Paul to be Chinese and say his name is Paul Jew because he spells it J-E-W. We were in New York, and well, in those days it's kind of hard to say, "My name is Paul Jew." And Paul Jew wouldn't sound good or wouldn't look good on the marquee. [*Laughs*] And so he changed it to Paul Wing, and so it was "Toy and Wing."

You've got to think about the public going to a theater and you want them to remember you. "Oh, that was Toy and Wing"—easy! You've got to think of the Caucasian way of thinking, not the Chinese way. Purely business—to sell yourself. And in show business, the most important thing is to sell yourself.

So most all the actors—whether they were Filipinos, Chinese, or Japanese—always used Chinese names because Chinese had very short names and were easy to remember. Nobody knew the difference; Caucasian people did not know the difference between Chinese or Japanese—your face is yellow and that's it; they didn't know what nationality you were. I mean, you're still an American, but they figure you're from another country.

I went to dancing school when I was young. I was dancing on my toes in front of my mother's restaurant in regular shoes, and the man across the street who owned the theater—it had vaudeville in those days—the manager said to my mother, "You know, you should send your daughter to dancing school." And that was the biggest mistake!

In Japan, dancing is the very lowest thing you can do. My mother's from Yokohama, which is a city in Japan, and my father was from the country, which is Waikayama, and they came over here many years ago. And she was much more modern than the other relatives that we had. My relatives did not like the idea that my mother was sending me to dancing school. All the people looked down on her.

In the Japanese community they wouldn't even speak to her. "What are you doing, sending your daughter to dancing school? That's very bad!" Girls were just...went to high school, and then after high school they got married and settled down.

The teacher thought I had big potential. I wasn't just a dancer on my points, I did all the things that he used to do when he was younger,

OPPOSITE: Toy and Wing (1930s). Photo by Maurice Seymour.

ABOVE, TOP: Dorothy Toy is interviewed by the author at her Oakland home (April 29, 1989). Photo by Arthur Dong. BOTTOM: Dorothy Toy (1930s). Photo by Bloom, Chicago.

ABOVE, TOP: "I always remember the Indian number because my mother sewed one hundred feathers by hand on this Indian outfit"—Dorothy Toy. Photo by Irving Archer of Hollywood (1929). BOTTOM: "Toy and Wing" on the Paramount Theater marquee, New York City (ca. 1941).

and he loved it. I did everything on points, and Russian dancing too. He took a special interest in me: he would come to my mother's restaurant with a pair of friends and he would eat so I could take lessons—that's the way he did it because we couldn't afford it. We were poor.

I was at the Ransdell Dance Studio in Los Angeles and they had about twelve or fifteen girls. All the girls were blonde—Caucasian, beautiful long legs—and I was the only Asian girl. And in the summertime the dance teacher would take us to Riverside and Pomona and work in these little theaters for experience, stage experience.

I always remembered the Indian number because my mother sewed one hundred feathers by hand on this Indian outfit. The girls are all sitting around like a powwow, you know. They had danced first, then I came out and at the end I did the splits, and they would carry me off the stage and it looked real sensational. And do you know the mothers complained? They didn't like to carry an Asian girl out; they didn't want to lower themselves. My teacher said, "We can't do that anymore and you have to dance off." But when you're young it's wonderful, it doesn't hit you. I just danced off! [*Laughs*]

I loved dancing. We [Toy and Wing] used to live in the rehearsal hall—we didn't do anything else but dance, and so we did well. But it wasn't easy climbing that ladder, it was very difficult. White people looked at us as a novelty—not an act—something they hadn't seen before, that they don't see often. You're different to them, and I could feel it. But when you're very, very young...I didn't know anything else, and I just accepted whatever it was.

We found that we had to be much better than the American dance team, the Caucasians, or else we wouldn't get the bookings. We had to be ten times better, not just a little bit better. Luckily, we worked very hard and we had sort of a charisma that helped people accept us when we were performing.

We were with the William Morris Agency and they would have about fifteen or twenty-five dance teams. If an owner of a theatre or a nightclub says, "I'm looking for a dance team," they'd go right down the line and look. But we had an agent that was taking care of us separately, and he would always..."Well, Toy and Wing is one of the best we have." So we were very fortunate that he pushed for us.

You do your act, an act they know they can depend upon—that's why they say "a standard act"—to open the show right. When I was at the Strand in New York City, they applauded with our first New York performance. They applauded and applauded and the bandleader was—I don't know if you heard of him, Leo Reisman, he was a big name, big band—Dinah Shore was the singer—they started to play "My Reverie." But [the audience] wouldn't stop clapping, so they had to stop the music and tell us to come out and take a bow because they weren't listening to his music. So we come out and take a bow so they'll stop. That's what they call a real showstopper. That's when Paul and I did our first appearance on Broadway; it was very important. The bandleader was furious—a very big name, an older man, very well known in society. He was so mad!

We would fly back to Chicago and play at the Chez Paree, and we would fly back to New York. And we went to the Palladium [in London]. You know, this is where you traveled. I remember when I was in Knoxville, Tennessee. My partner and I were playing a theater and we got on a bus—this is something that is very funny—we got on the bus and sat in the back of the bus and the bus driver got up and told us, "You can't sit here, you gotta go in the front, the back is for the blacks." We didn't know. We didn't know they were that way! That's how prejudiced they are with the blacks. But the Asians...they wanted us to sit in the front. And

we couldn't figure out which way they were accepting us; it was very confusing down South. There were some people down South that didn't like either the black or the Asian. They didn't have to make excuses in those days. That's one incident that I thought was very, very bad.

During World War II, when all the Japanese were being interned in California, my partner and I were in New York and we received an offer and a telegram. We got this big deal to go to Hollywood to be with Kay Kyser in this movie, and we were so happy over it because it would have been a big break in our show business life. We were travelling with the Chico Marx show—one of the places we stopped at was San Diego, and by the way, it was with Mel Torme when he was seventeen years old playing the drums and singing—and all of a sudden we get this phone call from William Morris Agency, which was handling us: "You'll have to leave because one of you are Japanese and we don't want any problems."

It just so happens that there was another dance team at the same time wanting this same job. I presume they just were jealous of us, I guess. *She* was just jealous of us because this girl went and called and told them that I'm Japanese. And naturally the agency gets very flustered, they got very upset, you know, and they didn't know what to do. The team that told on us hurt me more deeply because they were Chinese themselves. See, it was not a Caucasian team, it was an Oriental team. And they just told on us because they wanted our job, and so I feel that was something I could never forgive them for. The other dance team took our place, but it ended up in the cutting room on the floor.

I don't want to say anything more because we had a lot of problems because of that. I mean, you had to spend your own money to go all the way back to New York, and then we had to start from scratch again. And

TOP: Toy and Wing bring down the house at the Strand Theater, New York City (November 29, 1939). BOTTOM: Toy and Wing perform at an unidentified location (ca. 1939).

ABOVE, LEFT: Publicity still from *Deviled Ham* (RKO Radio Pictures, 1937). RIGHT: Forbidden City postcard (late 1940s).

it's not easy. You had to start getting dates way outside in Woodbury or some little town in Providence, Rhode Island. And it really...it was really very hard for us. We had to start right from the bottom again.

We came to Forbidden City as guest artists who performed for a couple of months. But it was so nice and it became a home base, and that's how we ended up staying there a year or two, because it was so comfortable. Traveling is not easy, and that's why a lot of these acts that were very good stayed right here in San Francisco. They didn't want that hassle of traveling, I guess, because they loved it here in San Francisco. They went to work every night and they had a steady job, and they can stay there and dance or sing.

You [should] never stay in one place that long because you get stagnant, you're stale, you get lazy. It was very bad for an ambitious person. Very bad. That was our mistake, I think, was staying in one place. It was nice, don't misunderstand me. It was nice working there, but for a career it isn't good to stay in one place that long. You must keep moving and going back East and going places where your competition is so you know what's happening, especially New York. Then I got married [to Leslie Fong, after divorcing Paul Wing], which I shouldn't have for the show business part.

It was only the Forbidden City and the Sky Room in the sixties; the rest of [the clubs] had all closed. You have to remember, they're no more: the Shanghai had closed, Kubla Khan had closed. People stopped coming when they closed the gambling—that's the main thing. It made a whole lot of difference; we needed those gamblers very badly. It's funny for me to say that because I'm not a gambler, but for business reasons it helped the people. [Now there was] no more work. You know how many people they used in these gambling houses? Did the gambling close around the fifties? I could get a better idea if I look back. It was all underground—they didn't show it, but [everyone] knew what was going on. The policeman on this route in Chinatown, in one year he'd be a millionaire and he could retire. Really! That's how much the payoffs were.

I was still working at the Forbidden City, and Forbidden City at that time was going through the change in hands, you know. It was hard times. That's why when I put my show into the Sky Room—when I went over to the Sky Room with my review in the sixties—'60 or '59, whatever it was—we had no business. It wasn't that popular. Did you talk to Andy? Andy Wong? I went there and I brought my show and I said to Andy, "I worked for Coby [Yee at Forbidden City] and I lost my shirt because I had Sammee Tong [there] and went on a percentage deal. And it was terrible because [the patrons] didn't come in to see Sammee, because he owed everybody money for gambling. And I didn't know that, I didn't know Sammee didn't pay them all back and they didn't want to come see him." So I said, "Oh my god," and I got out of there and I went to Andy and I said, "Andy, I'd like to put my show in here to help you out," because he only had three or four customers a night. He was dying; he needed something.

BELOW: Toy and Wing toured with the "China Doll Revue" during the early 1960s. L-R: Rita Adonis, unidentified, unidentified, Sheryl Lee, Paul Wing, Joe (Jue) Ming (of Ming and Ling), Mai Tai Sing, Robert Ling (of Ming and Ling), Dorothy Toy, two members of the Sing Lee Sing Trio, two members of the Three Tong Brothers, Jackie Wong, unidentified, Fawn Yee, unidentified. The children are Sing Lee Sing offspring. Photo by Bernard of Hollywood.

"THE SAMMEE TONG SHOW"

STARRING

SAMMEE TONG
"PETER OF T.V.'s BACHELOR FATHER"

• **TOY and WING**
INTERNATIONAL DANCE STARS

• **THE GRANT AVENUE TRIO**
Rhythm Folk Singers

• **SAMMEE TONG PLAYGIRLS**

and

INTRODUCING
THE LUSCIOUS

MISS
UNI-NA

United Nation's Choice Of 1963

So I brought my show in and I built that place up. We had the tours come up to the Sky Room. I built that place up so they had three buses coming every night and they had so much business. He did very, very well—we were taking the business away from Broadway [Street]. And at that time they had what they call "amateur strips," and I would hire these girls to come in and we'd have special nights—Thursday Night Amateur Strip—besides our show. And the crowd of people would come in. Andy made a lot of money.

Anyway, to make a long story short, he lost his lease and I said, "Andy! I thought you owned this building." And he said, "No, my lease is up and that's it." And I said, "After I built your business up this much and we're doing so well, you lost your lease?" I was so shocked! I was shocked! So we both closed at the same time. He had to close, leave the place, and I had to leave with my show, you see, at the last minute. Then I took my show on the road, but Andy had no place. He went and bought a hotel in Sacramento and it went under. The younger generation has to be sharper.

I worked at the Hyatt Union Square and then I opened the Hyatt Regency. I was the assistant manager of the discotheque, which was called Happenstance. And I was the assistant manager because they had a rock group in there and it was my cup of tea, you know, music and dancing. Anyway, they closed that room up and I became a hostess at that hotel for three years.

Try in '72 to say you're in show business and get a job in an office—it was different [then,] so we never mentioned show business. Never. We just faked our way through. When they say to me, "Do you know the register?" I'd say, "Yes," because they're going to teach you their system anyway. There wasn't anything I said no to. I said yes to everything. When we left show business, we never said anything [more about it]. We just went from one job to another quietly. ●

OPPOSITE, TOP: Marketing brochure for "The Sammee Tong Show" with Toy and Wing (1960s). BOTTOM: Toy and Wing's Oriental Playgirls performed with the duo at the Chinese Sky Room and on tour nationwide. Here they're joined by singer Jimmy Jay (Borges). From left: Arlene Wing, Kako Tani, Sisko Borges (Jay's then wife), Cynthia Fong, and Jennifer Pang (mid-1960s).

RIGHT: Toy and Wing (early 1950s). Photo by Milton Mann Studios.

To Arthur,
All Best to
You on
"Forbidden City
U.S.A."
Great working
with you!
Paul Wing
9/88 —

Paul Wing

1912–1997, Dancer, Toy and Wing

Excerpts from interviews conducted on
November 30, 1985; September 22, 1988; and June 12, 1989.

Fred Astaire—everything is Fred Astaire to me: the way he dresses, the way he talks, the way he moves. I flunked the fourth grade thinking about it so much. Oh, my father? Very much against it; he didn't want me to dance at all. See, we lived in Palo Alto, it's only two miles away from Stanford University, and he really want me to go to Stanford. So one day he walked in the kitchen—here I am practicing dancing with a chair as a partner. Now, he sees this and surprisingly goes to my mother and says, "You know our number one son? Something wrong somewhere!"

The time I went to the Varsity Theater to see *Top Hat,* starring Fred Astaire and Ginger Rogers, I went to see Fred Astaire so many times because they run it five times a day. And I stayed from noon to into the wee hours, ten o'clock at night. My mother sent the police looking for me. And I told her that I saw Fred Astaire five times at the Varsity Theater. She understands. Well, she was lenient to me. She says, "Well, that's the case, but don't tell your father!"

I met this colored boy when we were selling newspapers on the corner and he was dancing the Charleston and selling more papers than I was. I made friends with him so I could learn the Charleston so I could sell as much papers as he can. And right there I had an idea: making business and mixing it with pleasure.

Back in 1932 when I was still in high school on a summer vacation, I wanted to go to the New York Palace Theater just to see what it looked like, to see what it was all about. Drove my father's Dodge, 1922 Dodge. I told him I'm going to Reno a couple of days and drove it to New York. I took a piano friend of mine that played basketball, Don Collins, a college kid. He played piano and I danced all the way across in restaurants for money and food. They'd give us free meals—Chinese restaurants. This Irish kid didn't like Chinese food, so they had to cook him eggs; he ate ham and eggs all the way, I ate Chinese food.

He played piano and I danced; they thought it was great. We're only sixteen years old at the time. We can't play in the professional places or any places like that that require a birth certificate that you're over twenty-one. So actually, the Chinese places, they don't care how old you are. You got a lot of guts when you're young, sixteen, seventeen, and you look about twelve!

When we got to Brooklyn the car broke down, fall flat on its face. But we finally find the way to the Palace Theater. And boy was I happy!

OPPOSITE: Paul Wing photo (early 1950s), autographed to the author. Photo by Romaine.

ABOVE, TOP: Paul Wing at the Oakland home of Frances Chun (August 18, 1988). Photo by Zand Gee. BOTTOM: Toy and Wing (1940s). Photo by Bruno of Hollywood.

ABOVE: Toy and Wing (1930s). Photo by Bloom, Chicago.

It only cost thirty-five cents to sit in the balcony and it was pretty good, darn it, and we had a hell of a time. And boy, I'll never forget that day—to see the Palace Theater—and that encouraged me all the time, from 1932 to now.

I had to get back to finish school. I got into these dance contests in a theater—amateur. First prize was twenty-five dollars, and second prize was fifteen dollars, and third prize was ten dollars. So I'd win about three first prizes: one in Brooklyn, and one in the Bronx, and one over in Long Island. I had seventy-five dollars. Bought a car for sixty dollars, Chevrolet 1926.

You know something? We would sleep in Kansas City, and down there was thunder and storm and whatever. We had one blanket, soaking wet. We get to Gilroy [California] and the goddamn thing broke down. So we had to have Don's father tow us in; Don's father was a mechanic. And that's how I enjoy seeing the Palace Theater. [*Laughs*] Those were the days!

We graduated and that gave me a yen to travel, so I hitchhiked down to LA and got into show business. It wasn't that easy. When I got there I didn't know what to do, where to go to get a job as a dancer. But in Chinatown, around the grapevine, I hear that there's an audition out at the Grauman's Chinese Theatre for Chinese atmosphere: Chinese extras walking in a Chinatown scene—stage prologue before Joan Crawford's picture *Rain,* which started in the tropics and goes into San Francisco Chinatown and back into the tropics. That was the background of the picture.

So I went there and took an audition. Sid Grauman was the producer at the time. He was alive then and Evelyn Golla was his secretary. So I came out and did my dance. That's all I knew was one dance, that's all I learned. So I did my dance in a costume which my mother made. It was kind of homemade-ish, but there was Oriental style with a little *bok bok mouh*, you know, a Chinese hat. So he says, "Yeah, I like that dance; I have an idea for that dance. Yeah, we're going to use you." So all right. I find out later, a day or two, that he's going to use me in a Chinatown scene in San Francisco.

And I find out he thinks that another costume would be more appropriate for what I'm going to be: a Chinese laundryman, and with the tour guide asking me to do a dance right in Chinatown to the people on tour. Imagine me from the Chinese laundry, where I have been helping out my father back in Palo Alto, and here I get into show business and I do a dance as a Chinese laundryman? How about that?!

After the Grauman's Chinese Theater there was an Oriental revue being booked for Mexicali called the "ABC Nightclub." There was Korean girls, Japanese girls, Filipino men, one man was a comedian, and me as a Chinese. One of the girls, Korean girl, her name is Suzanna Kim. That's how I met Dorothy Takahashi—that's her name then—with her sister Helen Takahashi. They were called the Takahashi Sisters. And we did a few dance numbers together in the show. When we came back to Los Angeles we came out as the Three Mah Jongs.

We [Dorothy and Paul] were billed as "Toy and Wing," and the name itself implies we're Chinese, and your costume is all-Chinese and your music is all-Chinese. Our opening of Toy and Wing's act was we would be in robes. I would be in a long robe with a big Mandarin hat, it's all color and sequins. And my partner, Toy, would be in a gown of Oriental design and full sequins, all three-quarter length.

We'd come out together and we'd make a circle and I'd be in the middle, and they think we will be coming out to do some acrobatic and juggling. She'd come back in front of me and I'd take off her robe and she starts dancing.

ABOVE: The Three Mah Jongs (l–r): Dorothy Toy, Paul Wing, and Helen Toy, Dorothy's sister (1930s).

And then we go into a number where she does a partial ballet number with spins and turns and we'd start dancing a foxtrot, right into a swing number, which gives a surprise to the audience. They were thinking that we would be doing Oriental number, fantasy number of that sort, you see. And that's how we open into the variety of tap dancing and swing number. It's all production value.

We were Oriental, but still we considered ourselves Americans doing American dancing. To do an act you had to be very good—outstanding. I want to be not only a novelty but be more exceptional and be one of the top acts in the business. We had to have that in our mind.

To be performing to the American audience, you've got to be good, more exceptional than just being Oriental. They know ballroom dancing because they've seen their own race do it—the American people—and they know good and bad. Don't think they don't. But, however, to see Orientals do it, "They're either good or bad," they'll say. It's competitive; you've got to deliver. You know what deliver is? It's like football: you either play the ball right or you don't. You play the game, it's all in the game.

It took us a lot of energy, perseverance, and practice and grooming in various small towns to go play the big towns and to accumulate all the necessary ingredients of an act to make it a standard big-time act.

ABOVE, TOP: Ad for the Capitol Theater appearance of Toy and Wing, "Chinese Dance Stylists" (1930s). BOTTOM: "Toy and Wing" on the Chez Paree marquee, Chicago (1930s).

OPPOSITE, TOP: Toy and Wing at the Paramount Theater, New York City (1953). MIDDLE: Paul Wing, left, partners with Larry Leung as the Wing Brothers (1950s). Photo by Bruce Chin. BOTTOM: Paul Wing, left, and Larry Chan (1950s). Photo by Milton Mann Studios.

We had to play small places like New Jersey, some places in Massachusetts, some places I've forgotten. Small towns like Allentown, Pennsylvania—it's not small now, but it was small then.

You got to do shows every night, every night in front of an audience. You can't get as much benefit in front of a rehearsal hall, you've got to practice in front of an audience, that's the main thing. It's up to you to try to score with them, gaining the applause and so forth. You've got to practice your act up to be in tip-top shape so you'll look good, look professional. You pick out the bad points of an act and also make it look like big-time, so they could book you in the big houses—farm you out.

In Chicago we were trying to get the Chez Paree. And there were two owners, [Mike] Fritzel and [Joe] Jacobson, and one of the owners didn't want to have our act there because he mentioned that he had an Oriental acrobatic act in there and they came over to do the show in slippers, and they wore those white socks and Chinese pantaloons, and it didn't look very nice in a class spot like the Chez Paree at Fairbanks Court in Chicago, you see. So Jacobson, the other boss, said, "Why don't you give them a chance. I caught them at the Chicago Theater and they were really wonderful. Had a lot of class, top drawer. They know what they're doing and they had variety of dancing. They scored well with the audience." So they gave us an OK. So we opened at the Chez Paree.

The William Morris Agency at that time was the number one agency—still is—and mentioned that they're interested in us after they caught our act at the Chez Paree 'cause we had a very, well, good reception. They were always pretty good to us. They booked us all over: Europe and London; clubs, theaters, conventions, big convention halls like in Philadelphia; Boston Metropolitan Theater; the Biltmore Hotel; the Biltmore Bowl in Los Angeles—we played there; the Islander Club in the Roosevelt Hotel—that's in Los Angeles; and the Hotel Barkley—they call it Barkley over there, that's in England, that's in London. We were fortunate enough that they all enjoyed us in various places like Rio de Janeiro, London at the London Palladium, New York Broadway—all around the world. Like in the Radio City Music Hall, where we were with a big line called the Rockettes and they'll build a production around us.

There were other Oriental dance teams, Oriental acts, singers, single acts, [but] they don't get the bookings we get because they just haven't got the caliber or the qualifications to play the Loew's State or the Capitol Theater, or the Paramount Theater. I know a lot of acts that got in the business and got out soon as they got in because they didn't know which way to turn, they didn't know how to develop an act. [The agency] farms you out and [the clubs] look at it and it doesn't work out. They don't think it's bookable, they won't play it. I know some of them, they're my friends. I'm not going to mention their names—they didn't make it.

When the war was on, we were playing the Brown Hotel in Louisville, Kentucky. They thought we were Japanese when we were walking, and people in the street called us Japs and so forth. We overlooked it, we kept walking. But when they come upstairs to the room of the Brown Hotel and see us perform and they enjoy us— they applaud us and really appreciate our work—and they say, "They must be Chinese." As if the Japanese couldn't do what we could do, dancing, like to entertain them. So unbeknownst to them that one of us is Japanese, which is Toy. She's Japanese and they didn't know. So what's the difference? "I didn't throw a bomb at you." Hell, I'm more American than they are; I was born in Palo Alto! Anyway, we were too young to understand any discrimination of who's Japanese and who's Chinese at that time.

We signed some contracts for RKO Pictures with the *Around the World* picture with Kay Kyser. During the Pearl Harbor days, the Japanese had to go to internment camps. Whoever enters into California had to go to the camp, or they will have to leave California. We didn't know about that, so we played some dates before we opened at the RKO Studios for the picture. And we're playing at the Orpheum Theater in San Diego and we receive a phone call and the immigration officer mentioned that, "Understand that Toy, your partner, is Japanese. You must leave California or she will have to go to internment camp—that is the law now." So what we did, we went to Lake Tahoe. William Morris booked us right away to Lake Tahoe. We lost all our contracts.

We were booked into Forbidden City about 1946, the first time was...I think it was after '48 that we played Forbidden City because in '48 Sammee Tong was emcee at the Club Shanghai—that was for Fong Wan, he owned the club. We played there for about three months— Club Shanghai on Grant Avenue; that was the first time we played a Chinese club.

Could be about '49 that we played Forbidden City. When we do have open time, like we're on our end route to the Biltmore Bowl in Los Angeles, we'd wire Charlie [Low] and he'd fill us in three months, or three months with option, and so forth. We enjoy playing the exotic club and we like Charlie Low so well as a host. It was just a feeling of feeling good because we were in a show of our own race. It's comfortable enough: we'd go out and eat, all Oriental, they're all having fun. One is a singing act like Frances Chun or Larry Ching there. And acrobatics: they're fast and furious, they're very clever. And other dancing acts like

Jackie Mei Ling, the Tai Sings...that's really fun to be in an Oriental show. It's like a family.

You can safely say that the Chinese nightclubs in San Francisco Chinatown really groomed these guys. Like Sammee Tong. In *Bachelor Father*, he was the valet to John Forsythe. Remember that TV series? Jack Soo made it, bless his soul. Pat Morita got in front of the Chinese Sky Room and did his comedy and nobody laughed because he was ahead of his time—jokes, you know. Now he was in a series. He was a cook—*Happy Days*. Wherever he got the karate, I don't know, but he's sure pretty good at that karate bit that he does on the screen [in the *Karate Kid* movies]. And Bob Ito, he's a good singer and dancer— Chinese Sky Room. He was what you call a singer and dancer and he does well with the production number, and turned out to be a very good actor in *Quincy*.

It doesn't matter if you're Chinese or what nationality, as long as you have the talent and you rehearse for the talent and you practice for it and really worked on your act, you could perform around the world like we have, almost three times around the world. I'd always dreamed of this since the fourth grade. I said I'm going to do the best I can, whatever way, what, which, where...I'm going to make it count. I'm going back to Stanford Stadium with a camel hair coat and watch the football game—be that successful. I did already on Thanksgiving Day—with a camel hair coat! ●

ABOVE: Paul Wing performs at the world premiere of the documentary *Forbidden City, USA,* Palace of Fine Arts, San Francisco (November 15, 1989). Photo by Bob Hsiang. BELOW: Brochure for the "China Doll Revue" at the Hotel Thunderbird in Las Vegas (early 1960s).

OPPOSITE: Toy and Wing (1930s). Photo by Bloom, Chicago.

Bloom
Chicago

Toy Yat Mar

1920–1997, Singer

Excerpts from interviews conducted on
February 6, 1986, and September 30, 1988.

I am known as a southpaw, which my mother was not aware of when I was an infant. As mothers normally do, they have a rattle for the baby, and she placed the rattle in my right hand, which I dropped immediately. She placed it in my left hand and I shook the dickens out of it. Now, you know, in old-fashioned, strict Chinese families, you sit down at a table and use chopsticks with your left hand? No way! But she let me because she figured, "Well, that's the way she is, she's going to be a southpaw, a left-hander." So I grew up unfettered by tradition.

I was born in Portland, Oregon. I grew up in the city of Seattle and spent all my years in Seattle until I left there in 1937. The Chinese in my generation lived very much within their community or within their own gatherings. In our days—and I'm speaking of our race—we made the most of it, and if we wanted more, we put ourselves out to do more to achieve more—and by golly, I think the majority of us did.

In our own quiet, passive manner, we would accomplish what we set out to do without saying, "You owe me because my father laid a railroad tie." Which my father did, OK? But you don't see me screaming, hollering, "Yeah, you owe me because my father was a coolie." He came over replete with a pigtail and the whole bit. He made his way speaking no English: managed to buy a nice home, raised us, and went back to heaven, without creating any disturbances.

We did have a Victrola, wind-up one. We used to have records, Chinese records. And then she [my mother] bought us a radio. I heard music, I heard plays, I heard dramas, and I would sing along with the radio. I thought, "Gee, this is pretty snappy!" And I kept it a secret of my desire to sing—never sang in public.

The first time I sang in public was in high school. There was a little Chinese club that was called the Cathay Club for Chinese students. And the high school which I attended put quite a bit of emphasis on productions by the students. I had as a friend a black girl who was a pianist, and we rehearsed a couple of songs. Or was it one song? I believe it was "Dinah," and I came in second. And with that, all my friends descended upon me and said, "Gee, we didn't know you could sing. Where did all this come from? God, you're great!" You know, I became sort of a mini-star. Well, that encouraged me.

Sometime later—this is sometime after my father passed away and Mother was not having a very good time economically speaking—she

OPPOSITE: Toy Yat Mar (1950s). Photo by Romaine-Skelton.

ABOVE, TOP: Toy Yat Mar is interviewed by the author at her Fresno home (February 6, 1986). Photo by Arthur Dong. BOTTOM: Toy Yat Mar photo (1940s), autographed to the author. Photo by Romaine.

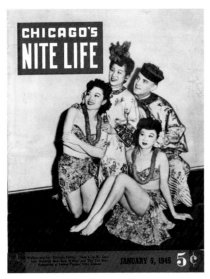

CHICAGO'S NITE LIFE

JANUARY 5, 1946   5¢

[Mother] approached me this once and asked me if I would be interested in going to work in a check room in this roadhouse out on the highway in Seattle for $2.50 a night. "Sure, why not? It's a job. I think I can handle it."

In the roadhouse they had a three- or four-piece band, and on Saturday nights they had live entertainment, a couple of acts. And between shows I would go strike up a conversation with the acts, asked them questions, many questions: "How do you get started?" "What do you have to do in order to get doing what you're doing?" And the people who owned the roadhouse were aware of the fact that I was somewhat of a singer and encouraged me to sing with the band when they were playing dance music. So that was, more or less, my first appearance before a regular public.

Well, I found out that in order to get bookings one had to go to agents, which I did. Young as I was—in my bobby socks, beanie cap, the whole high school bit at that time—I walked into these agents' office. "Well, don't call us, we'll call you." Well, that didn't deter me.

Finally walked into the office of this one man—I'll always remember him: a decent man, very pleasant, kind face. His name is Louie Kohler, his secretary's name is Helen. "OK, can you go to work?" "Who, me? Sure!" "Well, you know it's in an all-night spot in Seattle's Chinatown." I asked my mother if it was all right, and she was rather hesitant, and I told her...I made the one statement to her and she never questioned me from there on in for the rest of her days. I said, "Mama, I would never do anything that I would consider wrong or you would consider wrong, and you can trust me." So I went to work there for $12.50 a week.

They usually had a strip person on the bill. It was a two-piece band—piano player and drummer—the entertainment consisted of me and a stripper. In those days, in that type of club, when a customer comes in, you were supposed to go over and hustle him for a song so that he would tip. "Hi, how are you? What would you like to hear?" Well, I wasn't very good at that. I used to stand next to the drummer and he would nudge me, "Go on, get out there. Ask them what they want to hear. Go on out." So that lasted, I'd say, about two weeks.

I got other bookings and went to little towns [in Washington state] like Wenatchee, Yakima, Longview—I've played them. With just a few weeks under my belt, there was an opportunity to join a small company of entertainers going out on the road, doing what they call one-night stands, playing little theaters. I was the only Chinese entertainer. We had two acrobats, we had a couple of comedians. I was with them for about a year. We traveled clean across the country.

When I say one-night stands, I *mean* one night! There was an advance man who was always ahead of us booking little theaters, little tank towns, little milk stops. We'd be traveling in autos at night and it would be so cold you'd put your feet into paper sacks or wrap them in newspapers to keep them warm 'cause the heater wouldn't be working in the car and you could not afford a hotel room.

The company went on to Canada, and I couldn't go on to Canada because of my race. They didn't have the money to put up a bond for me, so I was stranded [on the border] for six to eight weeks, I believe it was. Fortunate as I was, the Lord was with me. This couple took me in and took care of me until I got word from the company to join them in some little town in New York state: Plattsburgh, New York. So I stayed with them for a while, went to Detroit, and they had to go to Canada again, and there I was: dumped again. And I was stranded in Detroit.

For seven months it was just scratching for a living, I mean absolutely scratching. Wound up washing dishes in order to pay for a bus ticket to go home, which I did. Took a bus ride from there to Seattle. Got back there and thought maybe I'd better go back to school because I had dropped out of high school to go on the road. Wasn't there but a few weeks, got another call to join another company all the way back in Boston. Hippity hop, I went off again!

After traveling around, I finally wound up in San Francisco because I heard about this Chinese club, which featured Chinese entertainers, and it was called the Forbidden City. So I thought I would give it a try and I went up there and I auditioned for Charlie Low. And he liked me, hired me. In fact, I was the first female singer in there besides his wife, Li Tei Ming. She was the reigning queen. She was pretty fair but very impressed with herself—very prima donna.

Working for Charlie had its ups and downs. He is the good ol' "Charlie Chinaman" like the white folks like: always obliging, acquiescent, obliging the white people. Like it or not, white people still like it when a person of another race kowtows to them. He did a lot of kowtowing for the sake of his business. I feel you don't have to—to me it lacked sincerity.

Charlie was for Charlie, everything was for his own gain. Demanding—didn't know how to interact with his employees. He was on a power trip, carried away by his success. It got to him. I remember he was always coming back demanding that the girls go out and entertain his customers. That got to be old hat. He never bothered me, mostly the chorus girls. When you're treated that way it is only a natural reaction to balk—the girls did. He would get literally black in the face from anger; he's very dark, and he got black because they would take their time doing it. There was so much tension between him and the employees. I felt that it didn't have to be, but it was that way all the time. He was always going around complaining that the girls were ungrateful. I said, "Charlie, when you want somebody to do something for you, there is a way of asking."

OPPOSITE, TOP: Toy Yat Mar (1930s). Photo by Romaine. MIDDLE: Cover of *Chicago's Nite Life* magazine with the "Chinese Follies" (l-r): Mary Mammon, Toy Yat Mar, Ken Walker, and Dottie Sun (January 5, 1945). BOTTOM: Toy Yat Mar (1940s).

ABOVE: "I was a southpaw....I grew up unfettered by tradition"—Toy Yat Mar (photo 1940s).

In San Francisco they called me the "Chinese Sophie Tucker." Maybe it was because I sang one song that was associated with her ["Some of These Days"], or possibly it was my style of singing. In those days when I sang a song, I belted it. When I sang a song, I was strong—a male strength in your delivery. I really didn't care too much for the label, so to speak, although I was flattered because I considered her one of the great entertainers of all times, the last of the red-hot mommas. But it was commercial, so I stuck with it.

People in those days thronged Forbidden City. Especially after Forbidden City gained international fame, international publicity. Place was just crowded with people. It's one of the spots that they had to go to when they came to San Francisco. It was quite a treat for them, it was something unusual. Then the other clubs got on the bandwagon.

The group of us at the Forbidden City, we got along very well. There was a great deal of camaraderie, we did things together. One favorite spot for quite some time was Vanessi's in North Beach. When we showed up it was royal carpet. The treatment was such that when we came in and sat down to eat: "Steaks?" "Sure!" "Butter?" "By the quarter pound!" Stuff like that was rationed during the war. Bob's Steakhouse—the same thing. Bob opened up a special room in the back for just theatrical people. We were recognized throughout the city.

[Still, we faced discrimination.] There were incidents, like in San Francisco Chinatown, where the town would be teeming with military personnel and you always had your red-white-and-blue rednecks who can't see beyond their noses. And the moment they spot an Oriental face, the first thought was: "Jap, what the hell you doing here?!" I encountered that in Chinatown.

I had occasion when I was traveling—I think it was in Memphis—I had occasion to ride a public bus. I boarded the bus, and no sooner had I boarded the bus than I realized this is segregated. "Where do you sit, Toy?" I looked in the rear, I looked to the front. Fortunately there was something open in the middle of the bus. "OK, kid, go for it!" So I sat down in the middle of the bus. But nobody sat down beside me. I said, "Oh well." One learns to let it roll off of you when you feel discrimination is staring you in the face.

Another time in Las Vegas I needed to have my hair done, went to a beauty shop. A woman must have worn out her appointment book looking to see if there was an opening, and I could see her flipping empty pages. "Sorry. I have nothing open." Oh well.

Working in the Midwest, Chicago area, Des Moines, places like that, I used to have people come up to me after the show and say, "Where in the world did you learn to speak English?" Most customers were people who never had any contact with, any knowledge of Chinese Americans— what kind of people we are or what our capabilities are. And we're just as human as they are.

I never felt that I was different being Chinese. I grew up with [different] ethnic groups, and the thought of being Chinese never entered my mind. I was as American as apple pie, and that is the way I grew up. However, I didn't lose any of my feeling for my heritage, being that my parents didn't speak English very well or very much English at all. We weren't as badly discriminated against as the blacks; they were having a rough time.

During the fifties—on the onset of the fifties, I would say— business started to decline. Then we depended on Gray Line Tours—their salvation, their bread ticket. These people were just a one-shot deal:

OPPOSITE, TOP: Forbidden City postcard (1940s). MIDDLE: Toy Yat Mar at the Forbidden City with unidentified woman and service members (mid-1940s). BOTTOM: "It's Oriental, Gay, and Exciting!" Ad for the "Chinese Follies" at Amato's Supper Club in Astoria, Oregon (clockwise from top left): Jadin Wong, Toy Yat Mar, Hazel Jay, Mary Mammon, and Dottie Sun (mid-1940s).

ABOVE: Toy Yat Mar (1940s). Photo by Romaine.

businessmen from Dubuque, Iowa, and Omaha, Nebraska. They take this Gray Line Tour of the city, and included in it is a trip to one of the world's most famous Chinese nightclubs where you see it all. Sometimes [audiences would] be very enthusiastic, and sometimes it was so slow that you'd think we wouldn't [have to perform that night]—but no, the Gray Line Tour was coming and we'd have to do a show just for them.

And then that declined to a point where Charlie felt it was time to bail out, shall we say. At which time he sold the establishment to Coby Yee. And Coby made a very good effort, a very brave effort to keep the club going. But the times were not with her. If my memory serves me right, at that time I think the topless era came into being and entertainment such as we offered was more or less passé. I was still working at Forbidden City at night but working as a file clerk during the day. You can't let pride get in the way—I had no qualifications, no education really to speak of. The topless bars were taking over and it declined to the point to where [Coby] finally bailed out too.

ABOVE: Toy Yat Mar performs at the world premiere of the documentary *Forbidden City, USA*, Palace of Fine Arts, San Francisco (November 15, 1989). Photo by Bob Hsiang.

OPPOSITE: Toy Yat Mar at the Forbidden City, accompanied by Harry Abramson and his band (ca. 1946). Photo by Leslie I. Hause, Jr.

So I made an effort to find employment in the other world, so to speak. I felt that I didn't want to go back on the road again. I progressed to other office jobs and then reached the point that I needed security because of my age, so I went into the post office. I stayed with the service for nineteen years. Retired about almost three years ago.

I threw out most of my arrangements—they were packed away just getting old and dirty. You must think I'm real far out. It's been so long ago...I haven't wanted to be a part of it. It's past, it's gone. I'm the type of person that when I'm on the stage in back of the footlights, I'm on. But when I'm not there, I'm not on.

I moved down here to Fresno to get away from San Francisco, which I would consider Sodom and Gomorrah now. And I love it down here, I love the living here. Been here eleven years now—happy as a bird dog. ●

Walton Biggerstaff

1903–1995, Producer, Choreographer

Excerpts from an interview conducted on
February 15, 1986.

I'm an ex-school teacher [from] the state of Washington. I took up dancing against everyone's wishes that I knew—young men do not go in for dancing and ballet dancing. I was born and raised north of Seattle and had my first studio in Bellingham, Washington. I decided to go to San Francisco, where I opened my own studio.

Jack Mei Ling was a handsome young Chinese boy who had been studying with me, and I would always argue with him because he was so lazy and so talented. One night he called up and asked me to come down to the Lion's Den, and I became the producer there. It was the first Oriental club below the surface of the ground, and the place was very small but it was popular because it was below ground. All Oriental and quite different.

It was down in the basement and had only three dancers at that time: Mary Mammon, Dottie Sun, and Mel [Got]...whose name I've forgotten, as she didn't work with me. She had family trouble and all—she left. So we had, on a stage the size of a postage stamp, the two girls and two orchestra men. And everything was going on fine. I was very busy trying to make a show with two dancers and a singer and an emcee who was a Caucasian, and he would crack wise to entertain the inebriated people.

And then Jack Mei Ling came by one day and said, "I've got something for you to do: go with me over to Forbidden City and see Charlie Low." And we went to the famous Forbidden City. I met Charlie, and with the instigation of Jack Mei Ling, he got Charlie talking to me about his show. And I couldn't tell him how bad it was—or how "ordinary" would be a better word.

And finally Jack talked to him in Chinese and I found out Jackie had been selling me as the next choreographer to Charlie Low. Charlie knew nothing of my ability other than through Jack, but he knew for months that I have been at the Lion's Den, which was not an important club but it was one of the few [Chinese American nightclubs].

And so I was engaged by Mr. Low to do one show with the possibility of two shows. Each show was to use the girls and do three shows a night, and the first and last show would be the same. I handled the costuming department with costumers that I would discuss the costumes with. That became a long engagement with Mr. Low, and I was his producer. And I stayed at Forbidden City for fourteen years.

OPPOSITE: "This picture shows how Biggerstaff trains chorus girls and specialty dancers at his 'China Doll Factory.'"
—photo caption (Acme Photo Service, April 14, 1944).

ABOVE, TOP: Walton Biggerstaff is interview by the author at his San Francisco flat (February 15, 1986). Photo by Arthur Dong. BOTTOM: Walton Biggerstaff photo (1940s), autographed to the author. Photo by Romaine.

There was quite a strange feeling at Forbidden City when the woman who was the previous producer left; the office didn't seem to know what to do with a man being producer—Caucasian as well. Frank Huie was our maître d', and he was very friendly and told me that he would have a little opposition from old-timers who would come up there to see a show done by a man, and especially a Caucasian.

There actually wasn't any animosity as far as I can tell, only some of the people who would come up and watch rehearsals—some of the parents or boyfriends of the girls. And they would be a little upset to find that a man was there, and I would be going in and out of the dressing room and maybe adjusting costumes on the girls, and there would be a slight disturbance there. But no real problem at all, it was just one big, happy family.

But I was scared to death because I had never used Oriental girls in a routine. First of all, you had the parents' objection, or their husbands or their boyfriends, to get them to come to rehearsals. The girls had to be told that they'd wear abbreviated costumes, not streetwear, and some girls would get up and leave. And I found out afterwards that Mr. Low's been going through all this for many months due to the fact that the families objected to the girls going into theatrical productions. Especially when they use the word "dance"; dance was synonymous with prostitution, and it took a long time for that to be broken down. But one of the tricks was you never hired the girls as dancers—you hired them as waitresses, and within two or three nights you kind of coax them to take a lesson with me, as I had my own studio. And many of the girls would come and take dance lessons.

In fact, I had to produce a show in two weeks, so we worked every day for the first week. I called the girls on stage and they didn't know anything except having been [at] American nightclubs. So I started out, first of all, just having them walk to see they had no, say, impediment in their walking. Then I had them turn only once because many of them haven't heard of taking a turn unless they were in some game.

But the main thing was to get them to come from the dressing room down onto the stage without any casualties—having high heels and all of that, and it was slippery. You'd have to get them to the top of the stairs and have them look above your head and then walk down the

ABOVE: "I took up dancing against everyone's wishes that I knew—young men do not go in for dancing and ballet dancing."—Walton Biggerstaff. Photo by Romaine (1940s).

five steps, which they had never done, since they usually look [down] for their stepping. And they would have to learn to turn without falling or without looking like they were losing their balance, which many of them did.

The Chinese girls, all of them had two left feet, and one especially: Dottie Sun had unusually large left feet. Not large in size but in problem. And we later capitalized on that, and I think the other producers would have done too.

The girls, when they were frustrated, would turn to me and say, "We don't have any rhythm. You know, Orientals have no sense of Western rhythm, so we can't follow your routines." And I said, "Any child can follow mine." And they finally found out that my routines were not difficult, but they were theatrical and you had to project your personality as well as the steps. And the steps were not difficult. And I told the girls who were listening, "Now you girls will have to work." And they would not go into the show until they had taken a look at some of the productions and saw how beautiful the girls were. Of all the things, Mr. Low insisted they were beautiful.

The great success of Charlie was the fact that he was presenting beautiful costumed Oriental girls. And these girls were amazed themselves to see how stunning they were. And then Charlie had one thing in his great favor and that was it was an entertainment for the family. Not only the food was good but the whole family would come there, and while we did have bubble, fan dancers, and semi-nude, they were not offensive. And we had a large military [clientele]. All the branches were coming there, and they would not come individually but whole groups of them would come in. Many of the men [in the audience], who were from the Middle West, had never seen Oriental girls.

Noel Toy was new to me. I had never heard of her and I found that there were very few Oriental soloists and I expected to see a full routine. But here the lights went out and a beautiful but short Oriental girl...nice body: Noel with a gigantic balloon, hiding everything except her ankles and arms and head on up. And she sauntered down the stairs like she was walking on glass, being extremely careful, and her legs were beautiful. Noel would leave everything off so that she just had the balloon and herself. And Jack had to check her night after night to see that she had underpants on, or what the girls called— I think they call it a strap. And she always wore her—I'd forgotten the word now—pasties...I'd forgotten that.

We have a law here, in San Francisco anyway, that girls cannot be completely nude. They must wear pasties. And Noel took advantage of that and would have a little patch, which was required. All the girls would always think of that. But Jack had to see that she didn't make it too realistic-looking. This is a little aside, but Jack told me that she felt, "Why fool the public?" If they wanted to see a nude body, she would show them. So she would draw a crease down her little triangular patch

ABOVE, TOP: *Laff* magazine photographed Walton Biggerstaff in rehearsals with Dottie Sun, left, and Fay Ying at the Forbidden City (June 1948). BOTTOM: At the Club Shanghai (l-r): Robin Wing, Walton Biggerstaff, Mary Mammon, unidentified, unidentified, unidentified, Lynne Wong, unidentified (1950s).

ABOVE: Ads for just two of the shows that Walton Biggerstaff produced and choreographed at the Forbidden City over a period of fourteen years. He also worked at the Chinese Sky Room, the Club Shanghai, the Kubla Khan, the Lion's Den, and the New Shanghai Terrace (1940s).

OPPOSITE: Showgirls send off Walton Biggerstaff as he embarks on a trip to Honolulu (l-r): Jeannie Chang, unidentified, Louise Leung, Walton Biggerstaff, Barbara Yung, unidentified, unidentified (1940s).

that she would wear, which would satisfy the law but would also satisfy the customer.

The creative side of me must have been very great because I had to do a different show—three or four routines a show—every month. I had to do things that not only fit the girls but pleased the audience, satisfied Charlie Low, as well as satisfied me. I must say that Charlie Low was the most amazing boss that I had ever had. I use the word "boss" because I'm used to people telling you, "This is what you do and that's what you do, and that's that!" Charlie didn't tell me what to do except "produce me a show," and a show that's better than they have been.

I studied everything Oriental, though I didn't do any strict Oriental shows. I always thought that Charlie would give me permission to do a Chinese show, and while most of my training has been in the Japanese culture, I still knew something about the Chinese dance and would make it entertaining—[although] not trying to imitate the Chinese theater, because that I wouldn't be able to. Charlie never quite said "no," but especially he would go around the bush and would let me know that he didn't think that would be popular with the audience.

I spent at least ten years trying to find out how I could get Mr. Low in the show himself, as his personality was just magnificent. And his own friends would scarcely get to see him, as new customers were always bidding for attention, "Come to my table, come to my table." Finally I made a chorus boy out of him; I got him to appear with the girls in one of the routines. His great appearance was in Forbidden City's version of the "Gay '90s" revue, and Mr. Low let it run four or five months.

Now, we thought that [Charlie] would pick up a great deal of business from the Oriental world, and he did, but nothing in comparison to the American, the Caucasian group that would come there. People would come night after night, not necessarily to see the show but to come to an Oriental atmosphere. And the food was extremely good and the acts were always good.

I was bowled over by seeing not only the results, which were quite fine, but that Charlie Low's business had picked up so tremendously. And then the fact that he gave me an introduction into the psychology of the Chinese theater—not the real, authentic theater, but the fact that Chinese people could do Western dancing and put it across—not only singing, which they always knew, but they could make theatrical appearances and prove it profitable to them as well as to their producers.

Now that I'm all through with dancing and Forbidden City, I look back at it and wonder how I could have satisfied them as well as me. When I think back, I think that there must have been some bad moments where I could have done something strange that wasn't pleasing. But as a rule, I must have been very inventive and would take ideas from other people. And I got a lot from the girls, who would show me what I had shown them and it would be quite different, and that would become the beginning of a new step. ●

The Clubs

Andy Wong's "Chinese Vanities of 1954." Front row (l-r): Julianne Lew and Mae Lacsamana. Middle row: Hana Abe, Sheryl Lee, Jackie Mei Ling, Jeannie Chang, and Pat Chin. Back row: Lily Pon and Dinky Lee.

China Doll

357 51st Street, New York City

China Doll, New York

Talent Policy: Floorshows at 8, 12 and 2; continuous dancing. Operator, Tom Ball. Publicity, Milt Rubin. Prices: $2.50-$3.50 minimum.

New club is basically the same as the recently departed Club London. Color scheme has been changed a bit and Oriental doodads have been hung around.

Show itself ran smoothly, even for an opening night, and displayed some gorgeous Chinese gals (9) billed as the China Dolls, who do their routines like they knew them. Costumes are full of color, featuring tremendous stylized headgear and Chinese robes. Lee Mortimer, who was supposed to have obtained some of these kids from the Coast, including some who were never in showbiz before, came up with a group of sloe-eyed lookers to set tongues wagging.

Only act familiar on the Stem is Ming and Ling, Chinese hillbillies, who get excellent results with their Sinatra-Crosby stuff. Team was way ahead when they decided to come back for *Eli-Eli* and followed it with a crack, *Glad You Like Our National Song*. From then on they were dead.

Best returns were given to the Tai Sings, a Chinese ballroom team. Couple are just fair dancers, but class and gal's delicate features sell heavily. Did three numbers, walking off to a goodish samba. Iris Wong, canary, did okay with special stuff set to *Little Green Shack* and *Jennie*. Voice is small but figure and costuming get attention. Florence Hin Low, acro and contortionist, did a lot of pretzel bends. Started on the floor, where she was lost, and then moved to a platform. Good hand, but act was too long and found crowd restive. Mara Kim, line girl, comes out to do an acceptable toe ballet.

Show starts with a book number by Rogers and Prince showing a bus hustler shilling Chinatown residents to see the sights uptown. Idea is novel and well presented. From then on customers are supposed to be seeing the Stem and the acts that follow represent the hot spots. Three productions are well handled and kids work like they enjoy it.

Chavez cuts a good show. Four Sins (Chinese ork) relieves.

Mara Kim, the Chinese ballerina.

Chin Wan, an oriental juggler.

Ming and Ling, Chinese hillbillies.

Iris Wong, the Chinese blues singer.

ABOVE (clockwise from left). *Billboard* review of "Slant Eyed Scandals" at the China Doll (April 13, 1946). Postcard of the China Doll club; the caption on the back reads: "Three revues nightly featuring 20 slant-eyed China Dolls" (ca. 1946). Photos from "Slant Eyed Scandals" (page from a magazine, source unknown, ca. 1946).

OPPOSITE (clockwise): Program for "Slant Eyed Scandals" featuring (l–r) Iris Wong, unidentified, Ming and Ling, the Tai Sings (Jessie Tai Sing and Wilbur Tai Sing), and Mara Kim (April 1946). Drinks list from a menu (ca. 1946). Ad for the "Maid in China" show (October 10, 1946). Program cover (1946).

TOM BALL
presents
"SLANT EYED SCANDALS"
produced by DONN ARDEN
with MING & LING, TAI SINGS, FLORENCE HIN LOWE, IRIS WONG, MARA KIM, CHIN WAN
AND
LEE MORTIMER'S CHINA DOLLS

Costumes: Mme. Berthé   Decor: Kaj Velden Studios   Publicity: Milton Rubin

Music By CHAVEZ, MANDARIN OF THE RHUMBA and the EXOTIC FOUR SINS

1- **AT PELL AND MOTT STREETS: Introducing**
"Take the Bus Uptown," by DICK ROGERS and HUGHIE PRINCE with MARA KIM, CHIN WAN and LEE MORTIMER'S CHINA DOLLS.

2- **CHIN WAN**
China's No. 1 Juggler.

3- **FLORENCE HIN LOWE**
The Orient's Outstanding Acrobatic Dancer.

4- **IRIS WONG**
San Francisco's Favorite Chinese Nightingale.

5- **PARADE OF THE CHINA DOLLS: Introducing**
"China Doll," words by LEE MORTIMER; Music by HARRY PUCK. With MARY MON and MARA KIM and
The China Dolls

Mae Dong	Lily Pon	Clare Lee
Tchow Lin Wong		Ko Fu Gee
Muilana Wong	Lue Mae	Mae Lin

6- **THE TAI SINGS**
Suave, Smart, Sophisticated.

7- **MING & LING**
Famed Chinese Hill Billies.

8- **FINALE: HOT CHINA, entire company.**

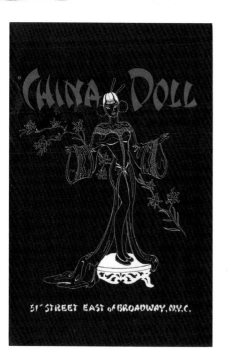

CHINA DOLL

51st STREET EAST of BROADWAY, N.Y.C.

Premiere Tomorrow Thursday

"MAID in CHINA"
Produced by DONN ARDEN
MING and LING
Famous Chinese Hillbillies
FRANCES CHUN
Chinese Singing Sensation
TAI SINGS
China's Foremost Dancers
FOUR CANTON BROS.
American Premiere
MUI SONG • LOY YOUNG
Continuous Dancing to
JOSE CURBELO & HIS RUMBAS
JACK FRASE ORCHESTRA
20 LEE MORTIMER'S **20**
CHINA DOLLS
"The Most Beautiful Chinese Girls In the World"
3 GREAT SHOWS NITELY
at 8—12—2:30
DINNER SERVED 'til 9:30
NO COVER EVER
TOM BALL'S

China Doll
RESERVATIONS CI 5-8980
51st STREET at BROADWAY

Chinese Sky Room

605 Pine Street, San Francisco

Well, I'll Be Darned, If It Ain't a Chinese Sinatra!

ANDY WONG
presents
FIRST TIME
IN AMERICA

A Chinese-Japanese Musical

"HOLIDAY
IN THE
ORIENT"

★ The Changs
★ Helen Chiyo Toy
★ Barbara Young
★ The Geisha Girls

Chinese Sky Room

GRANT & PINE STS.   NO COVER CHG.

MEMBERS OF DINERS — AMERICAN EXPRESS

MISS HELEN TOY

PRINCE GUM LOEW

Andy Wong proudly presents

THE CHINESE SKY ROOM'S

''PRE-SUMMER REVUE''

With

NOEL TOY, KIM WONG, HELEN KIM
ELIZABETH JEAN, PRICE GUM LOEW
and HELEN TOY

P R O G R A M

(Subject to Change)

(a) KICKING THE GONG AROUND .
. . . . The Wongettes

(b) MISS HELEN TOY . . . .
. Singing Mistress of Ceremonies

(c) CHINATOWN'S GREATEST DISCOVERY
PRINCE GUM LOEW
The Merry Musical Mimic

(d) CHINO SOY — Chinese Rhumba . .
. . . . The Wongettes

(e) THE ONE AND ONLY . . . .
N O E L T O Y
in
A Chinese Girl's Impression of
Gypsy Rose Lee

(f) LA CONGA . . . . . The Wongettes
(Follow the Leader)

Presented under the personal supervision of Mr. Andy Wong
Dances by Marah Hoobing -:- Music by Sammy Wong
Exploitation by King Howard

THE 'WONGETTES,' dancing debutantes. Reading upwards they are Kim Wong, Helen Kim and Elizabeth Jean.

Telephone: CHINA 2163

The CHINESE SKY ROOM, Cor. Pine St. and Grant Ave., San Francisco, Calif.

ABOVE (clockwise): Program. Ad, photos by Tigard. Postcard (all images 1940s).

OPPOSITE (clockwise from top left): Singer Dudley Lee swoons Randy Cromwell at the Chinese Sky Room: "Well, I'll be Darned, If It Ain't a Chinese Sinatra!" (magazine source unidentified, June 1944). Marquee (ca. 1959). Patrons dance to the Hal Schutz Trio (ca. 1956). Ad for a "Chinese-Japanese Musical," most likely from before Japan's 1941 bombing of Pearl Harbor and prior to the internment of West Coast Japanese; dancer Barbara Yung holds a "bubble" with a Chinese New Year greeting.

The Brightest Spot in Chinatown

ANDY WONG Proudly Presents
THE MOST TALKED ABOUT FLOOR SHOW IN THE BAY AREA
Starring
★ **THIDA LOY** ★
Sensational Chinese
★ **FAN DANCER**
with
HELEN TOY
Singing MISTRESS OF CEREMONIES

DANCE to Sammy Wong's MUSIC MAKERS

Never a Cover Charge

ANDY WONG'S **CHINESE SKY ROOM** GRANT AVE AT PINE

Andy Wong packaged a show from his Chinese Sky Room programs and took it downtown to the Tivoli Theater in 1949. It was one of the Tivoli's last shows; the theater closed its doors that same year and was later demolished, having been in operation since 1913.

ABOVE: The Tivoli Theater, 70 Eddy Street, San Francisco (1949).
OPPOSITE: Display at the Tivoli Theater for Andy Wong's "Chinese Sketchbook of 1949: San Francisco's First Chinese Vaudeville."

LEFT: Before the Chinese Sky Room formally opened, Andy Wong and his partners operated the space as the Chinese Penthouse (Southern Pacific Railroad photo, 1930s).

TEASE TIME REVUE

Oriental eyefuls please variety-seeking nightclubbers on the West Coast

Shanghai Club is plushest cabaret in San Francisco's Chinatown. Customers begin arriving at seven, last ones leave at three in the morning.

ABOVE (clockwise): Stanley Toy and Jeannie Chang (1950s). *Scoop* magazine reports that Club Shanghai customers "begin arriving at seven, last ones leave at three in the morning" (February 19, 1954). Gladys Ng Gin serves drinks (late 1940s).

OPPOSITE: Front row (l-r): Ethel Lau, Fawn Yee, and Lynne Wong. Back row: unidentified, Club Shanghai owner Fong Wan, unidentified. (late 1940s).

FOLLOWING PAGES: Postcard (1950s).

FONG WAN'S
Club Shanghai

THE TAI SINGS

Fabulous
FONG WAN
Presents

*CHINA
DARLINGS
of 1950*

453 GRANT

Lovely
BARBARA YUNG

YOUNG
CHINA
TROUPE

The CHINA
DARLINGS

MAY LEE

VENUE   SAN FRANCISCO

Forbidden City

363 Sutter Street, San Francisco

Forbidden City, San Francisco

(Sunday, August 11)

Talent Policy: Floorshows at 8 and 10. Owner, Charlie Low; manager, Frank Huie. Prices: $2 minimum.

Spot has been completely remodeled following a fire which destroyed rear, kitchen and part of dining room. Beautifully done, room has been enlarged and walls hung with eight rare Chinese drapes.

Show, with an all-Gershwin music theme, is tops. Line (8) started show off in a lively mood.

Wing Brothers followed. New dancing duo is fast, acrobatic and plenty smooth. Great mitt.

Frances Chun, back after an Eastern tour, sings pops. Has a pleasing voice and presentation. Did *Juke Box Serenade*, a stopper. Mimics of Hildegarde, Kate Smith, Fannie Brice, Sophie Tucker and Helen Morgan were goods.

A trio (boy and two girls), on next, did a fast number, which brought on Larry Ching, the Chinese Sinatra. Lad is a fave here. Has good looks and a pleasing personality.

The Mei Lings, terp team, did a great job of ballroom and lifts. Nattily garbed, pair did four numbers.

Fluorescent finale is a gorgeous bit staged by Producer Walton Biggerstaff. Entire cast takes bows.

Henry Abramson's ork (7) does a good show job. Capacity house (250).

ABOVE (clockwise from top left): *Billboard* review for the "Gershwin Revue" (August 11, 1947). Forbidden City performers (l–r) Fay Ying, unidentified, Hazel Jay, Mary Mammon, Dottie Sun, Rose Chan, Mae Dong, and Lily Pon (1940s, photo by Romaine). Marquee (*Carnival Show* magazine, March 1941). Forbidden City interior, page from a program (ca. 1942).

OPPOSITE: Dancer Jessie Tai Sing (of the Tai Sings) on a program cover (ca. 1942).

FORBIDDEN CITY

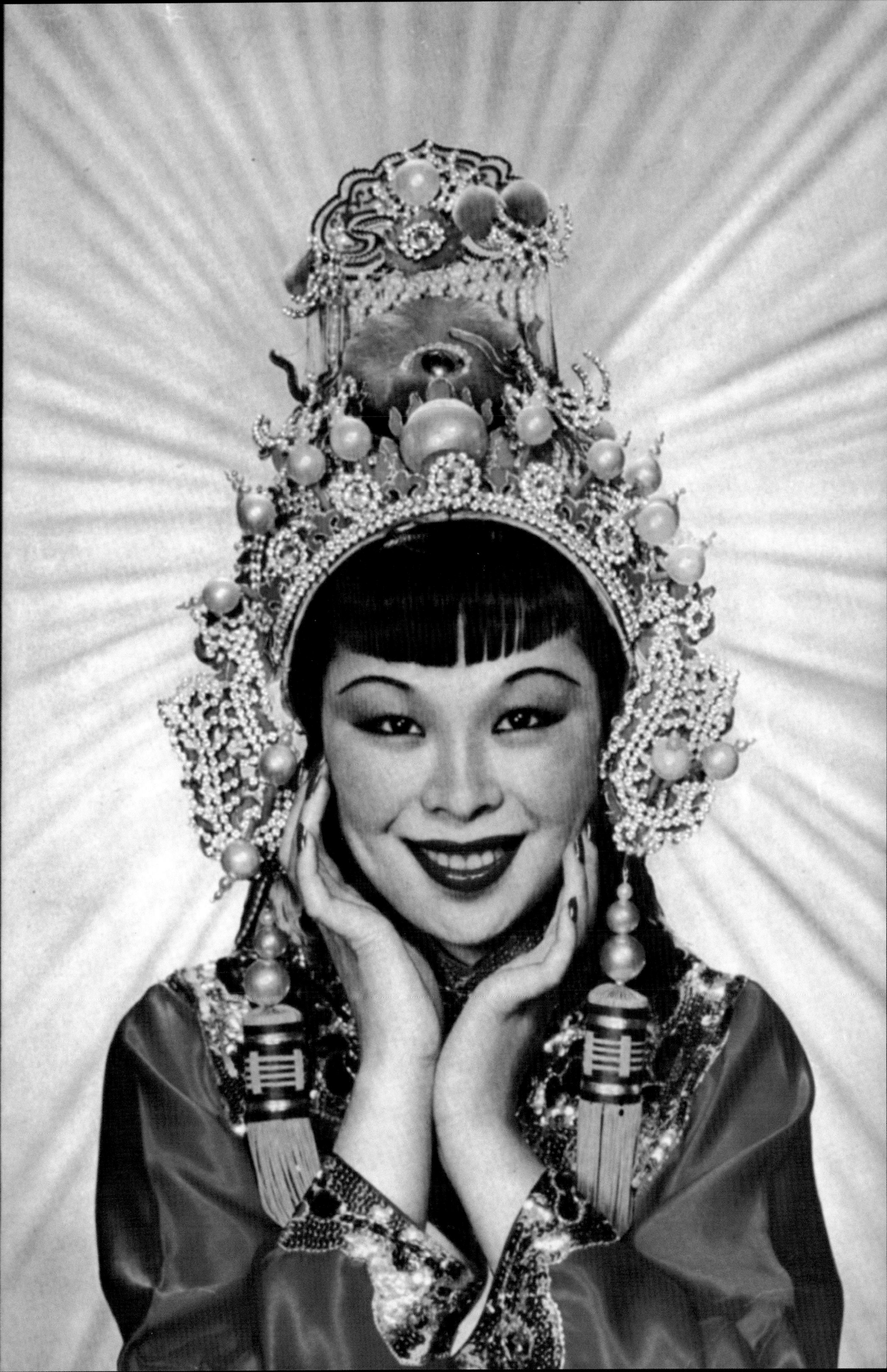

Charlie Low Presents
America's Greatest Chinese Revue

"Summertime Revue"

Shows 8:15 - 12:45

1. EVOLUTION OF THE DANCE
   Glamour Girls
   Review of Charleston, Ballin' the Jack, Black Bottom, Truckin' and Suzy-Q, Big Apple, Lambeth Walk, Shim Sham and the Jive

2. Our Favorite Singer of Songs
   HELEN TOY

3. Rhapsody in Taps
   TONY WING

4. SUMMERTIME POLKA
   Glamour Girls

5. Song Stylist Supreme
   LARRY CHING

6. China's Greatest Acrobatic Quartette
   SING LEE SINGS

7. HAWAIIAN FANTASY
   Glamour Girls and featuring Tony Wing, Helen Toy, Larry Ching

GLAMOUR GIRLS

1. Lily Pon   4. Ethel Lau
2. Diane Shinn   5. Dorothy Sun
3. Sue Mae Lee   6. Mary Mammon
7. Vicki Lee

CREDITS
Produced by Walton Biggerstaff
Costumed by Taziner Costume Shop

MUSICAL DIRECTION
Joe Marcellino and His Society Band

South American Holiday

Showtime 10:30

1. FIESTA TIME — Señores y Señoritas
   1. Bolivia — Mary Mammon
   2. Colombia — Dorothy Sun
   3. Venezuela — Sue Mae Lee
   4. Argentina — Lily Pon
   5. Uruguay — Ethel Lau
   6. Peru — Vicki Lee
   7. Chile — Diane Shinn
   8. Mr Brazil — Tony Wing

2. HELEN TOY

3. TONY WING, Whirlwind on Taps, in "Malaguena"

4. VOODOO MOON — Las Señoritas

5. LARRY CHING

6. Amazing Chinese Acrobats
   Sing Lee Sings

7. AFRO-CUBAN RITUAL
   Las Señoritas and featuring Tony Wing and Diane Shinn

Charlie Low's FORBIDDEN CITY
363 SUTTER STREET • SAN FRANCISCO

DOuglas 2-8648
DOuglas 2-4012

OPPOSITE (clockwise): The Mei Lings, Jackie Mei Ling and Jade Ling, dance to Harry Abramson and his band (1947). The Forbidden City bar (*Carnival Show* magazine, March 1941). Forbidden City exterior (ca. 1942).

ABOVE (clockwise): Program (mid-1940s). Airman Roger Chase and fiance Shirley Davis (US Air Force photo, 1954). Harry Abramson Band (l-r): Fritz Jensen, unidentified, unidentified, Freddie Higuera (drums), unidentified, and Harry Abramson (ca. 1946).

Kubla Khan

414 Grant Avenue, San Franciso

Kubla Khan, San Francisco

(Sunday, October 6)

Talent Policy: Floorshows at 8, 10 and 12. Owner-Manager, Eddie Pond. Prices: $2 minimum.

Based on Cole Porter tunes, show is best seen here in some time. Has an all-Chinese line with an American band, Bill Oetke's Rumberos (9). Opens with gorgeously costumed (by Frances Hill) *Night and Day* number, with the line, Jadin, Koby Yee and Owner Eddie Pond mixing in a gay routine. Miss Yee stays on to do a baton dance. Very clever.

Larry Ching, billed as the Chinese Crosby, sings *Night and Day* and several other Porter hits. Has a strong, deep voice and plenty of personality. Off to a good hand.

Line and Yee girl on next in a cute *My Heart Belongs to Daddy* routine, which brings on the Sing Lee Sing Troupe, show stars, with some daring acros and stunts. Swell work in a small space. Troupe is terrific and earns a heavy duke.

Mae Lee, pleasing soprano, clicks with *I Love You* among others. Then the line, again gorgeously gowned, in *Begin the Beguine,* which introduces Jadin and Li Sun, neat-looking dance duo. Oetke crew cuts the show and plays for dancing. Near capacity. Room is a 225-seater.

EXOTIC SPLENDOR OF THE KUBLA KHAN

ENTRANCE

CORNER OF LOBBY

BAR

CORNER OF COCKTAIL LOUNGE

DINING ROOM

RECREATION AND REHEARSAL HALL

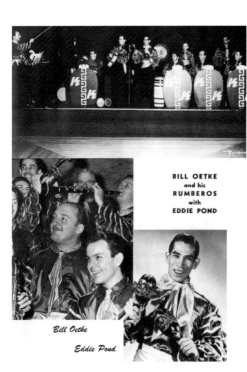

BILL OETKE and his RUMBEROS with EDDIE POND

Bill Oetke
Eddie Pond

ABOVE (clockwise from top left): *Billboard* review (October 6, 1946). Program showing Kubla Khan interior. Program showing owner Eddie Pond and the band Bill Oetke and His Rumberos. Program cover (ca. 1944).

OPPOSITE (clockwise): Program (mid-1940s). Cast (back row, l–r); unidentified, Eleanor Young, Gladys Wong, Louise Leung, Barbara Yung, unidentified, unidentified, and Hazel Jay; (front) Li-Sun, Jadin Wong, May Lee, and Eddie Pond (mid-1940s). Ad for opening night (1944).

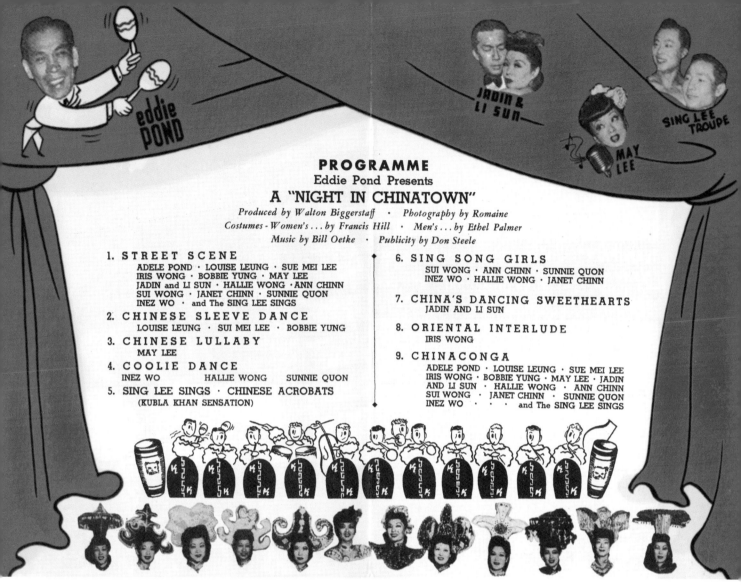

PROGRAMME
Eddie Pond Presents
A "NIGHT IN CHINATOWN"

Produced by Walton Biggerstaff · *Photography by Romaine*
Costumes - Women's . . . by Francis Hill · *Men's . . . by Ethel Palmer*
Music by Bill Oetke · *Publicity by Don Steele*

1. **STREET SCENE**
   ADELE POND · LOUISE LEUNG · SUE MEI LEE
   IRIS WONG · BOBBIE YUNG · MAY LEE
   JADIN and LI SUN · HALLIE WONG · ANN CHINN
   SUI WONG · JANET CHINN · SUNNIE QUON
   INEZ WO · and The SING LEE SINGS

2. **CHINESE SLEEVE DANCE**
   LOUISE LEUNG · SUI MEI LEE · BOBBIE YUNG

3. **CHINESE LULLABY**
   MAY LEE

4. **COOLIE DANCE**
   INEZ WO   HALLIE WONG   SUNNIE QUON

5. **SING LEE SINGS · CHINESE ACROBATS**
   (KUBLA KHAN SENSATION)

6. **SING SONG GIRLS**
   SUI WONG · ANN CHINN · SUNNIE QUON
   INEZ WO · HALLIE WONG · JANET CHINN

7. **CHINA'S DANCING SWEETHEARTS**
   JADIN AND LI SUN

8. **ORIENTAL INTERLUDE**
   IRIS WONG

9. **CHINACONGA**
   ADELE POND · LOUISE LEUNG · SUE MEI LEE
   IRIS WONG · BOBBIE YUNG · MAY LEE · JADIN
   AND LI SUN · HALLIE WONG · ANN CHINN
   SUI WONG · JANET CHINN · SUNNIE QUON
   INEZ WO · · · and The SING LEE SINGS

Lion's Den

946 Grant Avenue, San Francisco

ABOVE (clockwise from top left): Ad featuring Dottie Sun (July 19, 1941). Ad featuring Eleanore Yung (Eleanor Young) (August 1942). Performers and band, including dancer Suzanna Kim, far left, others unidentified (1940s). Customer's souvenir photo in folder (mid-1940s). Souvenir chopsticks (handwritten date, December 27, 1946). Entrance at the center leads to "San Francisco's only underground night spot" (November 1947).

OPPOSITE: Ad in *San Francisco Social Life* magazine features Cheri Lynn, "San Francisco's Most Exotic Oriental Dancer" (October 1945).

LIONS DEN
946 GRANT AVENUE   CHina 0946
San Francisco's Only Underground Nite Club

Presents
A Galaxy of Stars

Featuring
JACINE LEE
Oriental Song Stylist
and
Mistress Of Ceremonies

CHERI
Exotic Dance Star

TOY LING
Vivacious Fan Dancer

MAILE
Torrid Island Dancer

MUI LON FON
Bubble Fantasy

WING CHAO
Magician

ADRIAN
Creative Dance Artist

and

DARLYNE DUNKER
And Her Rhythmic Trio

3 Shows Nightly
CHina 0946

Open Every
Night

The LIONS DEN, San Francisco's only Underground Nite Club, 946 Grant Avenue, offers a very smart all-star Oriental floor show in exotic surroundings that are intriguing to behold. Spacious floor with convenient tables for your cocktails in full view of the shows, also good view from the bar, as well as dining room service on the Foyer where the three nightly shows are presented—all designed to meet the pleasure of the visitor, whatever his desires may be. It's a delightful setting electrified by an unique Oriental fantasy of thrills and excitement. Many charming Chinese girls who serve your cocktails and entertain you are always in evidence to add glamour to the otherwise colorful setting.

—PHOTO BY ROMAINE

CHERI—San Francisco's Most Exotic Oriental Dancer currently at the Lions Den.

Oakland Clubs

New Shanghai Terrace Bowl: 421 10th Street, Oakland, California
Club Oakland and New Shanghai Cafe: 425 10th Street, Oakland, California

樓海上新當舖

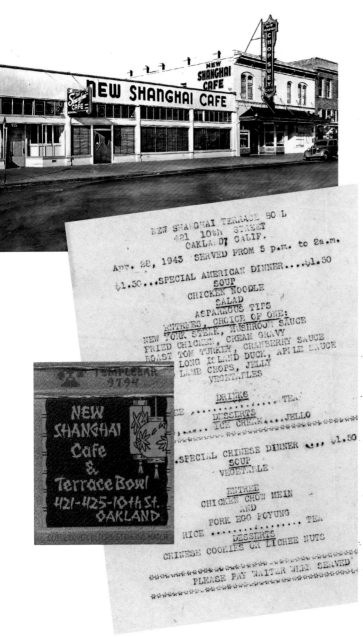

From 1927 to 1950, Fong Wan operated Oakland clubs under
three different names in several adjacent buildings (in addition to
his Club Shanghai and Chinese Cellar nightspots in San Francisco).

ABOVE (clockwise from top left): Fong Wan's buildings (ca. 1937). Ad featuring (clockwise) Fong Wan, Jennie (Jeannie) Chang,
Sherry (Cheri) Lynn, and Barbara Yung (1949). Menu insert for the New Shanghai Terrace (April 28, 1943). Matchbook cover (1940s).

OPPOSITE (clockwise): Ad for the New Shanghai Terrace grand opening (July 2, 1940). Photo folder cover (ca. 1940s).
Customer's souvenir photo in folder (1940s). Program for New Year's Eve show (December 1941).

FOLLOWING PAGES: Ad for the Shangri-La (June 1942). PHOTOGRAPH INSET: Shangri-La entrance (1942).

NEW SHANGHAI TERRACE BOWL

re is a view of the New Shanghai Terrace Bowl. 415-417-419-421 nth Street, which will hold its grand opening for diners and dancers tomorrow evening. Dr. Fong Wan (inset) is owner of the New Shanghai Cafe and the Terrace Bowl. Three floor shows will be presented nightly.

— Souvenir Program —

Happy New Year To All . . . . .

Open All Night on New Year's Eve . . . . $3.00 per Person

$500.00 Reward to anyone who has seen all these wonderful acts in any other place.

NEW SHANGHAI CAFE | **TERRACE BOWL**
425 - 10TH STREET | 421 - 10TH STREET
OAKLAND, CALIFORNIA | OAKLAND, CALIFORNIA

GLencourt 8838

SAMMEE TONG
Master of Ceremonies

The FONG WAN Chinese Acrobatic Troupe, and Man Lai Fong

The MEI LINGS Chinese Dance Trio

ZIGANIA Girl Rubinoff

TOY YAT MAR Singer

TED THOMPSON Orchestra Leader

GEORGE WRIGHT Organist

The SEN WONGS   Chinese Dance Team

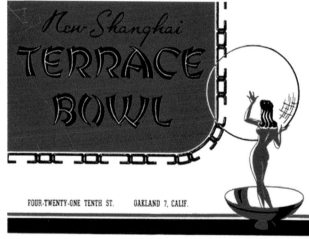

New Shanghai
TERRACE
BOWL

FOUR-TWENTY-ONE TENTH ST.   OAKLAND 7, CALIF.

FOUR TWENTY ONE - TENTH STREET

new

SHANGHAI

TERRACE

bowl

OAKLAND, CALIFORNIA

HOME OF "THE WONGETTES"

ANDY WONG'S
CHINESE SKY ROOM

LEFT: New Shanghai Terrace souvenir photo
folder cover (1940s). ABOVE: Sugar cubes
from the Chinese Sky Room, "Home of 'The
Wongettes'" (l–r): Elizabeth Jean, Kim Wong,
and Helen Kim (1940s).

MATCHBOOK COVERS

Background: Detail from a Forbidden City matchbook cover (1940s).

830 GRANT AVENUE SAN FRANCISCO
Chinatown's Unique
Cocktail Lounge
PHONE CHINA 033

CHINESE
PAGODA

CLOSE COVER BEFORE STRIKING MATCH

CHINESE
VILLAGE
CHINATOWN
SAN FRANCISCO

702 GRANT AVE.

CLOSE COVER BEFORE STRIKING MATCH

SAN FRANCISCO, CALIF.

DINING - DANCING
ENTERTAINMENT

Ed Pond's
DRAGON'S
LAIR
521 GRANT AVE.

IN SAN FRANCISCO'S
CHINATOWN

CLOSE COVER BEFORE STRIKING

158 Waverly Place
Cor. of Washington

San Francisco's
Unique
Cocktail Bar

Phone
China 1580

TWIN
DRAGON

CLOSE COVER BEFORE STRIKING

TELEPHONE CHINA 1543
CLUB
MANDALAY
720
WASHINGTON ST.
in
San Francisco
Chinatown

CLOSE · COVER · BEFORE · STRIKING

CLUB MANDALAY

Where
the West
Meets
the East.
Where
Good Food
and
Fine Drinks
are
a Tradition

CLUB MANDALAY

CLOSE COVER BEFORE STRIKING

425 - 10th St.
OAKLAND, CALIF.

New
Shanghai
Cafe

Floor Show Nightly

DINE and
DANCE

453 GRANT AVE - CHINATOWN
SAN FRANCISCO

CHINA 0789

NEW
SHANGHAI CAFE

AMERICAN and CHINESE
DISHES ... Cocktails

new
Shanghai Cafe

DANCING

MUSIC & DANCING
EVERY EVENING

MENUS

ABOVE (bottom right): Forbidden City menu cover. OPPOSITE (top left): Chinese Sky Room menu autographed by singer Sophie Tucker.
BACKGROUND: Pattern from the back cover of the New Shanghai Terrace Bowl menu.

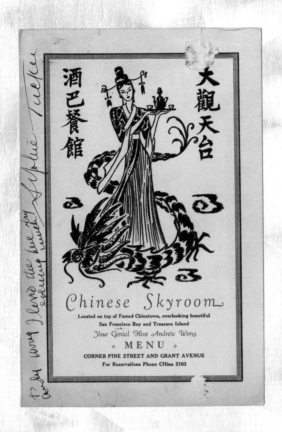

To Jru Wong I love the love for
evening much. Julia Tucker

大觀天台
酒巴餐館

Chinese Skyroom

Located on top of Famed Chinatown, overlooking beautiful
San Francisco Bay and Treasure Island
Your Genial Host Andrew Wong

MENU

CORNER PINE STREET AND GRANT AVENUE
For Reservations Phone CHina 2163

和樂園

Lions
DEN

946 Grant Avenue
San Francisco

The "Chinese Folies-Bergere" of the Americas

FONG WAN'S
Club
Shanghai

QUEEN MAE TAI SING
CALIFORNIA STATEHOOD
CENTENNIAL CELEBRATION 1950

At the Gateway to Chinatown

NEW
SHANGHAI
TERRACE
BOWL

LIQUOR LIST

CHINESE DISHES

AMERICAN DISHES

CHINESE MENU

SPECIAL CHINESE DINNER 2.75
6 to 11 P.M.

RELISHES

MANDARIN SOUP
CHICKEN CHOW MEIN CHICAGO STYLE

FRIED PRAWNS   PORK EGG FOO YEONG
GREEN CHOW YUKE   CANTON FRIED RICE

CHINESE TEA   ALMOND COOKIES

A la Carte

CHOW MEIN WITH CRISP OR FRIED NOODLES

CLUB SHANGHAI SPECIAL CHOW MEIN (for one) 2.50; (for two 4.00
Special Chinese Style Chow Mein, Diced Vegetables, Water Chestnuts, Lotus Seeds, White Mushrooms, Bamboo
Shoots, Fine-Sliced Boned Chicken, Chopped Almonds and Fried Noodles

FRESH VEGETABLE CHOW MEIN 1.35
Made only with Fresh Vegetables—No Meat

PLAIN PORK OR BEEF CHOW MEIN 1.40
Sliced Tenderloin of Beef or Roast Pork, Bean Sprouts, Peppers, Onions, Water Chestnuts and Noodles

TOMATO BEEF CHOW MEIN 1.75
Fried Noodles with Tomatoes and Sliced Tenderloin of Beef, Green Peppers, Onions, Tomato Sauce and Noodles

CHOW MEIN, SWEET AND SOUR SAUCE 2.00
Sliced Chicken, Pineapple, Bean Sprouts, Bamboo Shoots, Onions, Water Chestnuts and Noodles

SHRIMP OR CRAB CHOW MEIN 1.50

CHICKEN CHOW MEIN 1.50

SUB GUM CHICKEN ALMOND CHOW MEIN 2.00
Diced Chicken, Diced Vegetables, White Mushrooms, Water Chestnuts, Toasted Almonds, Sesame Seeds,
Special Sauce and Noodles

EGG FOO YEONG

CHICKEN 1.50
Sliced Chicken, Chinese Vegetables,
Bamboo Shoots, Water Chestnuts,
White Mushrooms, Green Onions,
Bean Sprouts and Eggs

BARBECUED PORK 1.40
Barbecued Pork, Water Chestnuts,
Mushrooms, Green Onions, Bamboo
Shoots, and Eggs, made omelette
style

CRAB OR SHRIMP 1.50
Sea Food, Bean Sprouts, Mushrooms,
Bamboo Shoots, Baby Green Onions,
Ham, Eggs and Water Chestnuts.

CHOP SUEY

CLUB SHANGHAI SPECIAL 2.00
Boned Chicken, White Mushrooms,
Water Chestnuts, Bamboo Shoots,
Vegetables, Bean Sprouts, Sesame

SUB GUM CHOP SUEY 1.75
Diced Boneless Chicken, Bamboo
Shoots, Button Mushrooms, Water
Chestnuts and Celery

ALMOND DICED CHICKEN . . . 1.75
Diced Boneless Chicken, Bamboo
Shoots, Button Mushrooms, Water
Chestnuts, Celery and Toasted
Almonds

CHOW YUKE

CHINESE GREEN 1.25
PORK OR BEEF 1.50
SHRIMP OR CRAB 1.50
TOMATO 1.35

FRIED RICE

CHICKEN FRIED RICE 1.50
BARBECUED PORK 1.25
CRAB OR SHRIMP 1.50
HAM FRIED RICE 1.35

CHINESE SPECIALS

BARBECUED PORK SPARE RIBS CANTON STYLE 1.50
WOR SUI OPP (MANDARIN DUCK) SWEET & SOUR SAUCE 2.50
FRIED JUMBO SHRIMPS 1.60
PEKIN CHICKEN EGG ROLL 2.00
PINEAPPLE PORK SPARE RIBS 2.00
BROILED SQUAB, CHINESE FAMILY STYLE 3.50
FRIED WON TON CHEF'S SAUCE 2.00
WOR WON TON WITH CHICKEN 1.50
BARBECUED PORK NOODLES 1.00
CHICKEN NOODLES 1.25
CHINESE PORK BARBECUED 1.25

OTHER NATIVE DISHES UPON REQUEST

Not Responsible for Lost or Stolen Articles

AMERICAN MENU

DELUXE AMERICAN DINNER
6 to 11 P.M.

The Price of Entree Determines Cost of Dinner

Relishes   --   Soup Du Jour   --   Shanghai Salad

N. Y. CUT SIRLOIN OR FILET MIGNON . . . 3.00
ROAST TOM TURKEY CRANBERRY SAUCE . . . 2.75
CHICKEN A LA KING EN CASSEROLE . . . 2.50
FRENCH LAMB CHOPS WITH GREEN PEAS . . . 2.75
PORK CHOPS WITH APPLE FRITTERS . . . 2.50
FRIED HALF SPRING CHICKEN ON TOAST . . . 2.50

Vegetables   Potatoes   Rolls & Butter
Coffee, Tea or Milk   Ice Cream   Homemade Pie

A la Carte

SALADS

SHANGHAI GESTURE 1.50
Tomatoes, Egg, Pineapple, Cottage Cheese, Anchovies, Peppers, Celery

SPECIAL CHICKEN SALAD 1.50

HONGKONG FRUIT SALAD 1.50
Choice of Mayonnaise, French, Thousand Island, Cream or Roquefort Dressing

KING SALAD 1.50
Half Avocado, Pineapple, Grapefruit and Peaches, Chef's Dressing

CRAB OR SHRIMP, LOUIE 1.75

SALADE COSMOPOLITAINE 1.75

STUFFED FRUIT SPECIAL 1.75
Half Pear, Peach, Pineapple, Assorted Fillings

STUFFED AVOCADO, MANDARIN 1.75
Stuffed with Crab or Shrimp Salad

STEAKS AND CHOPS

GRILLED FILET MIGNON 2.75
GRILLED NEW YORK CUT 2.75
FRENCH LAMB CHOPS 2.25
FRIED PORK CHOPS 2.00
FRIED SPRING CHICKEN 2.25
HAM STEAK 2.25
HAM AND EGGS 1.75

SANDWICHES

MANHATTAN 1.40
GRILLED STEAK 1.75
SPECIAL CLUB HOUSE 1.50
CHICKEN 1.25
HAM AND EGG 1.25
MONTE CRISTO 1.75
TUNA FISH OR SARDINE 1.25

SOUPS
CONSOMME 75
CLAM CHOWDER 75
VEGETABLE SOUP 75

POTATOES
FRENCH FRIED 50
AMERICAN FRIED 60
SHOESTRING 60

BEVERAGES
COFFEE 25
TEA (Small) . . . .30; (Large) . . .50
MILK .25   HOT CHOCOLATE . . .40

DESSERTS
PASTRIES 35
ICE CREAM 30
PRESERVED FRUIT 50

We Reserve the Right to Refuse Service to Anyone

PHOTOS (l-r): Club Shanghai (l-r): unidentified, Mr. and Mrs. Andy and Penny Wong, and Sammee Tong. Forbidden City:
Mr. and Mrs. Tom and Mae Chan, and Judge and Mrs. Delbert and Delores Wong. Club Shanghai: unidentified sailors.
China Doll: unidentified customers. Forbidden City: unidentified service member (all photos 1940s).

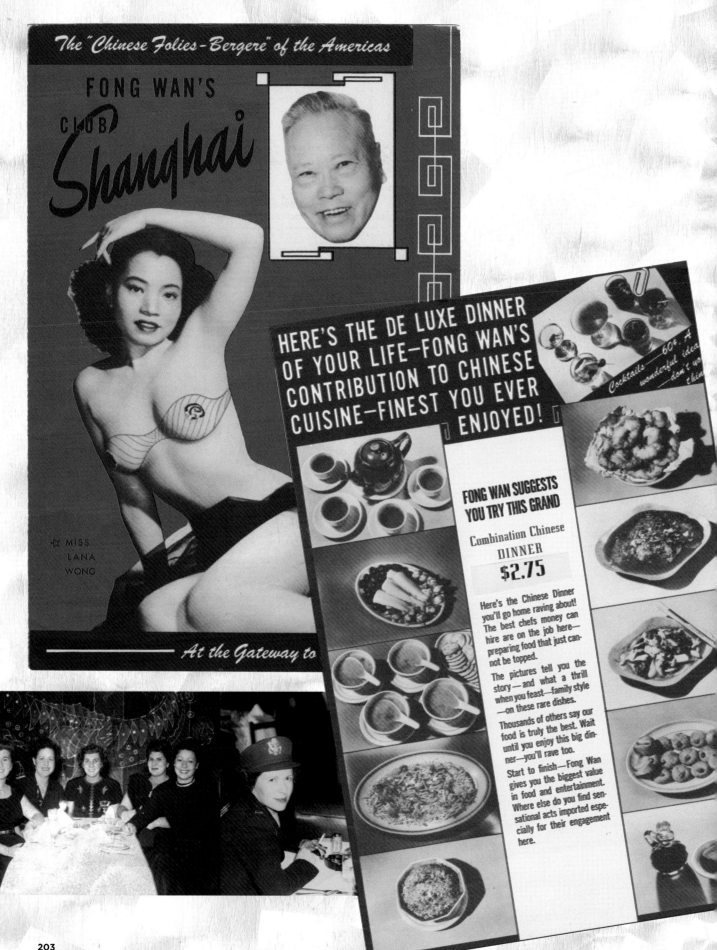

203

COCKTAIL NAPKINS

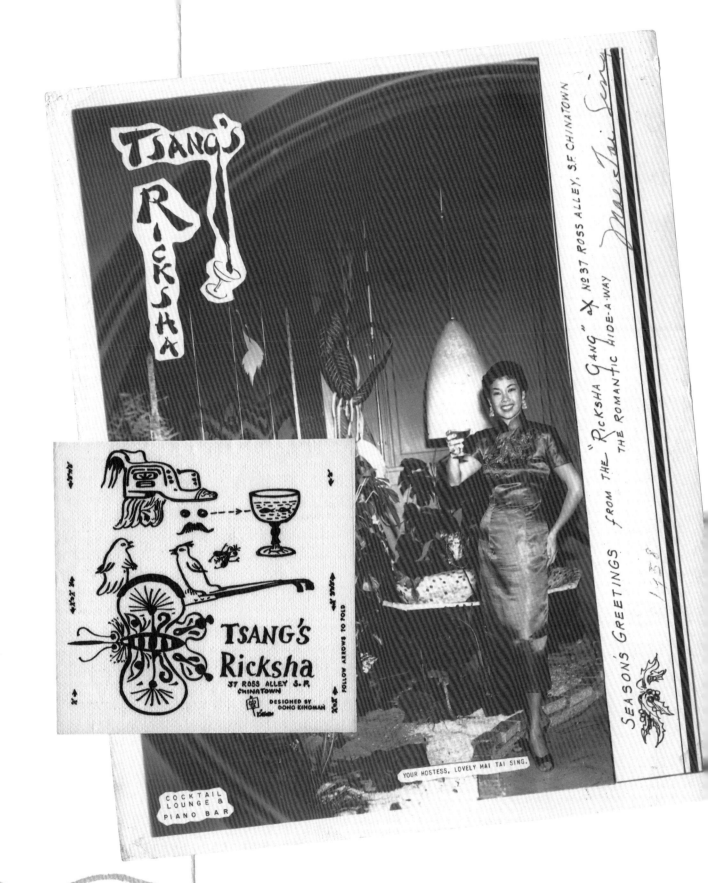

TSANG'S RICKSHA

TSANG'S
Ricksha
37 ROSS ALLEY S.F.
CHINATOWN

DESIGNED BY
DONG KINGMAN

FOLLOW ARROWS TO FOLD

COCKTAIL
LOUNGE &
PIANO BAR

YOUR HOSTESS, LOVELY MAI TAI SING.

SEASON'S GREETINGS FROM THE "RICKSHA GANG" at Nº 37 ROSS ALLEY, S.F. CHINATOWN

THE ROMANTIC HIDE-A-WAY

ABOVE: Mai Tai Sing retired from dancing in nightclubs as a featured performer and as a partner of the Tai Sings to run the Ricksha bar with her brothers from 1959 to 1970. In between, she also starred in the TV series *Hong Kong,* with Rod Taylor, before moving to Hawaii to manage the Trappers club at the Hyatt. The Ricksha cocktail napkin was designed by her uncle, noted watercolorist Dong Kingman (photo ca. 1958–1959).

PHOTO FOLDER COVERS

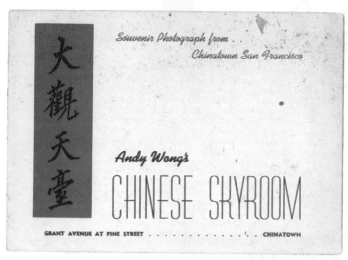

BACKGROUND: Detail from a Buddha Cocktail Lounge ad (January 1953).
FOLLOWING PAGES: Forbidden City postcard (ca. 1940s).

List of Clubs

The date ranges listed below are for each venue's years of operation. Research on some dates was based on limited information and/or listings that were found in archival city directories, which are incomplete.

China Doll
357 51st Street, New York City
April 1946–1948

Chinese Sky Room
605 Pine Street, San Francisco
December 31, 1937–1964

Club Mandalay
720 Washington Street, San Francisco
dates unknown, ca. 1940s

Club Oakland
425 10th Street, Oakland
July 29, 1946–1950

Club Shanghai
453 Grant Avenue, San Francisco
ca. 1941–1947 (under D. W. Low)
June 19, 1947–ca. 1954 (under Fong Wan)

Forbidden City
363 Sutter Street, San Francisco
December 22, 1938–December 1962
   (under Charlie Low)
December 1962–1970
   (under Coby Yee and family)

Kubla Khan
414 Grant Avenue, San Francisco
1944–1950

Lion's Den
946 Grant Avenue, San Francisco
ca. 1940–ca. 1960s

New Shanghai Cafe
425 10th Street, Oakland
March 22, 1927–1946

New Shanghai Terrace Bowl
421 10th Street, Oakland
July 3, 1940–1946

Shangri-La
960 Bush Street, San Francisco
June 1942–August 1942

SAN FRANCISCO CHINATOWN BARS

Buddha Cocktail Lounge
901 Grant Avenue
ca. 1952–present

Chinese Pagoda
830 Grant Avenue
ca. 1939–1970

Chinese Village
702 Grant Avenue
1936–ca. 1971

Dragon's Lair
521 Grant Avenue
ca. 1944–1948

Jade Palace
842 Grant Avenue
ca. 1938–1962

Li Po
916 Grant Avenue
1937–present

Ricksha
37 Ross Alley
ca. 1953–1982

Ricksha Bistro (Rickshaw Bistro)
453 Grant Avenue
ca. 1965–1980

Twin Dragon
158 Waverly Place
ca. 1940–closing date unknown

Map of Chinatown from a tourist brochure (San Francisco Convention and Visitors Bureau, 1950s).

Selected Resources

Chang, Iris. *The Chinese in America: A Narrative History*. New York: Penguin Books, 2003.

Chen, Yong. *Chinese San Francisco, 1850–1943: A Trans-Pacific Community*. Stanford: Stanford UP, 2000.

Cho, Jenny, and the Chinese Historical Society of Southern California. *Chinese in Hollywood*. Charleston, SC: Arcadia Publishing, 2013. Images of America.

Chun, Gloria Heyung. *Of Orphans and Warriors: Inventing Chinese American Culture and Identity*. New Brunswick, NJ, and London: Rutgers UP, 2000.

Dong, Arthur, dir. *Forbidden City, USA*. Los Angeles: DeepFocus Productions, 1989. Documentary film with study guide.

——, curator. *Hollywood Chinese: The Arthur Dong Collection*. Exhibition catalogue with essay by Renee Tajima-Peña. Los Angeles: Chinese American Museum, 2009.

——, dir. *Hollywood Chinese: The Chinese in American Feature Films*. Los Angeles: DeepFocus Productions, 2007. Documentary film with study guide.

——, Lorraine Dong, and Irene Poon, curators. *Chop Suey on Wax: The Flower Drum Song Album, The Arthur Dong Collection*. Exhibition catalogue with essays by Renee Tajima-Peña and Ben Fong-Torres. San Francisco: Chinese Historical Society of America, 2006.

Fleming, Ann Marie. *The Magical Life of Long Tack Sam: An Illustrated Memoir*. New York: Riverhead Books-Penguin Group (USA), 2007.

Flower Drum Song. Music by Richard Rodgers. Lyrics by Oscar Hammerstein II. St. James Theatre, New York. 1 Dec. 1958. Musical.

——. Screenplay by Joseph Fields. Music by Richard Rodgers. Lyrics by Oscar Hammerstein II. Universal Studios, 1961. Film.

——. Book by David Henry Hwang. Music by Richard Rodgers. Lyrics by Oscar Hammerstein II. Mark Taper Forum, Los Angeles. 14 Oct. 2001. Musical.

——. Book by David Henry Hwang. Music by Richard Rodgers. Lyrics by Oscar Hammerstein II. New York: Theatre Communications Group, 2003.

——. *A Musical Play*. Book by Oscar Hammerstein II and Joseph Fields. Music by Richard Rodgers. Lyrics by Oscar Hammerstein II. New York: Farrar, Straus & Cudahy, 1959.

Kwong, Peter, and Dusanka Miscevic. *Chinese America: The Untold Story of America's Oldest New Community*. New York and London: New Press, 2005.

Lee, Anthony W. *Picturing Chinatown: Art and Orientalism in San Francisco*. Los Angeles and London: U of California P, 2001.

Lee, C[hin]. Y[ang]. *The Flower Drum Song*. New York: Farrar, Straus and Cudahy, 1957.

Lee, Robert G. *Orientals: Asian Americans in Popular Culture*. Philadelphia: Temple UP, 1999.

Lewis, David H. *Flower Drum Songs: The Story of Two Musicals*. Jefferson, NC, and London: MacFarland and Company, Inc., 2006.

Lowe, Lisa. *Immigrant Acts: On Asian American Cultural Politics*. Durham, NC: Duke UP, 1996.

Moon, Krystyn. *Yellowface: Creating the Chinese in American Popular Music and Performance, 1850s–1920s*. New Brunswick, NJ: Rutgers UP, 2004.

Moy, James S. *Marginal Sights: Staging the Chinese in America*. Iowa City: U of Iowa P, 1993.

Peretti, Burton. *Nightclub City: Politics and Amusement in Manhattan*. Philadelphia: U of Pennsylvania P, 2011.

Robbins, Trina. *Forbidden City: The Golden Age of Chinese Nightclubs*. Cresskill, NJ: Hampton Press, Inc., 2010.

See, Lisa. *China Dolls: A Novel*. New York: Random House, 2014.

Shimakawa, Karen. *National Abjection: The Asian American Body Onstage*. Durham, NC, and London: Duke UP, 2002.

Tchen, John Kuo Wei. *New York before Chinatown: Orientalism and the Shaping of American Culture, 1776–1882*. New York: Johns Hopkins UP, 2001.

Waggoner, Susan. *Nightclub Nights: Art, Legend, and Style 1920–1960*. New York: Rizzoli, 2001.

Walker, Stanley. *The Night Club Era*. Baltimore: Johns Hopkins UP, 1999.

Yung, Judy. *Unbound Feet: A Social History of Chinese Women in San Francisco*. Berkeley, Los Angeles, and London: U of California P, 1995.

——. *Unbound Voices: A Documentary History of Chinese Women in San Francisco*. Berkeley, Los Angeles, and London: U of California P, 1999.

RIGHT: Chinese Sky Room performers read *The Young China* while club owner Andy Wong goes over musical arrangements (l–r): Andy Wong, unidentified, Robin Wing, Julianne Lew, unidentified, Vicky Lee, unidentified (1940s). Photo by Ivan Essayan.

Index

Source Index

BACKGROUND: Cover of *San Francisco Life* magazine (June 1947).

Credits

Willie Tsang, singer and dancer.
A self-taught draftsman, Tsang worked with his sister, dancer Mai Tai Sing, to design and run the Ricksha bar with two other brothers. He autographed this 1940s photo to his teacher, dancer Tony Wing.

Author: Arthur Dong
Foreword: Lisa See
Essay Writers: Arthur Dong and Lorraine Dong
Editorial Consultant: Oliver Wang
Copy Editor and Indexer: Lisa K. Marietta
Resource List and Research: Lorraine Dong
Cultural Consultants: Marlon K. Hom and Peter Mintun
Copyright Research: Joan Yoshiwara
Legal Counsel: Justine Jacob, Esq., Blyth, Lee & Associates

Book Design: Zand Gee

SPECIAL THANKS

Andy Young	Cynthia Fong Yee	Norine Murray
Arlene Wing Dark	Elise Capron	Pat Chin
Barbara Yung	Gayle Wattawa	Pat Mar Harvey
Bo Lee	Janice Quan	Penny Wong
Calvin Fong	Jen Abrahamson	Tony Contini
Cary Amo	Mark Wong	Victor Wai Ho Lim
Coby Yee	Michael Kan	Willard Fong

This book was supported in part by an Investing in Artists Grant from the Center for Cultural Innovation.

Forbidden City, USA was published in coordination with an exhibition about Chinese American nightclubs curated by Arthur Dong for the San Francisco Public Library's Jewett Gallery (April 12–July 6, 2014).

Library of Congress Control Number: 2014932571

ISBN: 978-0-9915733-0-1

Orders, inquires, and correspondence should be addressed to:
DeepFocus Productions, Inc.
P.O. Box 39548
Los Angeles CA 90039-0548
info@deepfocusproductions.com
www.deepfocusproductions.com

DeepFocus PRODUCTIONS, INC.

www.ForbiddenCityBook.com

www.facebook.com/ChineseAmericanNightclubs

Printed in the United States of America.